D0905097

K A T Y A

& The Prince of Siam

EILEEN HUNTER
with NARISA CHAKRABONGSE

To Lisba
In loving Memory

Acknowledgments

Eileen and Narisa would like to thank the following for their advice
and encouragment throughout: Zamira Benthall, Lesley Blanche,
Allen Levy, Robert and Rebecca MacDonald, Henry Maxwell,
Olga Petithuegenin, Valerian Skwarzoff, Desa Trevisan

First edition published in Thailand by River Books
and distributed in the UK by
White Mouse Editions
3 Denbigh Road
London W11 2SJ
Tel 0171 229 6765

A River Books Production
Copyright © Text: Narisa Chakrabongse and Eileen Hunter
Copyright © Collective Work: River Books, 1994

All rights reserved. This book or parts thereof may not be repro-
duced in any form without permission in writing from
the publisher.

Design by Supadee Ruangsak
Picture research by Pattara Khan
Editorial direction by Narisa Chakrabongse
Production by Paisarn Piemmettawat
Typesetting by Nicola Barwood

Printed and bound in Thailand by Amarin Printing and Publishing

ISBN 0 904568 76 8

CONTENTS

FOREWORD

After my father Prince Chula died when I was seven, my mother and I often used to spend the evenings at our house in Cornwall watching the many 16mm films they had shot together – films spanning a thirty year period from 1935 to 1964. We would sit together in the room called the 'Bira Bar' surrounded by my uncle's motor racing trophies. At the time I was not sensitive to the fact that these films might upset my mother, but perhaps in a way they comforted her and brought my father close to her again. For my part, I simply enjoyed asking who all the different people were and hearing the stories about them. Thus it was that I first saw a smiling middle-aged woman and was told that this was my Russian grandmother Katya. (Apparently, I was taken to see her once in Paris when I was about two years old but no memory remains.) In the films she moves across the lawn with the slightly speeded up motion of 16 mm, or sits sipping a cup of tea on a terrace. The weather is always fine and I could gain no conception of what she was like, or the life she had led.

On my mother's death eight years later, I was left with the daunting task of sorting through not only trunk loads of my parents personal correspondence, diaries and papers, but those of my father's parents as well. Those of my grandparents were a mixture of Thai and Russian, of which I could read the former but not the latter. In the same trunk were many old photographs and elegant cartes de visites inscribed with the names of photographers in Kiev, St Petersburg and Bangkok. I gazed at the faces of stern-looking bearded gentlemen, severe matrons or a young girl in nurse's uniform. On the backs in my mother's writing were scribbled the names of my grandmother's father, mother and Katya herself. I began to become intrigued and wanted to discover more, but not reading Russian and having to study for exams and later university, I had to put them aside for a while.

It was only 10 years later when talking with my aunt Eileen Hunter, the writer, in our favourite little Greek restaurant in Craven Hill that we decided that the story of Katya and my grandfather Prince Chakrabongse was one that should be told and that with my aunt's experience as an author and my research abilities we would collaborate on the project. I immediately began translating my grandfather's diaries written in Thai and searched out my grandparents' letters to each other. However, finding someone to translate them proved somewhat problematic, more than a few Russian specialists being able to deal with my grandfather's neat hand but finding my grandmother's script and style convoluted and indecipherable. In fact, it was only when I went to live in Thailand for three years in the mid-1980s that I found some translators – a shaky old Cossack living in an old people's home on the outskirts of Bangkok, a Scottish couple working as Russian specialists at the UN and finally a Pravda correspondent, who was probably in reality KGB. This latter man and his delightful wife seemed to develop an immense affection for me and the project while we worked together, but from the moment they left Bangkok despite numerous letters to them, I have never heard from them again.

While working on the translation I gradually became totally immersed in my grandparents' lives – their happiness and sorrow, trials and tribulations. In particular, I came to identify with my grandmother, a foreigner living in a strange land. For although I have a well-known Thai name and speak excellent Thai, my European appearance has always caused and continues to cause constant and intrusive questioning. But if it has been difficult for me to live and work in Thailand, how much more difficult it must have been for my grandmother all those years ago when Bangkok was nothing like the cosmopolitan city it is today? In addition, I identified with her as someone who had lost her parents at a young age and all the insecurities that this can cause.

Through working on the book I also learnt more about my father's early life. I came to sympathise with his traumatic childhood and understood some of the reasons why he might not have been able to be as loving a father as I felt he should have been. Thus in many ways working on the book has been a cathartic experience for me and enabled me to reach my father and my paternal grandparents whom I never had a chance to know.

It has also impacted on my personal life as well, as the first trip I undertook with my husband Gee Svasti-Thomson, before we were married, was to Istanbul in search of the church were my grandparents were married some 80 years earlier. Having to find an old priest to unlock the church and sitting together alone in the dark interior we could almost feel their presence beside us. Another connection is that both my father and Gee's grandfather were both in love with the same girl, who later married Gee's grandfather.

For my aunt, I think the book has sometimes been difficult. Just when she would think a particular section was finished I'd write or ring her with another letter, another diary revelation which I would insist had to be included. At other times with me in Thailand and her in England discussing the book has been problematic. Nevertheless, despite it all we've managed to stay good friends and produce a book which I hope does justice to my grandparents, who were both remarkable people in their own very different ways.

Narisa Chakrabongse

August 1994

Katya, Prince Chakrabongse and their son Prince Chula.

I

The Siamese Royal Family

*T*he story of Katya – Ekaterina Ivanovna Desnitsky's marriage to Prince Chakrabongse of Siam has intrigued me since I first heard of it in 1938, the year that their son and only child Prince Chula married my sister Lisba. Although there was considerable opposition to their marriage from my family, it was as nothing to the undisguised anger of the Siamese Royal Family when, in 1906, Chakrabongse, a son of the reigning monarch, chose a 'farang' – a foreigner – as his bride.

The Chakri Dynasty, rulers of Siam since 1782, had held to a strict tradition of consanguineous marriage among royalty 'to maintain the purity of the stock', and was shaken to the core, not so much by the fact that Katya was a commoner and an orphan without fortune, but because she was foreign. In the words of one of Chakrabongse's full brothers, Prince Prajadhipok, 'The marriage was a national dynastic catastrophe!'

To comprehend fully the intensity of this reaction on the part of his family, it is imperative to touch briefly on the background into which Chakrabongse was born in 1883.

Although his father, King Chulalongkorn, was said to have had ninety-two wives and seventy-seven children, his favourite wife was Queen Saowabha and Chakrabongse, one of her nine children, was one of his favourite sons. He was also the grandson of the great King Mongkut and the character and remarkable changes brought about in Siam by both his father and grandfather were profoundly to affect his own short life.

Mongkut, well known in the West through Anna Leonowens' book *An English Governess at the Siamese Court* and the loosely derived musical, *The King and I*, was in every respect a different character from his portrayal in both. He was born in 1804, the son of King Rama II, and when he was twenty – as was customary for all male Siamese princes – he entered the priesthood for what was generally a short period of about three months. But in his case this 'short period' was prolonged into a sojourn of twenty-seven years, for hardly had he stepped inside the monastery doors, when the King, his Father, died without having named an heir.

Mongkut being conveniently out of the way, his half-brother Prince Chesdah – some say aided by a scheming mother – was nominated by the Accession Council as King. This may well have influenced Mongkut to remain in the priesthood, for although Chesdah was his senior, Mongkut might have thought he had a prior right to the throne, as Chesdah was the son of a minor wife, whereas Mongkut's mother was royal. Whatever the reasons, the young Prince's motives for abandoning the world in the prime of youth for half a lifetime's submission to the disciplines of monastic life, was a decision eventually highly advantageous both for his own development and that of his country.

To begin with, his fellow monks were drawn from all ranks of society and as he travelled with them on foot all over his realm, he had the opportunity, unique for a royal prince of his day, of mingling democratically with people he would never have met otherwise, thus gaining first-hand knowledge of their lives and conditions.

Then, by learning Pali, the language in which Buddhist teaching is recorded, he acquired a rather more profound understanding of its tenets than he would have done had he left the monastery after only a few months. As it was, he was the only member of the Royal Family to have been awarded a first degree Doctorate in Theology.

He also learnt some Latin from the French Bishop Pallegoix with whom, as well as with English and American missionaries, he sometimes engaged in religious disputation, relaxed and friendly exchanges on his part, as he had the true Buddhist's tolerance of other faiths. But despite the lack of any encouragement on his side, the zealous missionaries still laboured to convert him, undeterred by his known pronouncement on Christianity – 'What you teach people to do is admirable, but what you teach them to believe is foolish!'

In 1844, when he was forty, he began to study English with some American missionaries, and made such progress that he came to regard it as his second language, speaking and writing it fluently with 'rather a literary tinge', as one of his teachers put it. Later he was to insist that his children spoke English too, and sent several of his sons to England for this purpose.

Even more important was the fact that his grasp of the language enabled him to read up-to-date scientific books on many subjects – astronomy was a special favourite – and these introduced him to a whole new world of modern thought. Thus, when the King, his brother, died in 1851 and at long last he was called to the throne at the age of forty-six, he was well prepared for kingship.

The discipline of his years in the priesthood, his great intellectual powers, and his contacts with ordinary people, had made him a man of remarkable balance and perception. He realised that his country, steeped in tradition, deeply religious, superstitious and with a respect for rank amounting to reverence, could only very gradually be guided into step with the modern world.

Soon after his own coronation, Mongkut appointed his full brother, Prince Chutamanni (known as King Pinklao), as *Uparaja* or second King, who was crowned in a ceremony only slightly less splendid than his own. He also had the good fortune to be blessed with an excellent *Kalahom* or Prime Minster, Sri Suriyawongse, so that his reign began under good auspices.

His power was absolute and government was by edict, each introduced by a recitation of the royal styles and titles, and commencing: 'By royal command reverberating like the roar of a lion …' There was also a palace gong that, if struck by a petitioner any afternoon or evening, ensured that the King would appear in person 'when not otherwise occupied in affairs of the realm, and provided that it will not be raining at the time'.

King Chulalongkorn and Queen Saowabha.

King Mongkut in his coronation regalia.

Worthy of particular mention is his edict on faith, not only for its fine word-ing, but because it reflects the wholehearted aversion to bigotry and religious per-secution that have always been an admirable feature of Buddhism: 'No just ruler restricts the freedom of his people in the choice of their religious belief by which each man hopes to find strength and salvation in his last hour, as well as in the future beyond. There are many precepts common to all religions.'

It is said that, during his reign, no less than five thousand acts of law were passed ranging from grave affairs of state to an edict entitled 'Advice against the inelegant practice of throwing dead animals in the waterways'. However, although alert to the benefit of contact with progressive Western ideas, Mongkut did not discard beliefs and traditions dear not only to his countrymen, but to him-self. He was highly gratified, for instance, to be presented with four white ele-phants during his reign and in fact found time to write a book on these rare creatures. He lists as desirable 'white hair and nails, and pink skin' and also praised an animal with a beautiful snore, but added reflectively that 'just as men have indi-vidual taste in women, this applies equally to elephants'.

According to some ancient writers, the swan, dove, monkey and elephant, when white, 'are nobler, purer creatures, reserved for the souls of the good and great in one of the stages of their soul's transmigration'. This reverence applies particularly to the white elephant, who was regarded as nothing less than a god. And King Mongkut's panegyric written on the death of one of them runs: ' ... his tusks like long pearls; his ears like silver shields; his trunk like a comet's tail; his legs like the feet of the skies; his tread like the sound of thunder; his looks full of meditation; his expression full of tenderness; his voice the voice of a mighty warrior; and his bearing that of an illustrious monarch.'

From the foregoing, it is therefore clear that a particularly flattering compliment was intended when the Chief of the Siamese Embassy returned from England and, recounting the Embassy's reception at Court, says of Queen Victoria 'One cannot but be struck with the aspect of the august Queen of England, or fail to observe she must be of pure descent from a race of goodly and warlike kings and rulers of the earth, in that her eyes, complexion and, above all, her bearing are those of a beautiful and majestic white elephant.'

The embassy in England was only one of many diplomatic exchanges during Mongkut's reign, and treaties were signed with so many nations that one of his sons, Prince Damrong, declared that his sagacious father had ensured in this manner that no one power could ever become of overweening importance. But at a time when all South-East Asia had fallen beneath the domination of the Western Powers, the value of Mongkut's adroit diplomacy cannot be over estimated. A most important treaty was with the envoy of Queen Victoria, Sir John Bowring, who arrived in Bangkok in 1855, and was agreeably surprised not only by the King's command of English, but by the fact that quite a number of Siamese officials spoke it as well.

Sir John, who brought gifts of a diamond watch and a travelling writing-case from his Sovereign, was well received by Mongkut, seated on a richly carved throne, robed in crimson and wearing a crown glittering with diamonds and precious stones. Yet despite this splendid formality – as Bowring recounts – 'the King offered me cigars with his own hand, while liqueurs, tea and sweetmeats were brought in.' The Englishman was also much impressed by Mongkut's Prime Minister, Sri Suriyawongse, whom he described as 'a most sagacious man, towering above every person we have met... of graceful gentlemanly manners and appropriate language.'

The treaty signed in April 1855 was, in most respects, similar to those which would be made with other nations later on. It provided for the nomination of a permanent British Consul in Bangkok. Siam agreed not to impose duties on British goods at more than three per cent ad valorem and accepted British extra-territorial rights in her own sovereign territory. In addition, Britons were to be allowed to buy land within four miles of the city walls.

Once this treaty was signed others followed with France, Napoleon III sending not only a carriage, but a pair of horses to the King; and with America, the

King Mongkut during his period in the monkhood.

King Mongkut processing to Wat Phra Chetuphon for the Katin ceremony.

Hanseatic League, Denmark, Portugal, Holland, Prussia, Sweden and Norway. Europeans were engaged to overhaul and reorganise government services. Learning was encouraged by the printing of books in Siamese and in English, printing presses having been introduced into Thailand by American Baptist missionaries. The King also initiated the building of ships, bridges, canals and roads, spurred on in this last by petulant complaints from more than one newly- established foreign consul, that 'their health was suffering as they were unable to take the air in their carriages of an evening, due to the bad roads in Bangkok.'

Mongkut also travelled about his realm, sometimes on horseback, sometimes in his paddle-steamer, showing himself to his subjects whereas, before his time, it had been taboo even to look on the monarch's countenance.

His austere, high-cheekboned face was clearly marked by his years in the monastery: remote, unsmiling, he had more the aspect of an idol than a man. Credited with an irascible temperament, he was also imperious and thought nothing of summoning to his presence, at dead of night, not only servants or courtiers, but missionaries and, on one occasion at least, the British Consul. Fetched from his bed, this official, as he hastened to the palace, revolved in his mind every combination of alarming event that could justify so untoward a command, but on arrival found the King, dictionary in hand, merely desiring his definition of a word.

Following the custom of those days, Mongkut was a polygamist; indeed he was credited with having thirty-two wives and eighty-eight children. This was naturally considered extremely shocking by the missionaries, one of whom, an American named Dr Bradley, reproached the King for placing an effigy of one of his wives in a temple but was rendered speechless by the Monarch enquiring how this differed from the Albert Memorial!

Mongkut's wives and children lived in a part of the palace – almost a small township – called not the harem but the 'Inside' which, far from being the scene of voluptuous debauchery, was as strictly organised as a finishing-school. Here were houses, gardens, shops, lakes and even the Inside's own law-courts and police-station. There was a Directress, who had various officials under her and, as each Queen had her own retinue of 200 to 300 women, which was increased if she bore a child, the total population of the Inside was somewhere near three thousand. This figure also comprised, in addition to wives and minor wives, the King's sons until they reached puberty, nurses, servants, women in charge of the King's kitchens, and a female police-force which guarded the gates, patrolling at night with torches and, should a man be admitted for repair or construction work, remaining closely at his side until he left.

Mrs Leonowens, the English Governess engaged to teach the royal children in 1862, despite her strong moral disapproval of polygamy, paints a most charming picture of the 'ladies of the harem, who amuse themselves in the early and late hours of the day, feeding birds in the aviaries and goldfish in the pond, twining garlands to adorn the heads of their children, arranging bouquets, singing songs of love or glory, dancing to the music of the guitar, listening to their slaves reading, strolling with their little ones through the parks and parterres, and especially in bathing. When the heat is least oppressive, they plunge into the waters of the pretty tiered lakes, swimming and diving like flocks of brown waterfowl.' As well as these diversions, there were theatrical shows, marionettes, card playing, gambling on the daily lotteries, and flying kites in March and April – the kite-flying season. Fed, housed and clothed, the Queens and their ladies, free from care though close-confined, seemed even to the censorious Englishwomen like denizens of an enchanted world.

Following his success in making English the second language of Siam, Mongkut decided it was an advantage that should be offered to the Inside, together with a light dusting of educational instruction. In the newspaper *The Bangkok Calendar* 1859, we read: 'His Majesty the King has requested the

Anna Leonowens.

Protestant Missions in Bangkok to furnish a preceptress for the royal females' and, this request being granted, 'No small amount of knowledge on various subjects was communicated to His Majesty's large and interesting family.' But alas, except for a very few, 'the royal females' showed but little inclination or aptitude for study and it was then that the King, recognising defeat, decided that his many children might make better scholars, and engaged the aforementioned Mrs Leonowens to be their Governess. A young widow of twenty-seven, she remained in Siam for that purpose for five years and, after writing *An English Governess at the Siamese Court* in 1870, followed it in 1873 by *Romance of a Harem*. However, it was not until 1945 that a novel by Margaret Landon, *Anna and the King of Siam* based on both these books, became a best-seller in America and led to its transformation into the musical 'The King and I'.

Although Mrs Leonowens was hampered by her imperfect grasp of the Siamese language, she gives a fascinating and charmingly written account of her unusual post, but one over-spiced by a liberal addition of imaginary melodramatic incidents which the eventual musical – as was only to be expected – exaggerated one hundredfold.

Her spontaneous response to the beauties of Siam, its people, architecture and moving ritual customs, is tempered by frequent denigration of 'paganism' and condescending pity for the 'heathen'. This ambivalence was largely due to the proselytising Christianity of that epoch for, in declaring itself the only true faith, its followers felt it their bounden duty to disparage all others, including of course Buddhism.

At one point, for instance, Anna describes King Mongkut as 'envious, revengeful, subtle and cruel', but at another pays tribute to him as 'the most remarkable of the Oriental princes of the present century ... the most progressive of the supreme rulers of Siam'. She also relates an incident that clearly demonstrates the 'pagan' monarch's typical Buddhist respect for the religious beliefs of others:

'Visiting a temple in company with the King and his family, I called his Majesty's attention to the statue at the Beautiful Gate as that of a Christian saint. Turning quickly to his children and addressing them gently, he bade them salute it reverently. "It is Mam's saint", he said; whereupon the tribe of little ones folded their hands devoutly and made obeisance before the effigy of St. Peter.'

A dark-eyed, strikingly handsome young woman – who might well be taken for an Indian – there is every reason to believe that her gift for veiling reality in clouds of fancy was already highly developed long before her arrival in Siam, for her story of her own past in Margaret Landon's book is, according to the painstaking research in William Bristowe's book, *Louis and the King of Siam*, an undoubted fabrication.

According to him, the facts are that her grandfather was one John Glasscock, a gunner in the Bengal Artillery, and that his child by an Eurasian or Indian woman, Mary Ann, was Anna Leonowen's mother, which would account for Anna's exotic appearance. In 1829 this Mary Ann Glasscock married Sergeant

Edwards, and they had two children – Eliza born 1830 and Anna (Leonowens) born 1831. Anna's version which imparted a high gloss of gentility to her antecedents and her past, recounts that she and Eliza were born in Wales, daughters of Captain and Mrs Crawford, their mother's maiden name being Edwards (her married name in reality) who came of ancient Welsh stock. In 1840 the two little girls were left in Wales with an aunt, while the parents went to India, Captain Crawford being ADC to the Commander of British troops in Lahore where he was killed in 1841.

When Eliza was sixteen and Anna fifteen, they went to India to join their mother, who was now remarried to 'a man in a senior position in the Public Works Department in Poona'. Anna's story was that she hated him because, although she was in love with a 'young officer'. Thomas Leon Owens, her stepfather tried to marry her to a rich merchant who, with Colonel Rutherford Sutherland (a non-existent character with a name straight out of Ouida), was joint-executor of her father's will.

She was then sent – rather strangely – 'on an educational tour of the Middle East with the Reverend Percy Badger' (in reality a well-known oriental scholar) and 'his wife'. Badger was in fact unmarried.

On her return, Anna married Thomas, whose second name and surname were now amalgamated into 'Leonowens', and they set up house 'with many servants on fashionable Malabar Hill'. After the death of her mother and their first child, the Leonowens set sail for England but, shipwrecked off the Cape of Good Hope, they were picked up by a vessel bound for Australia and landed there instead. Eventually they did reach England, where two children, Avis and Louis, were born in 1854 and 1855 respectively in St James' London.

After three years in London, Thomas, now promoted 'Major' Leonowens, rejoined his regiment in Singapore accompanied by his family. In 1857 Anna lost her small fortune in the collapse of the Agra Bank in India and, still worse, in 1858 Major Leonowens 'died of sunstroke, returning from a tiger shoot with brother officers'. Anna founded a little school for officers' children, but it only afforded her a bare living so when the post in Siam was offered in 1862, she was glad to accept it.

Meanwhile, her sister Eliza was edited out of the story as she had married a lowly Sergeant Major by whom she had six children, one of whom married an Eurasian widower called Pratt, an extremely able man who rose to be Assistant Collector of Salt Revenues in Bombay. Retiring in 1878, he settled in London, and three of his sons became highly distinguished. One was a Puisne Judge in Bombay, another a member of Bombay Legislative Council, and a third was awarded the KBE and CMG 'for distinguished services to the British Government'. Ironically this meant that they moved in circles to which their Aunt Anna had access only in fantasy. Eliza's youngest son, however, struck out in a quite different direction, for he became famous as Boris Karloff, who frightened a generation of movie-goers with his portrayals of sinister madmen, vampires and at least one Red Indian!

While the melodramatic inaccuracies in Anna's books are regrettable, there is undeniable pathos in her industrious weaving of falsehood about her origins, particularly as, in her true character, she was both enterprising and courageous, not entirely unworthy of Mongkut's alleged words of farewell when she left: 'Mam, you are much beloved by our common people, all inhabitants of palace and royal children. I am often angry on you and lose my temper though I have large respect for you. But you ought to know, Mam, you are of great difficulty and more difficult than generality ...'

Mongkut's interest in astronomy, shared by his Prime Minister, combined with his desire to demonstrate to his people the superiority of mathematical calculation over superstitious belief, caused him to welcome with enthusiasm the total eclipse of the sun, due on August 18, 1868. He therefore wrote on July 18 of that year to Henry Alabaster, Interpreter to the British Consulate at Singapore, requesting his good offices in urging acceptance of his invitation to the Governor, Sir Harry Orde and his wife, to be present on this occasion. An excerpt from his letter which begins, 'My Dear Familiar Friend', runs as follows:

> *'I have embraced good opportunity to communicate with Sir Harry Orde several times occasionally, his speech and tone of letter from him was very gracious and satisfactory to me indeed. Now he becomes familiar and intimate with me as well as his lady Mrs Orde, who was regardful to my fine noble ladies here ... The total eclipse of the sun will be most remarkable and interesting ... Please assist me to fulfil my desire according to your ability. I shall feel great obligation from you, your faithfully good friend, Mongkut.'*

As Siam lay directly in the path of the eclipse the King hoped to convince his subjects that, contrary to their belief, the eclipse would not be caused by the dragon Rahu making a meal of the sun and disgorging it only when frightened by beating of gongs and letting off fireworks, but could be predicted beforehand and explained by rather more rational methods.

A number of observers from Europe began to gather in the East for this event, including a French contingent which came directly to Siam. After calculations carried out by Mongkut himself, a wild and uninhabited spot about 140 miles South of Bangkok was selected for the viewing, and an invitation extended to all foreigners in that city, as well as the French expedition, to assemble there by 18th August. No trouble or expense was spared to ensure that all who came were treated with due respect and consideration for their every comfort. It was estimated that at least £20,000 from the privy purse was spent upon the enterprise. Jungle was cleared and a small township of temporary yet solid dwellings was constructed, covering about two miles. These included a shed with sliding roof, specially designed for rapid opening, to house the French contingent's telescopes.

Travelling overland (the Suez Canal not then being open) Monsieur Stephan, their leader, wrote: 'The King of Siam with all his court, part of his army and a

The compound of the Grand Palace during the reign of Rama V.

crowd of Europeans, arrived by sea on 8th August in twelve steamboats of the Royal Navy, while by land came troops of oxen, horses and fifty elephants.'

On August 16, the Governor of Singapore, Sir Harry Orde and Lady Orde, joined the party. But as August 16 was a Sunday and the Governor and his wife were devout Christians, they delayed disembarking till the following day, when they stepped ashore to an official welcome and a seventeen gun salute. Also present were two of Mongkut's sons, the Princes Chulalongkorn and Damrong, and a group of court astrologers, who could hardly be blamed if they concealed a certain lack of enthusiasm for a project which, if all went well, bid fair to supersede their own authority.

A pavilion hung with scarlet cloth and enclosed by a palisade housed the King with, next to him, the Prime Minister, the royal princes, the Governor of Singapore, the contingent from France, consular officials and European visitors, all accommodated with careful regard to precedent. Mongkut's hospitality was lavish for, in addition to native cooks, a French Chef presided over continental cuisine, wine was in copious supply, and not one but two brass bands played every evening.

The great and long-awaited day dawned bright and clear, but all hearts sank when by 10.22, when the first contact was due, clouds had gathered and completely obscured the sun. The French in particular, after many months of organisation and a journey of 10,000 miles, were utterly despondent at the apparent frustration of all their hopes. But as though by a miracle, only twenty minutes before the totality was due, the sky cleared, the sun appeared and was duly eclipsed at the exact moment calculated by Mongkut when, as Prince Damrong said, 'it became so dark, one could see many stars.'

Cannon fired, pipes and trumpets sounded and the King and his Prime Minster cried 'Hurrah! Hurrah!' in English, there being no such exclamation in Siamese. They were naturally both overjoyed by so splendid a vindication of their confidence in scientific calculation. A grand farewell party was given by the King that night, where the only guests who may have felt a trifle glum were possibly the court astronomers.

Most unhappily, Mongkut's triumphant return, delighted with the brilliant success of his progressive enterprise, ended in tragedy. For the exact line of totality where his pavilion was erected happened to be a low-lying malarial spot, and unfortunately it had occurred to no-one that it might be most unhealthy. Such was the case, and the King fell so gravely ill that very soon his life was despaired of, a fact which he accepted with dignity and resignation. Like the Buddha, he wished to die in full possession of his senses and, to prove to himself that this was so, he dictated a letter to the dignitaries of the Buddhist Council in Pali, spoke to his secretaries in English, and then took leave of the assembled princes and courtiers in Siamese regretting 'he could no longer serve his country'.

He would not allow his younger children to come near him, fearing they might distract him from willing relinquishment of the world and, having asked forgiveness for any pain and distress he may have caused by his hasty temper, he finally expired, aged 64, on his birthday, as the Buddha himself had done.

King Mongkut with his son, Prince Chulalongkorn, later King Chulalongkorn.

King Chulalongkorn.

Although it was his right, if he had so wished, to designate his heir as the two preceding Kings of the Chakri Dynasty had done, he chose not to do so, leaving this task to the Accession Council assembled for this purpose shortly after he had breathed his last. After lengthy deliberation, Chulalongkorn, Mongkut's eldest son, was elected. But because of his youth – he was only fifteen – the late King's Prime Minister, Sri Suriyawongse, was appointed Regent. This was most fortunate both for the young King and the country, for Suriyawongse, having worked closely with Mongkut, was fully aware of and in sympathy with his aims and ideals. Therefore, from the first, Chulalongkorn was encouraged to follow in his father's progressive footsteps.

As Chulalongkorn's mother, Queen Debsirindra, had died when he was nine, his great-aunt, Princess Lamom, described by Mrs Leonowens as 'a tranquil cheerful old soul', took her place and, together with other ladies of the Inside, instructed him in the elaborate court ceremonial and etiquette. His education had followed the usual lines except that, like his father, he studied English with a missionary and for a short time with Mrs Leonowens, so that he could read, write and speak it quite fluently.

The English Governess, generally rather sparing of praise, writes of him: 'For a Siamese, he was a handsome lad … figure symmetrical and compact. He was, moreover, modest and affectionate, eager to learn. He was attentive to his studies, serene and gentle, invariably affectionate to his old aunt and his younger brothers and, for the poor, ever sympathetic with a warm generous heart. He pursued his studies assiduously … with a resolution that gained strength as his mind gained ideas …' In person, Chulalongkorn resembled his father not at all, for his countenance was markedly open with a fine brow, a most engaging smile, and despite his lofty position, a charming simplicity of manner that endeared him to many, not only in his own country, but also abroad.

The Regent, although always present, had the great good sense to encourage Chulalongkorn to attend cabinet meetings, preside at religious ceremonies and give audiences from the first, so that, long before attaining his majority, he became well versed in the arts of government. He had also had the advantage of a grounding in diplomacy and state affairs by his father, who had freely admitted him into his confidence despite his extreme youth.

When he was eighteen, Chulalongkorn pressed the Regent to grant fulfilment of Mongkut's known wish that a return visit should be paid to Sir Harry Orde, Governor of Singapore, and the young Prince went there in 1871, following it by a trip to Java. Later that same year, he travelled to India, where he was well-received by the Viceroy, Lord Mayo, and returned home gratified by his reception in all three countries.

In 1873, when he was twenty, after only a token fifteen days in the priesthood, his coronation took place amidst scenes of great splendour. As was the custom, he himself placed the crown upon his head, thus signifying that no-one of superior or even equal rank existed worthy to perform this ceremony for the King. Robed and crowned, the Monarch addressed the prostrate throng from his throne: 'His Majesty has noticed that the great countries and powers in Asia where oppression existed, compelling inferiors to prostrate and worship their masters, have ceased these customs … They have done so to make manifest there shall be no more oppression. Those that have abolished these rigorous exactions have manifestly increased their prosperity … His Majesty therefore proposes to substitute, in place of crouching and crawling on all-fours, standing upright with a graceful bow of the head …'

At his words, all present rose to their feet and, drawing themselves erect before their sovereign for the first time, they made profound obeisance. As Prince Damrong wrote: 'It was indeed a most impressive and memorable sight.'

Aided by his Prime Minister, the young King, from the first, devoted himself energetically to further reforms, undertaken not only for their own sake but because he was convinced that his father had been right and that only by bringing Siam more into line with the modern world could he secure her continuing independence and freedom from further annexation and colonisation by the French or British. Nothing escaped his attention, from organising and enlarging the army, to improving postal and telegraph services, inaugurating railways, building palaces and laying out tree-lined boulevards bordered by cooling waterways in Bangkok.

'All children, from my own to the poorest, should have an equal chance of education', he announced when opening the Suan Khularb School, the first of many new secondary schools. He also determined that nobles and princes should be better instructed and founded a college for them in the palace itself.

Public health was not neglected and, in 1886, the first experimental hospital was opened under the supervision of an American doctor, Peter Cowan. But at first the hospital, though in full working order, was deficient in one respect – there were no patients! People still preferred their traditional remedies. In despair, Dr Cowan suggested filling the empty beds with beggars, whose sores and diseases he guaranteed to cure. But the beggars rejected the offer out of hand, claiming indignantly that a cure would deprive them of their livelihood. Eventually, members of the Hospital Committee were driven to order those of their servants who were ailing into the hospital and, when they emerged the better for treatment, general confidence was gained and there was soon a waiting list of patients.

In 1874 a Committee was convened to consider the abolition of slavery, when Chulalongkorn's opening address struck an unusual note for an all-powerful monarch; for he began: 'This is a task too great for one man. Please give me your advice, each one of you.' The word 'slave' or 'serf' conjures up a sad picture of inescapable bondage to the Western mind, yet, as Sir John Bowring, leader of the British Mission to Siam, noted in his diary: 'From what I have seen, I would be inclined to say that slaves are better treated here than servants in England; this is proved by the fact that whenever they are emancipated, they always sell themselves again.'

Chulalongkorn's first official consort was Princess Sunanda, the eldest of three sisters, the two younger being the Princesses Sawang Vadhana and Saowabha Pongsri, daughters of his father, King Mongkut, though by a different mother, thus making them his half-sisters. Such consanguineous marriages, though forbidden in the country as a whole, were still customary amongst royalty, with the object of maintaining purity of stock and blood for the succession.

Sunanda, his young wife, however, died in particularly tragic circumstances for, when she was only twenty-one and pregnant, she was drowned when the boat carrying her up river to the Royal Palace at Bang Pa-in, capsized. As the penalty for touching any part of the body of a royal personage was death, no-one dared stretch out a hand to save her.

Her death was deeply mourned by her bereaved young husband, but in due time he raised both her sisters to be Queens, though eventually it was the youngest Saowabha, who became Supreme Queen and favourite wife. It was she, and she alone of all the Queens and ladies of the Inside, whose rooms in the palace adjoined those of the King, and who was received even when unaccompanied by him, by the playing of the National Anthem. Saowabha bore him nine children, four of whom died in infancy, the remaining five sons being Vajiravudh, Chakrabongse, Asdang, Chutadhuj and Prajadhipok – Vajiravudh becoming Heir-Apparent in 1895 after the death of Queen Sawang's son, Crown Prince Maha Vajirunhis.

An innovation introduced by Chulalongkorn was to create some of his sons titular princes of cities or towns along the lines of the English system, thus Vajiravudh became Prince of Dwaravati (previously Ayudhaya, the old capital of Siam), and Chakrabongse, Prince of Bisnulok (a city known for a most noble and beautiful Buddha image, Phra Jinaraja). Both princes, like all Siamese, also had nicknames: Vajiravudh was 'Toe', meaning large, and Chakrabongse, 'Lek', meaning small.

Dr Malcolm Smith, who came to Bangkok in 1902, and practised among the European community for five years, also later attended the royal family, and while putting at their disposal the skills of modern medicine, judging by his delightful book, *A Physician at the Court of Siam*, was immensely taken with the charm of the country, its people, and the beauty of its religion, architecture and age-old customs. As Dr Smith possessed the immense advantage of speaking fluent Siamese, his account of daily visits to Queen Saowabha provide an affectionate yet clear-sighted character study of this remarkable woman.

He describes her as 'well-proportioned with delicately shaped hands and feet', and continues; 'the years dealt lightly with her, she retained her youthful figure, her face remaining almost unlined and her hair thick and black. She paid great attention to her appearance and spent a long time at her toilet every day'. She washed and bathed in scented water made from freshly cut flowers and aromatic herbs. After her clothes were washed, they were placed in a large earthenware jar, in the lid of which was coiled a long thin candle scented with musk and,

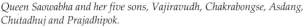

Queen Saowabha and her five sons, Vajiravudh, Chakrabongse, Asdang,
Chutadhuj and Prajadhipok.

Queen Saowabha.

the jar being closed, the candle was lit so that its aromatic smoke perfumed all her garments.

He took especial delight in her conversation, which was wide-ranging and included an exact knowledge of European monarchy about whom she spoke as though they were her relations. She talked well although she had received no formal education; her school had been her own experience and her shrewd and observant mind had made full use of it.

Dr Smith also notes that the cropped hair of Siamese women and teeth blackened by chewing betel-nut and polished with additional black pigment till they shone, rendered Siamese women in his day considerably less attractive to Western eyes than they would otherwise have been. But attractive they certainly were, for as Dr Smith remarks: 'Sexual indulgence by the Siamese is carried to a degree that to most Europeans is incredible. Between the ages of eighteen and forty, it is the over-mastering passion of their lives.'

One might well have thought that with so many queens and the Inside brimming with willing young creatures, whom a word from the King would bring to his bed, that no one woman in particular would be cherished above all others. But in addition to her titles and public position, there are many more charming and intimate mementoes of Chulalongkorn's special and abiding love for Saowabha, such as joint portraits and many ornaments and pieces of jewellery with entwined initials.

To quote Malcolm Smith again: 'Chakrabongse was always first favourite both with his Father and Mother. Much was expected of him, for he was regarded as the ablest as well as the handsomest of all the sons. With his dictatorial ways, his determination and his abounding energy, he was to me the only chip off the old block in the family. In complexion he was unusually pale, and his features had lit-

King Chulalongkorn and Prince Chakrabongse.

Seated from left: Crown Prince Maha Vajirunhis, the Tsarevitch, King Chulalongkorn. Taken at Bang Pa-In Summer Palace.

tle of the Siamese type of countenance …'. This last point would seem to be wishful thinking on Smith's part as in fact the prince had a dark complexion occasioned by frequent exposure to the sun during army duties.

In 1893 the Tsarevitch – the future Tsar Nicholas II – who had been visiting India, arrived in Bangkok. Although no two men could have been less alike than the diffident future Emperor and the genial Chulalongkorn, perhaps partly because they were so dissimilar, a mutual liking sprang up between them which later ripened into a firm friendship .

The Tsarevitch was gratified by his welcome and the charm and beauty of Saranrom Palace with its wonderfully attentive servants put at the disposal of him and his suite. He marvelled especially at the curtains hung at his windows, made of multi-coloured freshly gathered flowers, sewn together with astonishing skill and renewed daily during his stay.

Despite a life of intense and demanding activity, Chulalongkorn also found time for agreeable diversions such as a picnic – employing the English word – though the event had little in common with the simple meal in the open air or even the far grander aristocratic picnic, waited on by flunkies in England. For one thing, a picnic in Siam might last several weeks, when three or four thousand people set out in six hundred boats, each rowed by a dozen men standing to their oars like gondoliers. At nightfall, the party would land to be housed in pavilions, built to last but a day, some beautified by the entrancing curtains composed of flowers that had so impressed the Tsarevitch.

Sometimes a smaller party – a mere four or five hundred strong – would cruise in the royal yacht down the Gulf of Siam. Canvas screens on each deck divided the Outside from the Inside, but once ashore on the tiny uninhabited island of the Gulf, the ladies of the Inside enjoyed perfect freedom, roaming in the woodlands and bathing with their children in the pellucid waters of the little coves.

There were also less highly organised escapades when the King, like a prince from the Arabian Nights, – stories which he loved and some of which he translated – would move freely among his subjects in disguise, landing with a band of close friends from small paddle-boats in remote villages where they might attend a peasant's wedding or dine unrecognised at his table. These expeditions pleased Chulalongkorn mightily. So much so that in about 1902, on the further side of a canal called the Jade Basin, flanking the most delightful of his many palaces, Vimanmek, he constructed Ruan Ton. This was a group of modest traditional houses – a latter-day Petit Trianon – where, after leaving the palace dressed as usual, the King could assume a commoner's clothes, and move about his realm as an ordinary man. Sometimes the friends he made on these occasions were invited to a delicious meal cooked by their Sovereign, the dish-washing being expertly performed afterwards by the highest ranking nobility. For although regarded as a divinity and waited on hand and foot, Chulalongkorn was an expert cook and even wrote a cookery book!

He also found opportunity to see much of his many children, who often sat beside him at meal times or on the steps of his throne, though here they had to bear in mind, they might have to answer sudden searching questions about their studies which, if unsatisfactory, meant disgrace and demotion to a lower step.

Moreover, despite the enormous weight of state affairs and the many other matters demanding his constant attention, those of his sons being educated abroad received regular letters from him, in one of which he advised: 'The notion

Dusit Palace and its surroundings.

that you have been princes and can be comfortable in life without doing useful work is one which does not place you above the lower animals which come into life, eat and die!'

In 1897 accompanied by the Heir-Apparent Vajiravudh, Chulalongkorn set out in his yacht 'Maha Chakri' on his first grand tour of Europe, visiting crowned heads and heads of state in France, Italy, Austria, Belgium, Germany, Russia and England, where he stayed in Buckingham Palace and was entertained by the Prince of Wales, as Queen Victoria was resting at Windsor before the fatigue of her forthcoming Diamond Jubilee.

During his absence, Queen Saowabha had been proclaimed Regent, and as he wrote to Chakrabongse: 'Mother is upset at my departure and anxious over her heavy duties'.

The whole tour was an immense success, not least because Chulalongkorn was one of the first monarchs from South-East Asia with a fluent command of English, which enabled him to converse with most of his fellow monarchs without an interpreter but, in addition, his personality weighed heavily in his favour. Although an impressive figure on ceremonial occasions, he possessed an easy informality, rare indeed in those days, and his relaxed engaging expression in many of his portraits and photographs gives the impression of so lively and vital a personality that, over the distance of almost a century, one feels a warm admiration and affection for him.

*King Chulalongkorn in Russia, 1896.
Front row (left to right): HIH Grand
Duchess Olga Alexandrovna of Russia
(sister of Emperor Nicholas II). His
Majesty King Chulalongkorn, Her
Imperial Majesty Dowager Empress
Marie Feodorovna of Russia, His
Imperial Majesty Emperor Nicholas II
of Russia and HRH Crown Prince
Vajiravudh (later His Majesty King
Vajiravudh). Back row: HRH Prince
Svasti Sobhon (half-brother of King
Chulalongkorn), Count Muravieff
(Russian Minister of Foreign Affairs),
HRH Prince Jayanta Mongol (half-
brother of King Chulalongkorn) and
HRH Prince Chirapravati Voradej,
Prince of Nakorn Jaisri (son of King
Chulalongkorn).*

While undoubtedly stimulated and interested in such an extensive introduction to the Western world, the King, because of his already existing cordial relations with Tsar Nicholas, was particularly pleased to arrive in St Petersburg. Even the customary formal photograph taken with the Emperor and Empress, one of their daughters, Grand Duchess Olga, the Empress's Uncle, Prince Hans of Schleswig-Holstein-Sonderburg-Glucksburg, Prince Vajiravudh and two ADC's reflects his evident pleasure. Seated between the Empress and the Grand Duchess in that summer garden, he is smiling, holding negligently in one hand a rose he has picked, while his other arm is linked in an easy-going fashion through that of the Grand Duchess, looking touchingly *'jeune fille'* and timid in her high-necked white muslin.

This visit turned out to be fateful for Chulalongkorn's son, Chakrabongse, for it was then that the Emperor put forward the proposal that, should Chulalongkorn agree, he would be happy to receive one of his sons at the Imperial Court and make himself entirely responsible for his future education. The Tsar's offer must have been seen as a great opportunity by Chulalongkorn for, although he had many sons to choose from, his choice fell unerringly on his favourite Chakrabongse, as being likely to profit most from it and, in so doing, bring honour to his father and his country.

King Chulalongkorn and Prince Chakrabongse.

*Prince Chakrabongse in full dress
Hussar Uniform.*

II

From Bangkok to St Petersburg

*I*n 1896, the year before his father's tour of Europe and Imperial Russia, Chakrabongse had already been settled in England in the house of a Dr Yarr near Camberley, while his brother Crown Prince Vajiravudh was staying with a Colonel Hume, who was coaching him for entry into Sandhurst.

Chakrabongse was there to pursue his studies and perfect his English. He had with him his attaché, Nok Young, and a friend of his own age, Nai Poum Sakara. Poum was not a noble or a prince, but a brilliant student and winner of the King's Scholarship. He had been chosen to accompany Chakrabongse not only for companionship but because the astute Chulalongkorn considered that this clever hard-working boy would act as a spur and encouragement to the scholastic endeavours of his son.

Hardly had the two young boys begun to accustom themselves to life in so different an environment from that of their upbringing, when they heard from the king that at the Russian Emperor's invitation, they were eventually to proceed to St Petersburg where they would both become members of the elite Corps des Pages, and that, more immediately, steps would be taken to provide them with a Russian teacher.

Slight, small of stature, with fine dark eyes and a rather deprecating shy expression, Prince Chakrabongse must have been greatly cheered that his father

Phraya Mahibal, Prince Chakrabongse and Nai Poum.

had ordained that Poum, not unlike him in appearance and about the same age, was to accompany him from one already strange environment in England to the unimaginable country of Imperial Russia. For both the boys it was a great adventure, more so for Poum, unaccustomed as he was to the ceremonial of court life and etiquette that had surrounded Chakrabongse from birth.

Both of them – after all they were only thirteen years old – must have found the prospect of adding Russian to their already heavy programme of studies, already in a foreign language, rather daunting, and therefore awaited with some apprehension the arrival of Mr Ardachef, a recently-graduated Russian philologist. Unhappily, he proved a great disappointment as he devoted every second of their lessons to a relentless grounding in Russian grammar, and ignored completely their need to acquire conversational vocabulary. In addition, he could not have been said to have a vocation for teaching, as he was both impatient and bad-tempered. Fortunately, after three months, he was replaced by a Mr Petrof, with whom they made better progress.

In May 1898, they left for Russia via Paris, where they were joined by the Siamese Minister to Russia, Phraya Suriya, Phraya Mahibal, their tutor, and his wife. Sad to say, no record remains of their long journey to St Petersburg where they were welcomed by a Court Minister, and driven to the vast Winter Palace. There a magnificent apartment, reserved for imperial guests, had been placed at their disposal and must indeed have seemed a change from Camberley!

Next day, Chakrabongse and Poum were taken to pay their respects to the Tsar at his summer residence, Peterhof, a superb eighteenth century edifice some thirty miles outside St. Petersburg, surrounded by an enormous park, where a thousand shimmering fountains played, and the wide Samson Canal linked the palace with the Baltic Sea.

Warmly greeted by their Imperial host, the newcomers, after a further fortnight in St Petersburg were not sorry to leave their rather over-impressive quarters to spend the summer in a charming villa – the Villa Krassovskova – near Peterhof. Here they learned that the Emperor intended they should both be entered in the Corps des Pages forthwith, and summer uniforms without epaulettes were immediately provided for them. For the present, however, they were to enjoy themselves in the fine sunny weather and long nights, the famous 'White Nights', when the sun does not set till eleven or twelve at night and twilight continues until two or three in the morning.

They were given bicycles on which they ran races and swooped and zig-zagged along the well-raked paths of the park. There was riding, drives in the imperial carriages and, once a week, an evening concert where the court orchestra in scarlet tunics, a livery dating from the eighteenth century, played superbly in the open air. Some listeners would saunter in attentive silence, while ladies-in-waiting, old Generals and Aides-de-Camp with gold 'aiguillettes' remained seated in their carriages, their coachmen and footmen in scarlet, their collars embroidered with the imperial eagle. The two Siamese also had the company of their future companions in the Corps des Pages who, from their Summer Camp

Poum, Deguy, their personal tutor, another teacher and Prince Chakrabongse at the Corps des Pages.

Prince Chakrabongse whilst studying in the military academy.

nearby, strolled over to their villa and with much chatter and laughter and many questions encouraged them to talk in their still-halting Russian. Apart from a nasty riding accident when Chakrabongse's horse bolted, causing him to fall on his head and suffer severe concussion, time passed happily and too quickly.

In the last week of August, at the end of the short Russian summer, Chakrabongse and Poum returned to St Petersburg where, instead of boarding with the Corps des Pages in a building erected by Paul I for the Knights of Malta (because of this, the Pages bore the insignia of the Maltese Cross), they had been allotted more 'simple' accommodation in the Winter Palace: 'a roomy and very comfortable apartment on the Commandant's Entrance, with windows looking over the immense square – as large as the Place de la Concorde.' A staff of court servants and their own chef were also provided, and Captain Krulof of the Emperor's Lancers, was appointed their 'Gouverneur', responsible for their welfare.

Pages as a rule were recruited from sons of the nobility, high-ranking army officers, prominent statesmen and foreign royalty. A rigorous system of intensive education was designed to fit them eventually for entrance into the regiments of the Imperial Guard, for which a final examination result of at least nine points out of twelve was essential. Failing this, demotion to a regiment of the regular army for three years followed, before graduation to the Guards. At the same time, however, it was generally understood, though nowhere explicitly stated, that no student - high marks or not- could aspire to the Guards without sufficient means to maintain an extravagant lifestyle in this, the most elegant branch of the Service.

Phraya Mahibal, the Siamese minister in St Petersburg and his wife.

Prince Chakrabongse in Corps des Pages uniform.

At the school there were seven ordinary classes equivalent to a normal lycée curriculum, except for the inclusion of drill in addition to two classes devoted to Military Science. As Chakrabongse was not only a protégé of the Tsar, but himself a royal personage, a special staff of teachers had been recruited to give him and Poum the best tuition available. This was a vital necessity as, although placed in a class of their own age - fifteen - he and Poum had to catch up with the five years of tuition they had missed, in addition to studying in a formidable foreign language which put them under intense pressure from the first.

They rose at seven; mathematics at eight; lunch at eleven with Captain Krulof and conversation with him and their Russian language teacher. From twelve to two - more lessons. From two till four, drilling and gymnastics at the Corps des Pages. At four, back to the Winter Palace to study until five, then dinner with more Russian conversation. More work from six till nine, unless Captain Krulof had arranged an outing to the theatre, opera or occasionally the circus. Music, being a social accomplishment, was not really taken seriously. Nevertheless, piano, violin and balalaika were taught, Chakrabongse showing a strong preference for the balalaika. Their music professor was an enthusiast and managed to form a trio; Poum on the violin, Chakrabongse at the piano, and himself wielding the concertina.

Drawing took place in the evening, and every Sunday morning there were dancing lessons in the enormous salon of the Winter Palace, taught by no less a personage than the Regisseur of the Imperial Ballet himself. He also must have been an enthusiast, for he offered no scaled-down conventional ballroom waltzes and polka to his oriental pupils, but an ambitious repertoire that included the

The members of the 10 August 1902 Promotion (Graduating Class) of the Corps of Pages – Krasnoe Selo, May 1902. Forty graduated in 1902. There were two foreigners – HRH Prince Chakrabongse of Siam and his companion Nai-Poum, one Prince, three Counts, two Barons, twelve bore names of German or Swedish origin, twenty were not the first members of their families to graduate from the Corps.

polonaise, Pas-de-Quatre, Pas de Patineurs, Mazurka, Quadrille, Lancers, Chaconne, the Krakowiak, and an assortment of other picturesque Russian and Hungarian dances.

For the first year, Poum was obliged to take the lady's part, and an amusing picture is conjured up of the two of them whirling round the vast empty ball-room, performing these exotic steps! Later, doubtless to Poum's relief, lessons were held at the legation, where the daughters of the Brazilian and Spanish Ministers came to partner them.

Riding was at the Imperial Manège or at the Corps des Pages. On one Sunday a month in the winter, they would drive thirty versts (1.07 km) in a troika with Captain Krulof and others to hunt hare, partridge and quail, but shooting as a sport gave neither Chakrabongse nor Poum much enjoyment. This was probably because, although receiving a military education, as Buddhists they were averse to taking life.

After passing examinations in May 1899, Chakrabongse accompanied by Phraya Mahibal returned to Siam, mainly so that Queen Saowabha could see with her own anxious maternal eyes that her favourite son had completely recovered from his riding accident. Poum remained in Russia, where he spent the summer in the home of Captain Krulof.

As his father wished him to visit the Sultan Abdul Hamid and present him with the Order of the Royal House of Chakri, Chakrabongse returned to St Petersburg via Constantinople. Well-received, he would have more enjoyed his visit had he not been disconcerted by the fact that anything he saw, for which he expressed polite admiration, was promptly pressed on him as a gift. In this manner he acquired a number of magnificent rugs and carpets, and a fine Arab horse. No record remains as to how he conveyed this probably spirited steed to Russia. Another memento of his stay was the award of the highest Turkish Order, the Osmanieh, with a special diamond-studded star. This signal honour was paid him because, as the Sultan wrote to Chulalongkorn, 'I was deeply impressed by your serious-minded son, who, when conducted through my harem, did not even glance at its occupants!'

In spring 1900, after passing their examinations creditably, both Chakrabongse and Poum went to Paris, where the Great Exhibition drew thousands to the capital. Afterwards they went to Taplow near Henley-on-Thames, where the Crown Prince now lived. Punting and rowing on the river, riding and driving Vajiravudh's cars along the green English lanes, they must have revelled in their relaxation from the intense discipline of the Corps des Pages.

After a hard winter's work, their spring exam results were excellent. In fact, as they and two other pupils gained the highest marks, they became eligible for a special award – appointment to the '*Pages de la Chambre*', or pages-in-waiting to the Emperor and Empress. Chakrabongse was appointed to the Dowager Empress, Marie Feodorovna, and Poum to the Empress Alexandra. But at Chakrabongse's wish, they changed places, a change that must have been accomplished with considerable tact so as not to have offended the two august ladies. Thus arranged, it was Chakrabongse who attended on the Empress at all court functions, who carried her train and stood behind her chair at banquets.

Formerly it would also have been required of him to place each course of the menu before her, but this usage had been abandoned due to an unfortunate incident in the past, when a page, desperate at having spilled soup down her corsage, rushed at her with a napkin and scrubbed at her bosom with such embarrassing zeal that the Emperor was compelled to order him to desist.

In attendance at the presentation of ambassadors and notables, at gala dinners, soirées and balls, there were also lengthy religious celebrations of imperial birth and name-days, and four-hour Easter services in the Chapel of the Winter Palace. This, despite its dramatic ritual and glorious singing, must have seemed long to the five pages required to bear the enormously heavy trains of the Emperor, Empress and Empress-Dowager. There was, it is true, an interval in the proceedings though this was hardly a relaxation involving, as it did, the compression of the three royal personages, three trains and five pages into a tiny anteroom. And Chakrabongse gives an amusing insight into how their deportment and train-bearing was rehearsed: 'Lazerev was chosen to represent the Tsarina, wearing a towel as a veil, a uniform jacket as a cloak, and a blanket for the train – an extremely odd ensemble – and very strange he looked!'

On the Feast of St George, came Chakrabongse's first Court duty. 'Personal Pages in full uniform reported to the school at 8.15 in the morning, and proceeded to the Winter Palace to await Her Majesty and the Grand Duchesses. We bowed, took up their trains as had been assigned to us, and followed them through to the Gold Drawing-Room. There we went round and round in circles becoming quite giddy as the Tsarina keep moving to greet her ladies-in-waiting, who were scattered all over the room. She remarked to me, laughingly, "We must give you some practice!"'

Later in this lengthy ceremony, when the Emperor and Empress walked side by side, the Pages had considerable difficulty in manoeuvring themselves, the Imperial couple and their trains, through a series of doorways in one of which the Empress's train-lining was caught and torn, but happily was released before the august lady was pulled over backwards.

'By 5.30 that afternoon, we were all exhausted and famished with hunger! When in the service of the Court, it's best to forget completely about being a soldier and concentrate one's mind only on Court etiquette', he concludes sagely.

Despite many attendances of this kind in his capacity as *'Page de la Chambre'* and the arduous military studies and exercises in which he was so remarkably successful, Chakrabongse still found time for a full social life as well. He records enjoyment of numerous evening parties quite outside Court circles, where there were dancing or musical soirées to hear a quartet or a singer. 'The pieces by Arensky were very fine', he writes of one such occasion, 'and one aria in particular, with words by Lermontov - so moving and poetic - was quite wonderful.'

Frequent visits to the theatre to see Shakespeare or Molière, as well as Russian writers and opera, crowded his leisure hours with pleasure. He also enjoyed reading in several different languages and exclaims: 'I've just finished Turgenev's *A Nest of Gentlefolk* – what a superb novel!' He also mentions 'a boring afternoon when I felt bad-tempered as I had nothing to do, but then took up *Idle Thoughts of an Idle Fellow* by Jerome K. Jerome, which was so entertaining and funny that I quite recovered my good humour!'

Chakrabongse was particularly keen on the ballet as he was greatly intrigued by the famous ballerina Mathilde Kchessinskaya, who with Olga Preobrajenskaya, as Karsavina writes in *Theatre Street*, were 'idols of the Imperial Ballet School'.

Kchessinskaya, the mistress of the Tsar before his marriage, subsequently enjoyed liaisons with more than one Grand Duke, and eventually married Grand Duke Andrei Vladimirovitch. Karsavina describes her as 'small, pretty and vivacious, pleasure-loving and of a joyful nature, and the round of parties and late hours never impaired her looks or her temper. She had not only marvellous vitality, but enormous will-power, and within a month preceding an appearance, ceased to receive, trained for hours, was in bed by ten, kept to a frugal diet and would not drink even water for a whole day before dancing.'

Her romantic liaisons and her pre-performance routine were clearly reasons why she sometimes became inaccessible and did not answer Chakrabongse's notes or invite him to see her as often as he would have wished. 'Nothing is heard from K', he records disconsolately, 'though I've written and sent her a present for the New Year'. But the next day, she invited him to see her, 'and seemed really sorry for upsetting me, and made me promise to go and see her dance next Sunday'. This he did but 'unfortunately the Grand-Duke Serge (the Tsar's Uncle) was in the audience, and one was made aware of his presence by K's manner. She never bowed openly to me and only raised her eyes to mine, while bowing to the general public. The idea of his being jealous of me is simply ridiculous! But I admit she occupies a great place in my mind – such a pretty delightful woman, she cheers me up wonderfully!'

In early January 1901, Chakrabongse was cheered by the arrival of his full brother, the Heir-Apparent, Crown Prince Vajiravudh, his ADC, Siddhi, and one of their numerous half-brothers, Prince Yugala, on a short visit. Despite its brevity, the three of them organised a theatrical evening, the prime mover in this enterprise more than probably being the Crown Prince as, later on, when he became King, he not only often performed in plays at one or other of the royal palaces in Bangkok, but wrote many of them himself. As all three spoke English fluently, they chose to appear in two acts of Sheridan's *The Rivals* and one act of *My Friend Jarlet* (by Arnold Galsworthy and E B Norman – Vajiravudh later translated this into Thai under the name *Mit Thae* and subsequently *Puan Tai*). In the latter, Chakrabongse played a woman, Marie (a part acted by Vajiravudh in a previous performance), and was pleased that 'everyone found me very pretty and I made a good impression, except when I have to faint – I really don't know how to do it.'

Next day however, when he took Vajiravudh to see Kchessinskaya, 'who was in the gayest mood – awfully nice and cheery' and told her of his swooning difficulties, 'she promptly got up and showed me how it was done. She tried again and again to persuade Vajiravudh to stay longer in St Petersburg, raising her hands imploringly as we left, begging him not to go so soon. She also whispered to me, "Don't forget me!" On the whole, she's a good little thing and awfully fit to cheer one up', he added rather condescendingly.

After lunch on 6th January, they rehearsed *My Friend Jarlet*, which 'went off very badly, as we all laughed the whole time, Siddhi making funny faces and talking rot at inopportune moments. I have really not laughed so much for years'. But the dress rehearsal went better, though the seamstress was convulsed with merriment when Chakrabongse assumed his womanly guise and make-up.

Next evening, 'We had the acting. Oh, how nervous we all were while waiting to begin. However, as soon as I appeared and was greeted with applause it braced me up directly. In *The Rivals*, Vajiravudh was successful as Sir Anthony Absolute and, at the end, there was handclapping, cries of "bravo", and I was presented with some flowers. After it was over we joined the guests for supper. I received many congratulations and was told my fainting was good, as well. Because I had a fine teacher!', he records, and sent the flowers he was given to Kchessinskaya 'who said she was deeply touched'.

On 9th January 1901, Vajiravudh and party left for London on the next stage of their tour, and the day after Chakrabongse writes: 'I observe today as a day of rest, as I'm tired out after all the excitement for, while Vajiravudh was here, even when we went early to bed and not to a party, theatre or ballet, there was no end to what we had to talk about and we chatted half the night.'

*Chakrabongse in female dress for the
role of Marie in 'My Friend Jarlet'.*

The next afternoon, fully recovered, he went to *The Sleeping Beauty* at the Marinsky. 'K danced awfully well and was so pretty in the red dress'. The Grand Duke was obviously not present for Chakrabongse notes happily that 'she bowed to me many times'. But soon, alas, he received bad news from Bangkok. Phraya Suriya 'has written to Father about my friendship with K to prove I need stricter supervision and less freedom and independence. I'm sorry. Father, and Mother especially, will be troubled in vain. Phraya Suriya seems out to ruin me'. Fortunately no more is heard of this, but a little later he noted: 'K behaves in the most uncommon manner. Her complete silence continues. Really I suppose I should end our acquaintance as it's become known in Bangkok. It's extraordinary how people think that if one finds a woman charming and attractive, one is necessarily having an affair with her'. However, in view of the disclosures by the sanctimonious Phraya Suriya, it would not be surprising if it had not been tactfully hinted to the ballerina that the relationship should not be encouraged.

On 19th January, more tidings of a frivolous nature came about Crown Prince Vajiravudh in the form of 'awful news from England'. The prince while apparently seeing off a certain Mabel Gilman at Euston Station, was persuaded to travel as far as Rugby with her, and Siddhi was despatched to the booking-office to check that the train really did stop at Rugby and buy him a ticket if it did. Mabel and Vajiravudh awaiting his return, sat chatting in the carriage, when to their horror, the train moved off and, far from stopping at Rugby, turned out to be an express that carried them all the way to Liverpool! Chakrabongse comments, 'in this manner Vajiravudh went to Liverpool under unfortunate circumstances, and the incident is most regrettable because, if it becomes known, our enemies will make a capital story out of it'. He obviously feared that, like his interest in Kchessinskaya, the news would be carried even further than Liverpool – all the way to Bangkok in fact!

There were several houses where he and Poum were able to drop in casually – at Prince Constantine of Oldenburg, Prince Yourievsky, son of Alexander II by his morganatic wife, Princess Yourievsky, and above all at the home of Madame Chrapovitzkaya, where they were received as dear friends. This lady, the wealthy widow of a Hussar officer, was, from her portrait, a most delightful woman, utterly feminine with that elusive Russian grace and charm that casts a spell like music. 'In her apartment in the Machavaya Ulitsa, there were many rooms, fifteen servants and twenty-three birds.' Here, often jaded from overwork and the sometimes stifling etiquette of court life, the two young men met a lively society of artisits, writers, actors and singers, and young people of their own age who gathered at her hospitable table to enjoy themselves.

In March, Chakrabongse learned of the engagement of the Tsar's sister, Grand Duchess Olga, to Prince Peter Alexandrovitch of Oldenburg, news to which he reacted with surprising emotion. 'I must say I'm sorry for poor Olga, I don't think she's got much of a fiancé. Of course, it's her mother, the Empress-Dowager, who has arranged the marriage to keep Olga here by her side.' And next day, he added: 'Olga's engagement still troubles me – I hardly know why as I have no business to feel anything about it whatsoever. But I hate to hear of anyone concluding a *mariage de conveniance* and therefore feel much sympathy for her.' This sympathy, obviously prompted by strong personal feelings, reveals an attitude which is of interest in view of later events.

Chakrabongse's appearances at official ceremonies, and even at private luncheons *en famille* with the Tsar and Tsarina, were occasions when he had continually to recollect his position as a Prince and representative of his country, and there is ample evidence in his diaries that the obligation was accepted dutifully. But in more than one entry, as in his remarks about Grand Duchess Olga, a rebellious note is sounded: 'It's the worst of being a Prince – one is put under all sort of restraints and one can never act on impulse – everything one does and says is taken note of, and perhaps reaches Bangkok to cause trouble there!'

At the same time he also noted changing political events. On 22nd January he wrote: 'Something extraordinary has happened: the Queen of England is dead – she has reigned for so long, it's almost unbelievable – a great loss for her country and the world.' While later in March of the same year, he noted: 'Along the Nevsky there was great excitement as students had announced a day of disturbance and many people went there on purpose to see it. But we were told to take a roundabout route to the Manège and avoid the Nevsky. As far as I know, the students only walked about shouting, but they were charged by the troops, and I heard a Cossack was killed and an officer wounded, and the uproar continued all that day and late into the night. The Minister of Public Instruction, shot by a student in his office, has since died and his funeral is tomorrow. More disturbances are expected.'

The Socialist Revolutionary Party had been formed in 1901 – the combat section of which, under the young scientist called Gershuni, was entirely devoted to terrorism. Strikes, sporadic rioting, imprisonment without trial, exile to Siberia and summary executions, all added inexorably to the long account that would be rendered and paid off in tragic reckoning. But, for the present, the aristocratic ruling classes, despite occasional foreboding, found it expedient to ignore such events, as though they were happening in another world – a kind of underworld – beneath the surface where they elegantly disported themselves.

In May 1901, their last year as pages, he and Poum were again in camp, this time at Krasnoye Selo, where three weeks were spent in training and reconnoitring without instruments, studying military fieldcraft, gauging distances across open terrain and the strategy of troop placements.

In September, Chakrabongse came first in the final examinations. His name was therefore inscribed on the marble panel honouring pages past and present who had attained similar distinction. As an added honour, his mark of 11.75 was so high that it was a record in the history of the Corps. Poum came a good second with marks of 11.50. These results are quite astonishing when one remembers that Chakrabongse and Poum, on arrival in St Petersburg in 1898, had not only to cope with a full programme of studies and activities, but to make up on the five years of tuition they had missed. Moreover, they had to sit all their examinations in competition with native-born pages, in a foreign language as difficult as Russian.

Their last appearance as pages was at a great review to honour President Loubet of France, when they wore their uniforms of *Pages de la Chambre*, but with the addition of gold chevrons on the coat and sleeve, and a sword. That winter there were many royal visitors to St Petersburg, including King Victor Emanuel and Queen Elena of Italy, Ferdinand I of Bulgaria; but the most exotic personality was the Emir of Bokhara, whose impassive stance with one hand on his sword and the other holding a bouquet, in the face of every kind of entertainment, was such that he caused a considerable stir one evening merely by changing sword and bouquet from one hand to another!

The Pages were in attendance at all the various functions connected with these visits, then proceeded in June and July to manoeuvres at Tsarskoye Selo, and afterwards at Krasnoye Selo. During this period, so that 'they might live in comfort and quiet', Chakrabongse 'ordered a two storey cottage with stabling for six or eight horses, which was subsequently presented to the Regiment.' This 'order' with its airy suggestion of magical wand-waving, as though the cottage arose fully-furnished from the ground for a mere two months stay, would have naturally seemed nothing out of the way to Chakrabongse, or indeed to any aristocrat or royalty of those times.

After the manoeuvres, the long-awaited day arrived when, after certain formalities had been completed, they could expect to join the Hussars of the Imperial Guard. After the years of arduous training and examinations, and the candidate's announcement that he wished to join, practical matters would be looked into such as the status of his family, financial independence and so on. But above all, it was his character that was of prime importance, great stress being laid on modesty and tact 'for an officer of the Guards was expected to act nobly on all occasions'.

On the day of their promotion as sub-lieutenants – 2nd August 1902 – Chakrabongse and Poum, in full uniform, called formally on the thirty officers of the Hussars and also on Commandants of the Regiment, including the Tsar's brother, the Grand Duke Michael.

That evening, as was customary, a dinner was given at Ernest's, a well-known restaurant on one of the group of islands in the Neva river. This must undoubtedly have gone on all night, for it was not only held to reward the years of stern endeavour, but to celebrate the first appearance of the promoted Pages in a public restaurant, locales which had been out-of-bounds while in the Corps. Each was presented with the traditional steel, gold-lined ring engraved with the Page's name and date, and the words 'One of Forty' (there being forty members in their class). In addition, they also received a golden fob bearing the Maltese Cross in white enamel.

In the late summer of this same year, Chakrabongse and Poum left for England, where they joined Crown Prince Vajiravudh and, together with him, his tutor, aide-de-camp, and secretary, they sailed for the USA, where the New World must indeed have seemed new to them, fresh as they were from the pomp and ritual discipline of their life in Russia.

Arriving in New York, they stayed at the Waldorf Astoria, and were conducted by an official of the State Department on a round of sight-seeing and formal receptions, including a visit to the White House where they met President Theodore Roosevelt. Somewhere along the line of this rather conventional formal

Prince Chakrabongse and Poum in their Hussar uniform.

trip, Poum learned to dance the cakewalk, and they arrived back in St Petersburg after a stormy voyage in early November.

Once accepted in the Hussars, Chakrabongse and Poum savoured what was to be the final flowering of an elite and stylish military tradition. Founded by Catherine the Great in 1775, the Hussars played a brilliant part in the field, notably in the Napoleonic wars but, in time of peace, their duties apart, 'they led an elegant and joyful life'. Originally their uniform was a short green dolman and fur-covered shako, but this had been changed to blue on service, while dress uniform was either bright scarlet with gold frogging, or white – both trimmed with rich dark fur – and rightly described as 'the most showy and splendid in the Imperial Army'.

Their banquets and festivals were famous. 'Nothing was too good for them and expense was no consideration. Not only special carriages, but special trains were ordered for their guests, and the musical performers who enlivened their celebrations were of the same high quality – the best obtainable – as the catering and the cellar.'

Thus, not only their regular military obligations, but their social life as well demanded considerable stamina. On the regiment's fête day, for instance, the menu of the banquet set before them was as follows:

M E N U

'Zakuska' (hors d'œuvres)	*Vodka*
Soup	*Madeira*
Fish	*White Wine*
Roast Meat	*Red Wine*
Chicken and Salad	*Champagne*
Asparagus	
Entremets	*More Champagne*
Dessert	*Still more Champagne*
Coffee	
Liqueurs	*everything existing*

Later, between two and three in the morning, a light supper to assuage possible pangs of hunger was served:

    Soupe a l'oignon
    Quails and Partridge   Vodka
    Coffee and Liqueurs

During the evening there would be singing by a band of gipsies – singing, unique and unimaginable, according to the Baroness de Stoeckl, who heard them at a private party on the Islands at St Petersburg, and had often pictured 'these wonderful beautiful singers, for whom many young officers ruined themselves'.

But when they entered, she could hardly believe her eyes: 'the women were ugly; one squinted; another, with toothache, had her head wrapped in a kerchief. The men were surly and unkempt. Yet suddenly a voice of extraordinary sweetness rang out, softly followed by others. Then abruptly, wildness seized the whole troupe until the lovely pleading voice came forth again from the mad bacchanalian yells … I began to feel their influence, something one could not define, a feeling of hope, of a dream, as if one could go on for ever listening. Still they sang and danced and played, sometimes wildly, at others the melody could have made one weep'. Afterwards she asked someone: 'Tell me, what brings on this extraordinary rapture?', and he answered, 'The music in their souls.'

After eating and drinking, and being entertained in this style, followed by innumerable toasts drunk in champagne, on at least one recorded occasion, when these valiant fellows had fallen into bed at three a.m., the Grand Duke Michael had the 'Boots and Saddles' sounded at four. But, being Hussars, they were ready for inspection in fifteen minutes. 'Each man as firm in his seat as though he had slept eight hours'.

The Emperor took particular personal pride in the Hussars, in which every Tsarevitch was entered at birth, and dined with them every month, arriving at the Mess alone without even an aide-de-camp. He would take his place amongst them as a friend and comrade, and unless an earlier departure was necessitated by urgent engagements next day, he remained as a rule all night.

After dining, there were songs by the magnificent Regimental choir. The General then advanced, bearing the silver loving-cup studded with precious stones, filled with champagne and declaimed: 'Nikolai Alexandrovitch!', and the singers broke into joyful strains. The Tsar, taking the cup, drained it and cried: 'Your health, my Hussars!', and all the officers bowed low. The singers then seized their illustrious guest by his imperial legs and raised him above their shoulders. Every officer was then, after a toast and a song, held up in the same manner and passed, standing, to the singers. This ritual, obviously needing judgement and concentration even when cold-sober, must have presented some difficulty under the circumstances.

More singing, this time by the gypsies, ended the night, or rather the morning, except that sometimes impromptu entertainments followed, one of the most popular being Poum's imitation of an American negro doing the cakewalk - particularly enjoyed by the Tsar.

During the winter of 1902-03 there was much gaiety at court, including a sumptuous ball when the Hussars wore historical dress uniform, and where Chakrabongse and Poum doubtless did credit to the Régisseur of the Imperial Ballet. But it was still towards the Machavaya Ulitsa that the two young men made their way most eagerly, though now Poum sometimes went alone for he had fallen deeply in love with the charming widow – a love that was fully returned. And while he maintained the discretion of an officer and gentleman, Chakrabongse naturally knew of his happiness, though he himself was not so fortunate.

The Hussars at luncheon in Winter 1903 from left to right: Lieut Prut-chenko, Capt Oforunoff, Sul. Lieut Dmitrof, Khoonkaman, Sul. Lieut Ku-sheleff, Sul. Lieut Baron Fredericks, Sul. Lieut Prince Nakashidze, Capt. Grottan, Capt. Jufinovitch. This photo was taken by me

Prince Chakrabongse in 17th century infantry uniform for the costume ball in the Winter Palace.

One young girl who caught his fancy was a certain Natasha, who conveyed to him by tender glances and pressing his hand that she loved him, and with whom he had a gentle flirtation at a variety of social gatherings. When, at a lesson in Military Jurisprudence, he got top marks, he wrote: 'As Natasha had agreed to think of me during this class, I couldn't have got anything lower.'

In the spring of 1903, the annual Review took place on the Champs de Mars. Fifty or sixty thousand troops – Cuirassiers, Cossacks, Ataman of the Tsarevitch, Dragoon Guards, Mounted Grenadiers, Chevaliers-Gardes of Empress Marie, Gendarmes of the Guard, the Cossacks of the Emperor, the Hussars and many more – filed in glittering array before their Tsar. After an hour of brilliant manoeuvres, the Review ended with the traditional breathtaking Cavalry Charge. Withdrawing in perfect formation, a considerable distance from the Imperial entourage, which included the Empress and Grand Duchesses in open carriages, the Cavalry took up position. Silence fell, broken only by the clink of harness. Then a whip-crack command echoed from regiment to regiment and, helmets gleaming, lances glinting, the entire force thundered towards the Tsar but, within a few feet of him, at a shrill command, reined back, halted and stopped dead.

After this splendid finale to another phase of their life in Russia, Chakrabongse and Poum had special leave to visit their native land in the autumn and winter of 1903-1904. Received at Singapore by one of Chulalongkorn's aide-de-camps, they continued their journey in the royal yacht, and three days later were welcomed by the King with a state reception in Bangkok. Chakrabongse stayed with his brother, Crown Prince Vajiravudh, at Saranrom Palace – where the Tsar had stayed when Tsarevitch in 1893. He was given a commission in the First Infantry Regiment, King Chulalongkorn's own bodyguard.

All manner of lavish banquets, fêtes and entertainments had been planned to demonstrate his father's satisfaction with his excellent achievements in Russia, – satisfaction fully shared by his mother, Queen Saowabha. But when Chakrabongse fell more than a little in love with a pretty princess, one of his numerous half-sisters, Chulalongkorn was displeased and told him: 'Such marriages are out-of-date. You are heir-presumptive and can marry anyone you wish', meaning of course that his son could pick and choose among the highest in the land when the right time came for him to do so.

While consanguineous marriages were still commonplace, it is likely that Chulalongkorn felt they were no longer desirable and it is even more likely that the King considered that marriage at this point would interfere with his son's future prospects and progress in Russia. Chulalongkorn could not foresee how much he would regret his words and the interpretation that would be put on them in time to come.

Leaving Siam in January 1904, Chakrabongse and Poum arrived in Singapore in the royal yacht, and boarded the *SS Roon*, on their way to Russia via Genoa. The Secretary of the Siamese Legation in Tokyo, who was sailing with then, told them war was imminent between Russia and Japan – information which they disbelieved as did everyone else on board. Yet on landing at Genoa, they heard that two Russian warships had already been sunk by the Japanese at Port Arthur.

This conflict – most unpopular in Russia – had support from circles close to the Tsar, who thought that 'a small victorious war' would provide diversion from increasing revolutionary unrest. But, as it turned out, the war was a disaster and a great loss of prestige for the Russian army, while the flickering flame of revolution burned still higher and more steadily.

The repressive Minister of the Interior, Pleve had been assassinated in 1904 to be replaced by the more liberal Mirsky (a short lived appointment). In December 1904 a manifesto promising some form of nation-wide elections was drafted, and the highly charged atmosphere led in early 1905 to a general strike of Petersburg workers. On 9th January 1905, 150,000 workers, their wives and children, led by the priest Father Gapon marched to the Winter Palace to petition the Tsar to grant reforms, only to be met with unprecedented violence and repression with hundreds left dead or wounded. Hundreds of thousands of workers reacted with solidarity strikes and throughout January St. Petersburg was in turmoil.

Amidst such an atmosphere of political tension, in the early spring of 1905, Chakrabongse called at Madame Chrapovitzkaya on her 'At Home' day where, released from the formality of the Court and the rather enervating company of the sentimental young ladies with whom he danced and flirted at correct social evenings, he felt indeed more at home. For the people he met here had ideas and interests extending to wider horizons and their intelligent talk and banter refreshed and stimulated him.

It was here one day when, deep in conversation, he saw his hostess was greeting a late arrival – a young girl with glorious red-gold hair standing hesitantly on the threshold. He rose to his feet and bowed as Mme Chrapovitzkaya introduced her: Ekaterina Ivanovna Desnitskaya. The expression of her grey-blue eyes and her air of modest dignity and shy assurance inexplicably went straight to his heart. And now it seemed to him that the genial hum of talk and laughter receded, leaving him alone with her and, while they drank tea, he learned she was seventeen – an orphan – and that she and her brother had left Kiev, their birth place, for St Petersburg, where her brother was studying for the Diplomatic Service at university, while she had enrolled as a volunteer nurse at the Princess Marie Hospital and, upon qualification, immediately intended to leave for the Front.

Every intonation of her youthful voice, each fleeting glance of her candid eyes and movement of her small yet capable hands seemed inexpressibly important to Chakrabongse. His habitual reserve was crumbling, the restraints of rigid discipline in which his youth had been confided were breaking, so that he felt suddenly free as a madman – for if ever a man fell madly in love, it was Chakrabongse at this point in his life. In that instant of losing not only heart but head, the entire pattern of his future altered and, as Byron said: 'The fates changed horses'.

The idea that, so soon after their first meeting, she would be gone, that young and unprotected as she was, she might be maimed or killed, filled him with utter dismay. While she remained in St Petersburg however, he called on her almost daily, driving to the hospital situated on the Fontanka canal in an emblazoned imperial carriage, causing great excitement among the other student-nurses. But there was no weakening in Ekaterina's resolve to ignore her impetuous lover and continue steadfastly with her decision to go and nurse the Russian victims of the Russo-Japanese war.

Ivan Stepanovitch Desnitsky, Katya's father.

Maria Mihailovna Desnitskaya, Katya's mother.

III
Katya's Family

katerina Ivanova Desnitsky's father had been Chief Justice of the Lutz Tribunal in the Ukraine, where her mother Maria Milhailovna Khijniakoff's family owned several large estates. As both her father and mother had been married and widowed previously, Katya – as she was always called by her family – had seven half-brothers and sisters, but only one full brother, Ivan, two years older than herself.

According to family diaries, her mother was a considerable beauty whose first husband, Pyotr Vladimirovitch Verdi, a talented engineer, had matched her in his handsome demeanour and, romantic temperament. The two had been deeply in love. But in 1883, five years after his early death, although courted by many, she accepted the hand of Ivan Stepanovitch Desnitsky who apparently lacked both good looks and charm but made up for them by being 'serious and practical'.

In Lutz they lived harmoniously together and it was there that Ivan was born in 1886 and Katya two years later on 9th May 1888. Although an excellent mother to her step-children and children, whom she described collectively as 'yours, mine and ours', because her husband adored her, 'he would have no burdens laid on her'. He therefore engaged and instructed the servants and ordered the meals, while 'Maria read novels late into the night, rose at two and took no part in the running of the household.' In fact, one afternoon, having just risen from bed, she sauntered through the courtyard and, upon seeing a women unknown to her, the following exchange took place:

'What can I do for you, my dear?'

'Please M'am, I'm your cook.'

'Really, how nice; have you been here long?'

'Well, it's been about a month.'

Unfortunately for Maria, she was only too soon deprived of this carefree existence as, in 1888, after only five years of her second marriage, Ivan Stepanovitch died, leaving her once more a widow and this time badly off, as his death occurred before his full pension had been earned.

As Lutz now held only sad memories, Maria removed to an apartment in Kiev where she had relatives and friends, and it was in this beautiful university city with its superb cathedral and noble architecture that the little Katya, who had been only two months old when her father died, was brought up. Although circumstances were straightened, she had a happy childhood and retained a great affection for Kiev itself, for its wooded hill, shady streets and gardens overlooking the Dnieper river far below. There were also long delightful holidays when the whole band of children were taken to visit their mother's relations on their various estates – Krasnaya Sloboda, Kaptievka, Zubuyanaye, Trotstianka and Yurov.

In Katya's letters to her brother, written when she left for Siberia as a nurse in 1905, she often mused nostalgically about the happy times they enjoyed together

Katya aged 14.

Ivan, Katya's brother.

Maria (Katya's mother), Katya and Alla
(Katya's half sister).

Seriozha, Katya's half brother.

at the turn of the century. In addition, a fascinating memoir by one of Katya's maternal aunts contains many insights into the lives of the large extended family and of pre-revolutionary Ukraine. One of Katya's great-uncles writing of holidays in Yurov in the 1850s paints a picture which is typically Russian and had probably changed little by the time Katya was a girl.

> 'As a boy, I always anticipated our departure with excitement and joy, and recall those blessed moments when the trap was loaded, the horses bridled and my brother, sister and I rode out of Kiev. We had to travel sixty versts along the old post track and, leaving in the morning, we reached Yurov just after sunset. Sometimes Grandmama came with us, spending most of the journey dozing in the trap. With pillows piled around her, she would mutter occasionally in her sleep and then drop off again.
>
> 'In Yurov, warmly and joyfully greeted by Aunt Tatiana, Uncle Stepan and the whole family, we were led into the big wooden house at the back of a spacious courtyard. Behind the house was a park boasting an ancient alley way of limes, their branches meeting overhead, shady and fragrant on the hottest day.

'*Beyond the park was an orchard and an apiary. I sometimes used to spend the night sleeping in the old beekeeper's hut. I would turn up early while he was still cooking his supper, and would sit by the fire where he was baking potatoes. I would offer him a little flask of vodka and demand a story of the old days. And he would tell me of the Dnieper Cossacks and of how he himself had been a soldier in 1812, and chased the enemy out of Russia.*

'*I spent hours by the River Zdvzhi, rod in hand, fishing from the bank or from a boat. Even now at night, I recall those happy days and the familiar sounds of the river ring in my ears like music. We would go bathing and fishing several times a day ... But there were also the stables, a ride to take the horses to water, at the cattle yard and aviary, and a trip to woods and fields with the steward.*

'*In midsummer, starting early in the morning, we would go to the common, about twelve versts from Yurov, to pick mushrooms and berries in the forest. Auntie stayed with the baskets of food and the samovar, while we hurried off, exchanging cheerful calls, so that no-one wandered too far and got lost in the huge black woods. By evening whole traploads were filled with delicious mushrooms, fragrant forest raspberries, black-currants and red bilberries. After supper by the camp fire, on the way home I would curl up in the trap and fall asleep. Sometimes a bump in the road awakened me, I'd look up at the stars and fall asleep again – I never slept so well in my life.*

'*During the harvest, after the day's work, the mowers gathered to eat by the fire, telling tales of mystery and horror, and singing songs about the freedom of the Cossack life. I have also not forgotten the send-off always given to the Tchoomaks, Ukrainian ox-cart drivers, when they were sent to the Crimea for salt. Powerful short-horns drew the carts, whose drivers were selected for their health and strength. Assembled in the village square, they awaited the priest, who would offer prayers for their journey. When he arrived, arrayed in his vestments, they fell on their knees, praying ardently. Then they arose, and the eldest of them, loudly and ceremoniously addressed the crowd, "Farewell gentlemen, farewell one and all!" And this was not the end of it. Dozens of old*

A street in Kiev.

women would run and kiss the departing travellers with sobs of woeful lamentation as though they were going to their deaths. This also lasted a considerable time.

'*Finally the elder Tchoomak announced severely, "Let us now be gone!" Removing their caps, they turned towards the church, crossed themselves, and once more bowed to the crowd. The row of carts creaked off in a long line. The older Tchoomaks each took a handful of earth, tied it in a rag, and hung it round their necks, so that if one died on the road, his fellows would put this clod of home-earth with him in his grave.*

'*But alas, the joys of life in Yurov were shadowed by the cruel treatment of the serfs by the steward. Every day there was crude abuse, oaths, slaps and punches in the teeth, causing blood to flow from many mouths.*

'*My worst memory was the beating of offending serfs which took place on Saturday outside the steward's house. Then I used to retreat to a distant corner of the garden so as not to hear their cries and groans. On Saturdays, I was always late for supper and sat there unable to eat. Aunt and Uncle saw my state and tears, and understood. They were good people and I cannot recall them ever resorting to violence in the treatment of their own servants. But they saw the whip as a necessity and saving grace, although they never inflicted their views on me. But when I recall these things with living clarity, my lower lip trembles as it did sixty years ago, and tears of pity and indignation come to my eyes.*

'*The visits of the Priest Yefin Botvinovsky were a great treat for the younger members of the household. He would constantly be telling the most delightfully funny stories, and if he drank a bit over supper, he would sometimes throw off his cassock and present himself in loose trousers and a Russian 'poddyovka' (long-waisted coat) and dance with great enthusiasm. He would only do so when everyone assured him that Grandmama (of whom he stood in awe) had already gone to bed in her far-off room.*

'*But there were occasions when the situation was incorrectly assessed, and Grandmama would appear unexpectedly. Batya, executing the complex steps of the Trepak with great heat and effect, would fail to notice the fearsome spectre until Grandmama's voice would ring out furiously. The poor dancer would instantly look highly embarrassed and rush to kiss the old lady's hands, but she would tear them away and depart to her room, scowling and muttering fiercely.'*

Two of the Khijniakoff estates remained in the family's possession till the Revolution, but long before that, bad management, debts and fraudulent stewardship had set the rest on that well-worn path of melancholy decline so common in Russia. But in the case of Yurov – best loved of all – the end was more spectacular, for one day when Aunt Tatiana and her daughters had driven out to pay calls, on turning home in a sudden storm, they saw the glow of fire. Struck by lightning Yurov was ablaze, and all was lost including the splendid library.

In Kiev, life was far from easy for Maria Mihailovna in a household where her only helper was Marysya, the old nanny. But by 1890 her eldest stepdaughter was married, one stepson was in the army and two more at boarding-school, so that only one stepson, together with Alla and Seriozha, the children of her first marriage, and Ivan and Katya remained at home.

Seriozha, was their mother's special favourite and indeed was adored by all, being extremely handsome with the charm of both his parents combined. But he was a bit of a scapegrace, shockingly lazy and like his mother addicted to reading novels till dawn. This made early-rising for his studies trying in the extreme. He would therefore write a note in his mother's name to say he was ill, summon his dog Aidyl (trained by him for this purpose) and despatch him with the note to the school porter. Seriozha would then return to bed until two-thirty when his mother rose, and then pretend to be just back from school. Yet even though Aidyl was often called on to pad off to the porter's lodge, his master still managed to move up a class at the end of every year.

Seriozha was also a great flirt. Lydia was the name of more than one girl he had fancied and indeed had led to Aidyl's name – Lydia spelt backwards. One of his ploys when walking up the Kreschatka, the main street of Kiev, was to douse a handkerchief with scent and drop it at the feet of a pretty girl. 'Excuse me, is his your's?' 'No.' 'Oh, I'm so sorry, I though it was.' Then, when they next met, greetings could be exchanged and the acquaintanceship got under way.

'Eventually, however, he married one Mathilda Ivanovna, a pleasant modest German girl, quite different from all the Lydias who had once appealed to him. Sobered by marriage, he took a university degree but, most unfortunately, he yearned to own an estate and was encouraged by his mother in this ambition. And alas for them all, Duka, the contractor, made his appearance. He was a shrewd illiterate peasant, who saw profit in Maria Mihailovna's property and drew on her funds with such cunning and confidence that she would not believe her friends when they tried to open her eyes to his activities'. This situation, which damaged irreparably the family's already shaky finances, was compounded when Seriozha bought an estate near Kiev on credit and got in the words of Katya's aunt 'into a terrible mess.'

Far worse was to follow for, by the winter of 1903, Maria Milhailovna was dying of painful cancer, and Seriozha, with already two young children to support, fell seriously ill from stress and anxiety. Before she died, his mother told him: 'I am not saying goodbye to you for long!' Seriozha's poor wife also understood the way things were, for showing a relative some light-coloured material to make a coat, she said 'Its not worth cutting-out, I shall soon be in mourning.' Sure enough, nine months after his mother, Seriozha was dead.

This then was the sad insecure background from which Ivan and Katya, aged eighteen and sixteen respectively, having borrowed a little money from an uncle, set out to seek their fortune in St Petersburg.

It was a courageous decision and, although Ivan, like his Father 'lacked good looks and charm', he too was 'serious and practical' and in addition possessed great aptitude for languages, on which he based his hopes of making a career in diplomacy.

As for pretty lively Katya, not only was she fired by a patriotic desire to serve her country, but with nothing but her looks and youth to rely on, she must have feared that had she remained in Kiev, she might have become merely a poor relation, one of those figures that move though the pages of so many Russian novels and finally fade away as unregarded as the shabby furniture in a tolerant relatives household. In addition, tantalising glimpses of an infatuation with a certain Igor sprinkle her letters of this period and it is likely that his absence at the front was a further spur to her ambitions. In St Petersburg, she stayed with one of her mother's cousins, Aunt Sophia, who had married a doctor named Borodin.

Katya as a nurse in 1905.

IV
East meets West

It was in an atmosphere of extreme political and emotional tension that Katya left for Siberia in April 1905, where she served in a hospital train on the frozen Lake Baikal and, clearly, became a most competent nurse as, during the ensuing year, she was awarded no less than three decorations including the coveted Order of St George. Meanwhile in St Petersburg, Chakrabongse, having failed to obtain leave from his duties at the Military Academy in order to proceed to Siberia, had to content himself with bombarding her with letters and telegram

The sinking of 40 ships of the Russian Navy by the Japanese in May and lack of political reform in Russia, led the sailors of the Battleship Potemkin to rebel in June. However, the rebels lacked unity and organization and the government carried out swift and ruthless reprisals. Even when Russia accepted the mediation of America and the vastly unpopular Russo-Japanese war ended with the signing of the Treaty of Portsmouth (USA) in August 1905, it produced no amelioration in the ominous state of the country. Thus when Katya returned to St Petersburg that autumn, she found a city greatly changed – full of tension and disquieting rumour. However there had been no alteration in the intensity of Chakrabongse's passionate love.

At their first meeting, worn down by his suffering in her absence and tongue-tied – as so often happens – at seeing embodied in smooth rosy flesh the vision that had haunted him awake and sleeping, Chakrabongse, at a loss for romantic words in which to frame a proposal, suddenly blurted out: 'Do you dislike electric fans?' Katya, who had never heard of them, but did not wish to seem ignorant, answered that she liked them immensely. In the highly emotional state in which he had existed since falling so violently in love, her reply to this absurd question seemed positive encouragement and, without further ado, he asked her to marry him and live in Siam, where heat would be tempered by the said electric fans!

Though by now far from indifferent to her tempestuous wooer, Katya still hesitated. Chakrabongse, now a mature twenty-three, not only handsome, high-spirited and brilliantly clever, could also draw on an immense fund of determination to achieve any end on which his mind or heart – in this case both – were set. Not only did he entreat her in person, but he bombarded her daily with letters written from the Winter Palace.

> *'My dearest Soulmate Kaya*
>
> *Can't you understand that you do not have to doubt my feelings? I don't need anything but you. If only you can be with me, then everything will be marvellous and nothing can lessen my happiness. There is no question of a lessening in my feelings for you. Simply I have sometimes been afraid to tell you to ask you to be mine. Now if you really love me so much that you are ready*

*to leave with me no matter what, then don't be afraid, I am sure we will be very
happy. We must be in agreement, no matter what, we must hold together. Then
we tranquilly can meet the world head on. Only you must remember you'll
have to bear a lot. If you agree then remember we must be as one. Please talk
with you brother and make him agree.*
Your loving and hopeful

Lekya'

Such determination made him totally irresistible. Having consulted her dear
friend Elizaveta Ivanovna Chrapovitzkaya, and with the proviso that she must
have her brother's consent, Katya finally gave him her promise.

Armed with this, Chakrabongse, after long discussion, persuaded Ivan to
agree, but only on condition that his sister's marriage would be according to the
rites of the Russian Orthodox church. Although the university had reopened
briefly in September, in mid-October a strike of railway workers had developed
into a general strike involving some 1.5 million industrial workers. A Soviet of
Factory and Workers representatives had been set up and effectively was in control of St Petersburg. Witnessing such events at first hand and aware of the uncertain future that awaited his headstrong younger sister Ivan must have been more
receptive to Chakrabongse's wishes than he otherwise might have been.
Meanwhile, undaunted, his future brother-in-law set about abandoning his
Buddhist faith (for the time being) and being received into Katya's church.
Russian Orthodox, Hindu or Islamic, one feels it mattered not, as long as Katya
could be his, and letters reveal that, at one point, it was suggested that the marriage might even take place in the German Lutheran church. As for the traditions
of the Chakri dynasty, his royal parents who valued him so highly, the ramifica-
tions of his responsibilities to them and to the Russian Imperial family, who had
regarded him almost as a son, all such considerations had become of no account.

In fact, he decided to tell neither his father nor the Emperor, reasoning rather
speciously, that if they knew of his intended marriage and forbade it, he would
not be able to disobey, whereas if they said nothing, for the good reason that they
knew nothing, he felt free to do as he pleased. Similarly, Katya did not discuss her
plans with other members of her family, neither the Borodins with whom she had
lodged, nor her autocratic Uncle Vanya, her mother's brother, who, after the latter's death, had assumed a moral if not a financial responsibility for the young girl.
From all accounts he had disapproved of his late sister's extravagant life-style and,
latterly, his niece's decision to become a nurse. He was therefore hardly a sympathetic uncle who might have given her sound counsel on this decision.

Secrecy therefore was of prime importance and, a wedding in St Petersburg
being out of the question, it was arranged that it should take place in
Constantinople. This also meant concealment of his plans from the over-generous
Sultan Abdul Hamid, who might otherwise have wished to organise nuptials of
embarrassingly oriental splendour.

Chakrabongse's plans were apparently so well-laid and carried out with such military precision and attention to the smallest detail that no hint of them disturbed the orderly progression of his ceremonial passing-out of the Military Academy and his leave-taking of brother officers in his regiment. He duly paid his final visit to the Emperor, who created him honorary colonel in the Hussars, invested him with the Order of St Andrew – the equivalent of the English Garter – and bade him a fatherly farewell, quite unaware that his exemplary protégé was returning home with a young Russian bride.

Poum, who should have been returning to Siam with Chakrabongse, had decided not to leave Russia after all for, due not only to his close association with Chakrabongse but to his own marked abilities, opportunities were open to him in Russia that his humble birth precluded him from in Siam. He therefore applied to Chulalongkorn for leave to remain, but this was refused and he was ordered to return. Secure in his position and certain of further promotion in the Hussars in which he was extremely popular, he ignored the king's command, greatly angering the Monarch, who thenceforth regarded him as a 'deserter'. After some time he decided to be baptised into the Orthodox church, taking the name of Nicholas, the Emperor himself standing godfather, and thus he became a naturalised Russian. But although nothing was ever said about it openly, there had of course been another reason for his determination to stay on – his love for Madame Chrapovitzkaya. Although she was significantly older than him, this was an enduring love which ended only with her death, far from Russia, in years to come.

At the beginning of January 1906, Katya and Chakrabongse were seen off on the first stage of their journey to Constantinople by Ivan and Poum. They were accompanied by Chakrabongse's aide-de-camp, Surayudh, and his bride, Elena Nicholaievna, the daughter of the head of the St Petersburg Academy, the latter acting as chaperone for Katya until she should be married a few days later.

Elena Nicholaievna, who married
Prince Chakrabongse's aide-de-camp,
Phraya Surayudh Yotaharn.

For the lovers themselves it must have been an occasion fraught with conflicting emotions. Ivan, as his letters to Katya and Chakrabongse prove, was still deeply troubled as to whether he had acted rightly in entrusting his sister to her princely suitor and to life in a remote and unknown land. Poum, although he stood firmly by his decision to remain in Russia, would certainly have felt the parting from his close companion and friend for the last ten eventful years, especially since Chakrabongse would be returning to their homeland without him. And Chakrabongse, even though he was successfully carrying off the girl he loved so passionately, must surely have feared that his elaborate deception of all the key figures in his life would inevitably end in discovery hard to face and recriminations hard to bear.

For Katya, combined with the tremulous excitement of the elopement, must have been a fear of an unknown and unimaginable life opening in front of her. It is clear from her later letters to her brother and Madame Chrapovitzkaya that she had not realised how homesick she would be, not only far from her country, her friends and relatives, but also the comfort of her religion.

Therefore the nervous chatter, forced laughter, sudden silences and tension common to the most ordinary departures, were intensified, mingling with shame-faced relief as the engine got up steam, doors slammed, handkerchiefs were wept into and finally waved as the great train drew slowly out and on its way. En route for Odessa on the Black Sea, it would stop briefly at Kiev and one can imagine Katya's feelings as the train pulled out again and, craning from the carriage window to catch a fleeting glimpse of the city she had left only two short years before and might never see again, she pondered the extraordinary twist of fate that had presented her with a destiny so strange and so totally unforeseen.

Their marriage, which was duly celebrated in Constantinople, was not arranged without difficulty as Chakrabongse explained in a letter to Ivan dated only 1906.

> *'The marriage took place in the Greek church of St Trinity on Pera Street in the usual way without any special pomp. I went beforehand to see the priest and had a very long talk with him. It was extremely difficult to arrange everything in strict secrecy. Secrecy was necessary as, if my parents heard about it, there would be a huge scandal, as it is unheard of for a Siamese Prince, the son of the only Buddhist monarch in the world, to marry in a Christian church.*
>
> *'I therefore impressed on the priest that he must never talk to anyone about it and that if anyone should ever attempt to obtain information on the subject, he should not disclose any relevant documents or information from the church register, and in the last resort he must say that no such marriage ever took place. This secrecy is most important to me and I would not be able to sleep at night without having made these arrangements, for, as you know, Ivan Ivanovitch, intelligence gathering in the Orient is very well developed!*

> *'Now I feel confident that even the most ingenious and clever sleuth would be unable to extract a word about the marriage of the Prince from Siam in Constantinople!'*

Here Chakrabongse displays not only remarkable confidence in his own powers of persuasion, but also in the discretion of a priest, who probably suspected that the bridegroom's conversion to Christianity was merely a matter of temporary expediency. Meanwhile, in a more informal letter to Ivan, Katya wrote from the Hotel Savoy in Cairo on 12th February:

> *'Cairo is a dream. The city is beautiful, the weather is fine, it is not too hot but warm and agreeable'*

much to be preferred in her opinion to Constantinople which she considered

> *'dirty and dull.'*

She continued,

> *'To-morrow we will go up the Nile to the North for five days and, after one night in Cairo, we will leave for Port Said and then on to Siam. I am frightened and cannot understand why. The worst thing for me is that there is no Orthodox Church in Bangkok. Think of it! It is terrible to lose it forever!*
>
> *'This morning I went on my own to a Greek church service which began at eight a.m., but it was rather different from ours and the singing was terrible.'*

Undaunted, she went again a few days later with her husband but, unfortunately, they had been misinformed about the time of the service, which had already taken place. However, this disappointment was mitigated when a Chernogorian from the Ukraine spoke to them in Russian. *'Oh what a joy! It was*

Cairo.

such a pleasure to hear our native tongue. People mostly speak English here, which of course I cannot understand. I am afraid it will be terribly difficult for me in Siam. Being apart from Russia is harder than I supposed. But I cannot do anything about it now. I had no choice then.

'Now I must encourage myself', she continued bravely, 'with the thought that I am married to a man who loves me and whom I have made happy.' This last sentence, with its note of feminine resignation and no mention of her own feelings, is sad but not surprising when one considers how closely young girls were guarded in those days and that everything around Katya was utterly strange including the realities of a passionate honeymoon.

Naturally a visit was made to the Sphinx and the pyramids, where Katya would like to have climbed right to the top, but was afraid of dizziness and also she shrank from being lifted by not only one, but three Arab guides, who were waiting to render that service to all visitors.

Many diplomats and agents called on Chakrabongse at their hotel, but Katya stayed in her room while they were received by her husband and one senses a feeling of foreboding:

> 'We do not want to announce our marriage as we are afraid it might reach the King, and it would also mean we should have to attend celebrations and balls. This would mean great expense as ladies here are very fashionable and we have no money to spare on buying ball-dresses. Besides we should then have to pay visits to all these ladies, and as they speak only English, I should not understand a word they say.
>
> 'I am missing books terribly. Chakrabongse has subscribed to some Russian newspapers for me but I beg you, Vanya, to send me any Russian magazines and books, or I shall go mad.
>
> 'Now that I have come to understand my future better, it begins to lose its rosy colour. Well, my husband was right when he told me in St Petersburg that it was a real sacrifice to go with him although not everyone would agree.
>
> 'What is going on in Kiev? I wish I were there even for a single day – I am really longing for it. Sometimes I feel so sad that I am almost crying, but I must not for Chakrabongse's sake, so I pretend to be cheerful. He might feel hurt if he realised there is a shadow darkening my happiness ... Already, we are both looking forward to our trip to Moscow in two years time. Chakrabongse claims he will not allow me to go to Kiev alone as he is afraid our relations might prevent me from coming back yet, if he accompanies me, he is worried as to how he will be received. It seems that his Adjutant – who also has a Russian wife – is ignored by her relatives. But I reminded him of the incident you told me about when he was referred to the authorities and he simply told them when they questioned him: "But I am Prince Chakrabongse". So when he told me about the Adjutant, I said "Well but you are Prince Chakrabongse" and we*

*both burst out laughing as you had done. I am happy that you appreciate him
and we are both really grateful to you for our being together now …*

'*Write to me how they have all taken my marriage in Kiev – I am dying to
know.*

'*You must understand, dear Vanya, I feel so sorry for my past and that all
was over between me and Igor. If we had not parted, I should not be going to
Siam now, where God only knows how I shall be greeted. Shall I survive in that
climate? Sometimes I feel really frightened.*'

She ends with a final entreaty to send her books and adds the touching post-
script:, 'Don't forget Katya.'

A week later Katya wrote again from Cairo that they had been shopping and
that suits and shirts for her husband, and 'a lot of blouses and bonnets for me have
arrived at our hotel. I can't recognise myself when I put them on – its so unfamil-
iar to me.'

'*Now I am alone. Chakrabongse is dining with the Russian Ambassador
and I have had dinner in my room. There is too much glitter and show – all
served in silver and each dish is more fancy than the one before. Even now I
cannot believe my life has altered so much and, to tell the truth, I don't feel at
ease among all these dressy ladies. My life has been too simple to adjust to such
a change so quickly, and although my husband is charming and is doing his
best to make me happy, sometimes it is inevitable that no-one can help me.*'

Thus while Katya's mind could accept that Chakrabongse must leave her and
go out to lunch and pay visits, her heart was hankering after the warmth and simplicity of her previous life. The language was also another major hurdle to be
overcome but she reported that the Siamese ambassador has agreed to teach her
Siamese, though warning he will be 'very strict'.

'*In Suez, Chakrabongse's adjutant, his wife and their two children will
rejoin us. Our ship will be huge and therefore most comfortable. Is it really me
who now stays in palatial hotels without any concern about luggage and so on,
when I used to travel third or fourth class with lots of trunks and parcels and
a cat?*

'*Chakrabongse is very worried that I shall not stand the climate, but I feel
heat is more bearable for me than cold – but there is no need to rack one's brains
beforehand, we'll see what happens when summer comes.*

'*I tease Lek – this is my husband's Siamese nickname and means "little" –
saying I shall lie in a cold bath all day and sleep at night under those famous
electric fans! Anyway when we get to Bangkok, I'm going to play the piano,
study Siamese and English, and go for drives as we'll have a car.*'

The Suez Canal.

Nevertheless Katya was unable to maintain this more cheerful note for long, making one of her characteristic, almost panic-stricken, modulations into a sombre minor key:

> *'What will become of all this later? It terrifies me. Everything happened too quickly. My poor one, how much you had to endure in January. Thank you for everything, dear Vanya. But if all ends unhappily, I'll take the blame because it was I, who undertook the whole thing. Let God be with you. Bless me too. Remember, from now on you'll have a sister in Siam. Kissing you tenderly.'*

On 19th February, Katya and Lek left Cairo and sailed for Siam via Port Said and Suez, where they were reunited as arranged with Chakrabongse's adjutant, his Russian wife, Elena Nicholaievna, their two children and two nursemaids. In a letter to Ivan, Chakrabongse writes: 'The trip was wonderful. The weather was good, and the sea was calm, so Katya didn't suffer and was in good health all the time.'

With each passing day as Russia and the West receded still further, and the sounds and scents of the Far East took over, it sometimes seemed to Chakrabongse that he had never been away, for they reminded him only too sharply of the elaborate ceremonial, the inflexible protocol and respectful obedience to the demands of his royal position that awaited him in Siam. To him it was a way of life familiar from childhood, but how would it seem to the young woman at his side whom his ardent love had torn away from her native land and brought many thousands of miles, not, as he would have wished, to a warm welcome, but to face shock, dismay and bitter anger from the King and Queen and the Royal family?

Far away in St Petersburg, his passion for her had blinded him, but now, trying to visualise his eagerly awaited return as an eligible prince of the blood, not alone as expected, but accompanied by an alien wife of a different race and creed, he unwillingly concluded that news of his marriage must be 'broken gently'. Therefore, after much torturous soul-searching, he decided to leave Katya with Elena Nicholaievna in Singapore and proceed to Bangkok without her. As he wrote to Ivan: 'It would have been absolutely impossible if we both came to Bangkok. A lot of ceremonies will be held especially for me, and Katya in this case would not be comfortable and her situation would be very complicated. So even though I want us to be always together and although my heart was broken at leaving her, I believe she had to stay behind for our common good.'

Although this parting may well have been for their common good, Katya understandably felt it deeply and, in a poignant letter of 19th March, intended to reach Elisaveta Ivanovna Chrapovitskya in time for Easter, she confessed her fears for the future and her impatience with her present situation. Unfortunately, Elena Nicholaievna (referred to in shortened form as El. Nick by Katya) had not proved to be a congenial or lively companion:

'I stay on in Singapore in anguish. It is the eleventh day so far. Although El. Nick. is a tender wife and mother, she thinks of nothing but her children and, during the whole day, I have to hear what they have eaten, when they will have a bath and so on. Occasionally we go for a short drive, but still always with the children who are often naughty and capricious. Otherwise she just sits on the terrace or in her room where she even has dinner as she is afraid to leave her precious children with the nursemaids. And, although I feel great respect of such an ideal mother, to tell you the truth I am almost dying in this nursery atmosphere, particularly as we have no idea when we will be leaving.

'She really amazes me sometimes for, although it's true she is twelve years older than me, she behaves like a woman of eighty, and if she hears words like "fool" or "hell", she turns red with embarrassment, and I realise I am shocking her ears all the time. But never mind, she must get accustomed to it. I'm not going to change myself. I feel we are from different planets and her presence is no help to me as, apart from missing her husband, she says she is quite satisfied to be here – I cannot stand this atmosphere much longer without life around me.

'Lek complains in his many telegrams that I don't write to him, but so far I've received no letters from him and I can't think why this is so.

'He promised me that I would be staying here only two weeks, but I shall be finished soon. He doesn't say a word about our departure in his telegrams. I am in despair. I would pay anything to escape from here and spend an evening with you, it would put life into me at once.

'In spite of all my love for Lek, Singapore seems a hell to me though, if he had been with me I should not have felt so sad, but I am not only far away from *others I love, but far away from him.*

'Lek and I always have plans for the future and our eyes burn with brilliance when we discuss our trip to Russia. I am sure we shall both be longing for St Petersburg when we are in Siam. I was so happy there and it was always such a pleasure, dear Elisaveta Ivanovna, to come to your house and to know I was loved there and that nobody looked daggers at me. I am afraid that is how they will regard me in Bangkok once they know I am the Prince's wife.

'Whenever I think of Easter without matins, my heart feels heavy.

'How will it be for me in Siam? Think of it, dear Elisaveta Ivanovna, being alone here without even letters everything seems worse and gloomier to me than it really is. I shall hope to write you a letter full of joy and happiness from Siam and indeed I am sure I will, for I shall be with my boy and everything will be all right.' ·

Nevertheless, Katya's next letter to Elisaveta Ivanovna was still from Singapore and was no more cheerful in tone. Written to arrive in time for the latter's name day she began:

'I am cordially congratulating you on the day of your angel and wishing you health and peace of mind.

'I am still in despair as on Thursday it will be three weeks since we arrived here and I have only received two of Lek's letters. And I have not heard anything from my home for two months. I have a terrible feeling that a terrible scandal will break out on my arrival in Bangkok and Lek is obviously afraid it will be worse than we expected. Everything would have been easier if we could have been together now.

'I have been praying the whole night asking God to prevent a misfortune and, although I have only known you a short time, I write without concealing anything, sharing my joys and griefs with you. I am sorry to trouble you with my letters, but frankly I have no one else to write to. My relatives do not know Lek and God knows what they would imagine if I write to them that I am still in Singapore without him and dying from sadness.

'Although we are staying in the best hotel, the accommodation is not very good. The bathrooms for instance are most uncomfortable, containing a barrel instead of a bath and a scoop to pour the water. No matter what they say the East is not civilised yet. The servants here are all Chinese, who speak only their own language, though notices in the hotel announce they speak English. I have to communicate with them by gesture, which is so expressive that Elena Nicholaievna begs me not to do it during lunch or dinner or she will die of laughing. In Siam I am to have a Siamese maid who has worked for the Europeans before, but here we have 'Fairy', who was sent to Elena Nicholaievna. She is Siamese and seems afraid of everything as though she never saw Europeans or their dress in her life. We cannot explain anything to *her as neither of us speak Siamese, so again I have to communicate with amusing gesticulation while Fairy relaxes comfortably in the rocking-chair in our presence and drinks from our glasses and understands absolutely nothing I am trying to convey.*

'Sometimes I think it will take some time to get accustomed to the life here; at other times, if all turns out well with my arrival, I think I shall be at home with the East quite soon.

'I read in one of Lek's letters that on 5th April, new style, there was a ceremony to open the palace where we shall live and all the relatives were present. I am very anxious to be in Siam by Easter since, though I have no opportunity to go to church for matins, I would at least like to be with Lek on this solemn day, and would be unhappy to spend this day on the ship.

'God takes care of us. I trust that I'll soon be able to send you a joyful message.'

Prince Chakrabongse.

V

Life Behind Palace Walls

*M*eanwhile Chakrabongse had been welcomed in Bangkok with joy and appropriate celebration, and soon became aware of the high regard in which he was held, and the added lustre which his years in the Russian Army and colonelcy in the Imperial Hussars had imparted.

He was appointed Commandant of the Military College, and his duties there and attendance at the numerous official social functions which his rank and importance imposed, occupied him to the full. For his residence, he was given Paruskavan Palace near Ampornsathan Palace, where the King lived.

The construction of Paruskavan Palace had in fact been begun in 1903 with 22,075 baht being paid for walls of 275 metres in length on 30th December. On 19th April 1904, 61,173 baht was paid upon completion of the walls excluding the roof. Originally three architects were involved but two became ill during the course of work (Mr Tamayo got cholera and had to return to Europe while Mr Scos got smallpox and died). This left Beyroleyri in charge until the work was finished at the end of 1905.

Chakrabongse threw himself into his work with his customary diligence and enthusiasm and many days passed, not one of them seeming to offer the ideal moment to broach the subject of his marriage. Indeed – as is often the case in such situations – he may have experienced a guilty relief as the sun went down on yet another day, during which time the disclosure of his secret had again been postponed.

However, one morning, after he had been in Bangkok three weeks, he set out to arrive – punctual as always – at the weekly private audience held by the King at Dusit Palace. Attendance was not obligatory, but it was unofficially understood that members of the Royal Family and important notables were expected to be present.

Unknown to Chakrabongse, however, gossip and rumour had been winging round the city like flocks of mischievous birds, twittering that there was a Madame Bisnulok staying in Singapore. Discounted at first as being unbelievable, the story gained credence and eventually reached the ears of the King. Therefore on this fateful occasion, it was not long after Chakrabongse had arrived that he was invited to draw nearer to his father. The Monarch was his usual genial self as he chatted to his son, and while still smiling amiably though watching him closely, said jestingly: 'Lek, I hear you have a European wife – is it true?'

Torn between consternation and relief that the dreaded moment had inescapably come to pass, Chakrabongse turned pale, and at a similar loss for words as when he had proposed to Katya, muttered hoarsely and ineptly: 'Very possibly'. A terrible silence fell. Then with a look like forked lightning, Chulalongkorn turned on his heel and left, terminating the audience and his hitherto complete confidence in his beloved son.

Chakrabongse's interview with his mother was more harrowing still, for she stormed and raved for hours, while he, deeming it his duty, listened in respectful silence, for she was not only his mother, but also the Queen. Late that night when she at last allowed him to depart, he felt so wretched that he dismissed his car and walked home in a downpour of drenching rain.

Subsequently when the King again reproached him for marrying so irresponsibly, he reminded Chakrabongse that his new system of succession (based on the sons of his chief wife, Queen Saowabha taking precedence over those by lesser queens regardless of age) meant that Chakrabongse was not merely an important prince but heir-presumptive – second in line to the throne after his elder brother Crown Prince Vajiravudh.

Worn and exhausted by the furore he had raised, Chakrabongse lost no time in arranging for Katya to leave Singapore. And without mentioning the storm of disapproval he had caused by his marriage, wrote cheerfully and reassuringly to her brother in a letter dated only 1906:

> '*In some days Katya will arrive here. I am awaiting her with impatience. My house is ready and it is very nice and cosy and also cool. My father himself gave all the orders about the furnishing and arrangements and told me this is the best house in Bangkok. I am very happy that Katya will have a home with all modern comfort and convenience. She is so pretty that I still can't get used to it.*
>
> '*I cannot tell you how lucky I am to have such a wife. She is also so happy and I hope it will remain this way forever.*
>
> '*We talk about you often and I want to thank you once more for all your help especially to me, who has stolen your sister and taken her so far away. With many thanks and love.*'

When Katya crossed the threshold of her elegant cream-coloured home, built in the style of an Italian villa, the assembled servants falling gracefully at her feet, she stepped into a seclusion as absolute as that of the 'Inside' in the days of her husband's grandfather King Mongkut. But whereas by now, the queens and wives of Chulalongkorn enjoyed some freedom outside the palace walls, it would be a whole year before Katya went beyond the gates of Paruskavan except for evening motor-drives along the tree-lined avenues of Bangkok. During this period, she met neither her father-in-law or mother-in-law, who had presumably decided that if they ignored their son's marriage it might somehow turn out to be untrue.

Fortunately Paruskavan and its immense gardens contained much to delight and interest her, while Chakrabongse, remorseful and concerned that she should not be isolated, took great trouble to indulge and please her in every way. Apart from the main building were separate servants' quarters, stables and a European as well as a Siamese kitchen.

Paruskavan Palace.

Katya in Paruskavan Palace.

*Prince Chakrabongse with his three dogs in
Paruskavun Palace.*

On the ground floor of the main house were a hall and formal reception
rooms, and on the floor above were Chakrabongse and Katya's private suite, and
a smaller dining-room, where they breakfasted and lunched when alone. High up
beneath the roof was a traditional Shrine-Room, where among the many Buddha
images, were also housed relics and the ashes of deceased ancestors in miniature
bejewelled gold cremation urns. These relics were honoured and remembered
with ceremony on the anniversary of death, and respects paid on leaving on or
returning from a journey. To this day, most houses feature such shrine rooms in

which devout Buddhists pray and prostrate themselves and offer fresh flowers daily.

Almost two hundred people lived in the compound, composed of roughly one hundred grown-ups and children and one hundred servants. Among the adults were many who had mysteriously become part of the household so long ago that no one could remember exactly how they came to be there. This state of affairs may have reminded Katya of her homeland, for as Princess Stephanie Dolgorouky wrote in her memoirs: 'The English week-end invitation for a short stay is unknown in Russia, where guests in country-houses especially, not infrequently remain for years. They sometimes bring with them members of the family and occasionally it happens they remain for the rest of their lives ...'

Children living under this hospitable roof were either orphans or offspring from one of the many large families of royal relatives, happy to have a son or daughter brought-up or even actually adopted by a prince of the first rank such as Chakrabongse – a common custom in Siamese princely families. Thus Katya reported to her brother about her various adopted children:

> *'John – a nice boy – my devoted slave – and Domol is our adopted son'*

and added that she teased her husband on this score:

> *'No sooner do I enter my new home than he introduces me to his sons – but he has an alibi; they must have all been born while he was still in Russia!'*

Outside there was garaging for eight cars and stabling for six horses that included Chakrabongse's Russian charger Ramushka, whom he had always ridden in the Hussars. This gallant old friend, to whom he was devoted was to be his mount at most official parades and lived to the advanced age of thirty-three.

From one of Katya's lengthy letters to her brother, written almost immediately after her arrival and dated 18-31 April 1906, it is clear she lost no time in settling down, and taking the measure of her life. Dealing briskly with Ivan's reproaches

Prince Chakrabongse's favourite horse, Ramushka.

Chakrabongse on Ramushka during military manoeuvres.

Chakrabongse on Ramushka leading a parade.

Chakrabongse at one of the innumerable ceremonies he had to attend almost daily.

for not writing from Singapore 'because I could have written only sad letters from there', she continued:

> *'Thank God, we are now at peace. All the storms are over though sometimes the Queen quarrels about money – it's her way of punishing Lek – but let us leave it to God. Meanwhile, we must cut down our expenses, but I don't think it will last long, she will soon be bored with it. Here we live in concord and I am surprised to find how quickly we have become close to one another – there is nothing more important to us than this.*
>
> *'You ask me what Lek is like here at home in his own country. I think he is kinder, nicer and gentler than in St Petersburg. For one thing he never shows irritation even with the servants, with whom he is always calm and I like this so much.*
>
> *'Our life is very quiet indeed and I sometimes miss society as it's a little dull for my lively character. But God gives and we'll have children and then I won't feel alone when Lek is out which, to our mutual regret, is very often. In fact*

he's at his office each day from twelve to five-thirty, and he has to see the King every other evening from eight to nine. This is when the King comes out onto the square before his palace where his subjects can see and speak to him, so that although they regard him almost as a God, they know that he cares for them. Though they are not bound to attend, most of the princes do so, including Lek, who, now that the King is not so furious and talks to him again, I am particularly anxious not to offend.

'There are however various ceremonies at which Princes of the first rank must be present such as a memorial service for members of the Royal Family, a Day of Prayer, or a National Holiday. On such occasions, the King is always angered by a Prince's absence, which he unfailingly notices.'

Considering Katya's unfaltering devotion to her own faith, her attitude to Buddhism is surprisingly receptive for she writes:

'The more I get to know Buddhist customs the more I like this religion. There are a remarkably large number of monasteries here. Monks wear yellow robes, their heads are shaved and they go barefoot. Every Siamese on reaching the age of 20 becomes a monk for a while and enters a monastery, usually for three or four months, but not less than three days. When Lek returned to Bangkok, one of his uncles – who is the Patriarch – asked him repeatedly when he intended to enter a monastery and was very puzzled when he received no reply – the real reason, of course is that Lek could not become a monk as he is already a married man!'

On the other hand, in common with the imaginative Mrs Leonowens before her, Katya expressed wholehearted disapproval of 'the position of women'.

'They are not educated at all and from early childhood taught to regard a man as a superior being. Polygamy, which I find disgusting, is widespread. Sometimes one man will have ten wives or even more. There is a favourite wife and all the others are practically servants, who have to crawl before their master and are afraid to utter a word. This arouses my indignation.

'I am sure you know that the King has many wives but the numerous Princes – sons of the King but not the Queen – rarely have more than one. While the Crown Prince is unmarried, Lek has me, and eight other children are not yet grown-up. I hope when the Crown Prince comes to the throne this custom will die out, as people always follow an example set by their King or Queen. It is known that the Crown Prince will only have the one wife because of his convictions and I like this very much in him. And the Minister of Justice also only has one wife!

'If rumours are to be believed, the Queen is less angry than she was. I am longing to have children, particularly as they will be the Queen's first grandchildren, and I hope will make up for Lek's marriage to a European woman.

'Anyway all has turned out better than I expected. Of course our marriage could not have passed off without scandal and, to tell the truth, it was an outrageous step on the part of Lek, when you consider that he is a Siamese, a Buddhist and a son of the King and was well aware of the ideas and prejudices of his native land.

'The Siamese also have a way of dressing that seems strange to us for, although they find a European décolleté indecent, when at home they are naked except for a scarf and odd-looking trousers like pantaloons, which are the national dress.

'Servants here come to a prince's house and ask to serve him without payment: this is most extraordinary, but when you realise that all our servants in this house are nobles, it seems more unusual still. However in the end, Lek decides how much he gives them. He is very generous and is much loved.

'I must admit it took me some time to become accustomed to the etiquette here, particularly as I have said, our servants are nobles. Even so, they never stand upright before a prince, but show respect by crawling with bent head. If I am sitting, they hand me my letters or a glass of water kneeling on one knee and move backwards when I stand. And even though I am European, as the wife of a Prince, I must be paid these respects. I confess that earlier I did not like it at all but, as protest is useless, I am now getting used to it …

'As for the language, there is nothing to worry about as I can clearly understand what is said and can speak on any subject I wish – my maid and I comprehend each other perfectly.

'I shall learn English next as it is most important to be able to speak it in the East.'

A Siamese woman.

Seek — искать
Pile — Куча чего нибудь
Reluctantly — Нерешительно
Pad — Что кладут при закладке бумаги
Stain — Пятно
Screened — Влиянием
Wrist — Запястье
Tapering — Суживающееся
Peremptory — Решительный
Clan (Kulin) — Несколько семейств вместе
Emphases — Съ настойчивостью
Prop — Поддержка
Wretched — Разбитый
Tarpaulin — Покрышка для вагонов
Execrable — Ненавистный
Feature — лицо или вид
Slunt — Номер, руки
Stumbled — Споткнулся
Crawled — Ползал
Whilst — Между темъ
Struggling — Борется
Flopped — Падал на землю

Damply — Мокро
Proximity — Близость
Naked — Голый
Blindfolded — Съ закрытыми глазами
Peevishly — Жалобно
Struggle — Борьба
Propping — Поддерживать
It... — Это значит
Hostile — Неприязненный
Jerked — Дернул
Bang — Бум
Predicament — Затруднительное положение
Inquest — Следствие
Searching — Искание
Investigations — Расследование
Transpired — Вышло наружу
Afforded — Дал возможность
Perpetrator — Совершивший
Reiteration — Настойчивое повторение
Testified — Свидетельствовал
Lurking — Шмыгал
Barely — Почти что не
Undergrowth — Растение растущее низко у земли

A page from the Russian-English dictionary that Katya wrote herself.

However despite her wish to acquire another European language, Katya was unequivocal about European behaviour in Siam, which she described forthrightly as:

> 'Disgusting, for though they are at service in Siam and receive enormous salaries from the Siamese, they consider them inferior and mock them. In other words they behave disgracefully, and as the wife of a Siamese and a Prince, I feel disgusted by them!
>
> 'The rainy season was over a week ago and we go for a drive every evening after dinner. Tiny phosphorescent insects dot the trees like stars and fly around our car. Old shady alleys look somehow magical where huge trees line the canals covered with lotus flowers. We whirl along as if in a fairy tale and I can quite understand now why Siam is called a fairy land. Elephants walk along the streets, there is plenty of delicious fruit and beautiful exotic flowers – it is really like being in paradise …
>
> 'As the car is open, the many gossips, anxious to see what I look like, can satisfy their curiosity.'

But evidently a car-drive in the cool of the evening was not sensational enough and, by the time an account of their outings came back to Katya, the story had lost nothing in the telling:

> 'They say I drive out alone in a two-wheeled equipage drawn by a white draught-horse with two footmen behind. Needless to say we have neither such an equipage nor such a horse!'

Whereas this absurd fabrication had at least a bizarre charm, another piece of gossip to which Katya devoted two pages in a letter to her brother, was typical of the small-mindedness often generated in court or near-court circles.

This incident was due to the Adjutant's Russian wife Elena Nicholaievna, who might by now have become friendly with her compatriot Katya, had she not become envious and therefore spiteful. For whereas, according to Katya, she had in Singapore 'played a lady of great importance', once arrived in Bangkok, their different status became a problem:

> *'And though she is a nice woman, she is terribly fond of boasting about her home, her relatives, her carriages, her life before she got married, while here she must lead a modest life. I on the other hand, being married to a Prince, live in a luxurious palace, I am a customer of all the best European shops. I have horses and a car while she has nothing of the kind.'*

While it is true that this patronising attitude on the part of the eighteen year old bride must have been extremely galling, Elena Nicholaievna made further mischief by insinuating to Domol, Chakrabongse and Katya's adopted son, that 'Katya was not a hostess in her own house and could not even go for a drive when she wished.' Domol reported back to Katya. Katya was hurt and told her husband. Chakrabongse told his Adjutant. The Adjutant told his wife, who the next time she came to dine, kissed and embraced Katya and told her that 'she had been waiting for Katya as for golden rain from heaven!' She accused Domol of lying. And Katya commented that 'I am sorry not to be close friends with the only other Russian woman here.'

Matters gradually improved between them but there were still occasions when poor 'El-Nick' found the going hard as when she was shown Katya's Christmas present from her husband, described in some detail in a letter to Ivan:

> *'I must tell you about Lek's Christmas gift: it is a bonnet or hat-pin. In front there is a whip and a horseshoe; the handle of the whip is decorated with green enamel and the rest is in diamonds. There are sixty-two diamonds in all. It is really a very beautiful thing and surely must have cost a lot of money.'*

Unable to resist showing off this marvel to Elena Nicholaievna, she records her as

> *'turning red with jealousy that it belongs to me!'*

Katya with one of her pet monkeys.

Katya and her dogs at Paruskavan Palace.

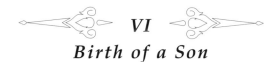

VI
Birth of a Son

*I*n April 1907, King Chulalongkorn decided to take a seven-month trip to Europe in order to seek the advice of doctors about his worsening kidney complaint. In his absence, Crown Prince Vajiravundh was appointed as Regent.

Following the departure of the King, Chakrabongse found time each day as usual to call on Queen Saowabha, but for many months, his ceremonial dismissal continued as before. After a time, however, it came to his ears that discreet enquiries were being made about Katya among members of his household. Feeling sure they had emanated from his mother, he suspected that feminine curiosity might at last have triumphed over her anger. In addition, he hoped that she might use the opportunity afforded by the King's absence to make a first approach to meeting his wife.

He felt certain that Katya, who had made admirable use of the year spent in isolation at Paruskavan, would now make an excellent impression, since she not only spoke fluent Siamese, but had learned the ritual salutations and postures of the intricate court etiquette. She had not however followed the fashion of most Siamese women and cropped her beautiful auburn hair. (This unbecoming treatment of 'a woman's crowning glory' originated from an incident during one of the Burmese Wars. The Burmese had laid siege to a town, which was temporarily undefended as its garrison had made a sortie to engage the enemy elsewhere. The wily Governor's wife, however, called on every woman in the town to crop their hair short and 'man' the ramparts. Astounded at the apparent strength of the defence, the enemy abandoned the siege and retreated in disarray.)

Nevertheless, one evening as Chakrabongse waited patiently in the Queen's ante-chamber, he was startled and then overjoyed when Khun Puey, Saowabha's chief personal attendant, bowed low and said the Queen would see him. Then in the course of the first interview they had for many months, she asked him to bring her a photograph of Katya, which request he duly complied with the very next day. Gazing at it thoughtfully in silence the Queen finally pronounced: 'What a pretty smile she has!'

Following the Queen's lead, Crown Prince Vajiravudh decided to call on Katya and declared his approval and support of his brother's marriage, and Prince Rabi, Minister of Justice and one of Chakrabongse's numerous half-brothers, brought Katya a present of a camera, 'fearing she must be dull remaining so much at home'.

A few days later an even bigger step in the slow process of reconciliation took place when the Queen suggested that Katya should abandon western clothes and adopt the baggy silk trousers, *jungraben* and lace blouse worn by Siamese ladies of the time. When Chakrabongse conveyed this remark to his wife, she cleverly suggested that the Queen should provide her with the material for such clothes and within a few days a pile of beautiful silks arrived at Paruskavan palace. A few weeks later, duly attired, the first meeting between Queen and Russian daughter-in-law finally took place – in the garden of Paruskavan. The Queen and Katya strolled around admiring the transformation and the latter cut a beautiful white rose to present to her mother in-law.

Not long after her satisfaction with Katya was to increase still further when she heard that by spring of the following year she would become a grandmother. Christmas was celebrated in some style in the Chakrabongse household and this year the Queen signified her approval by allowing seven of her nephews and nieces to attend the Russian celebrations, together with four children of Prince Chiraprawat, the Commander-in-Chief, Eltekov the Russian ambassador, and the Surayuts. Soon the baby would arrive and in the meantime Katya busied herself reupholstering furniture as she reported to her brother:

> *'One day, while I was busy with the furniture, my maid was sent to the Queen to give her roses (I have a lot of roses now). Can you imagine how surprised the Queen was when her questions as to what I was doing were answered by "She is making furniture". She said I was brilliant ... I feel very amused by the thought of how this would be received in Russia if they knew that I, with a house full of servants, had to do such things myself.'*

King Chulalongkorn returned from Europe on 17th November 1907. Perhaps Chakrabongse thought his father might now come round to meeting his wife but, throughout this time, although Chulalongkorn was duly informed of the altogether favourable impression made by Katya on the Queen and other members of his family and, though he must have been struck by the less rigid ambience of the English royal court, there was no change in his attitude towards his daughter-in-law. Later it is true, he would sometimes ask after her, he would express pleasure in hearing she admired the lay-out of Bangkok, for which he was responsible, and remark that he was interested that she shared his hobby of breeding Leghorn chickens. Otherwise to the end of his days, he remained firm in his resolve neither to meet her nor acknowledge her publicly.

It is probably true that if Chakrabongse had begged to be forgiven for his marriage, his father's attitude might have been different, but he was a proud young man and never brought himself to do so. In the course of one particular discussion the King reminded him that when marrying he should have remembered that he was second in the line of succession, and also enquired what titles he would expect a possible son of his to have. Chakrabongse answered roughly, 'Oh anything. What does it matter? Plain mister will do!'

This petulant remark ceased to be of mere academic interest on Saturday 28th March 1908, for at 11.58pm on that day, Katya gave birth to a son. The exact hour of this event is known as Prince Chakrabongse hoped fervently that his child would come into the world on a Saturday, as both he and the Crown Prince had done. Watch in hand, he was delighted when the infant obliged him — if only by two minutes!

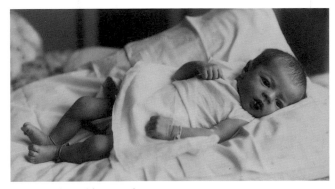

พระ ลำหนัก ปารุสกวัน

Prince Chula aged four months.

Letter from Prince Chakrabongse to Queen Saowabha about his new born son, noting his appearance and the exact time of his birth.

Two weeks later Katya had recovered sufficiently and wrote of the event to Ivan:

> 'The little boy is very pretty but he is already naughty and cries until he gets whatever he wants. He doesn't want to leave me and for the sake of everyone's comfort, we have to leave him to sleep with me. The labour was unbelievably difficult and lasted for a long time. First of all because the baby was wrapped around by the cord as if in a knot and this caused him to be in an abnormal position. After the two doctors had done much work they had to give me some chloroform and the baby was pulled out with forceps … he resembles Lek although perhaps his eyes are a little bigger. His hair is black and the colour of his skin is rather white… On the fifth day a Brahmin ceremony was held but it was private and not official. When he is a month old there will be another ceremony and a name must be given to him for which we will ask the Queen.'

Queen Saowabha, who now became a Grandmother for the first time, was overjoyed, a joy which may have been clouded by Chulalongkorn's disregard of the event, though he might well have been gratified since the Crown Prince, much to his and Saowabha's distress, remained an obstinate bachelor. The Queen, from the first, took a personal interest in all that concerned the little boy, even providing the cot and layette, which she remarked was better and finer than her own children had had, and Chom, one of her ladies-in-waiting, was frequently at Paruskavan with many royal recommendations on every aspect of infant welfare, together with numerous gifts for both the child and his mother.

This Chom, a lifelong companion of Queen Saowabha's since they themselves had been children, had become over the years confidante, Keeper of Keys and Jewels, and nurse to all the Queen's children including Chakrabongse. She must have been a most lovable creature as, although a nurse and two maids had already been engaged, Katya took such an immense liking to her that she begged Saowabha to allow her to be the supervisory nurse. She could obviously not have asked a greater favour, but it was granted instantly, and Chom became a beloved, never forgotten, figure both in the life of Katya and her son.

As a third floor had recently been added to Paruskavan to accommodate the baby, there was ample room in his nurseries for him and a bevy of adoring attendants. He grew into a most endearing dark-eyed child, his looks sometimes delightfully set-off by crisp white rompers trimmed with broderie-Anglaise, and a large muslin, somewhat nautical cap framing his black hair – a completely European outfit, probably ordered from London or Paris.

His grandmother at first gave him the name of Pongchak, being the inversion of chakrapong (the actual pronunciation of Chakrabongse). She also gave him the nickname of Nou meaning 'mouse'. Nicknames have always been common in Siam and particularly necessary in the case of princes with their lengthy titles. Thus Crown Prince Vajiravudh had the nickname of 'Toe', meaning large, while Chakrabongse was called 'Lek' (small) as Katya had earlier explained to her brother. Nou was taken to see his grandmother nearly every day, not always at the Grand Palace or Dusit Palace, but at a modest farmhouse near a rice field called Phya Thai. This was where, at weekends, the King and Queen, accompanied by a relatively small number of courtiers, went to relax and sometimes work in the rice fields with the peasants, enjoying welcome relief from the formality and ceremony of their ordinary life. Saowabha in fact grew to love Phya Thai so much, that later on Chulalongkorn built yet another palace for her not far from their farmhouse, where he drove to see her daily in his yellow electric car.

For at least 18 months, Queen Saowabha's delight in her grandchild was not shared by her husband, and Katya's feelings of rejection were clearly expressed in a letter written to her brother in the autumn of 1909:

'I don't know what to write about us. Lek is out of the house all day because to day is the anniversary of King Mongkut's death and they began the cere-

Phya Thai, where Chula often went to visit his grandmonther.

Prince Chula.

Chakrubongse and Chula aged six months.

*Prince Pong-Chak before his name
was changed to Chula.*

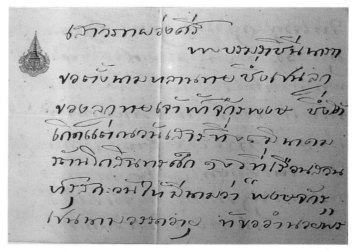

*Document in Queen Saowabha's handwriting naming Chula 'Pong-Chak'. This
was later changed to Chula Chakrabongse.*

Chakrabongse and Chula.

monies at 10 am and will finish in the evening with various breaks in between. But Lek will not return before evening, as the Survey Department, which dispenses a lot of money but doesn't do anything at all, has been placed under the command of the General Staff, giving Lek a greatly increased work load. There are about 30 English people in the department but no real discipline. Lek will have to organize it so that everything is in order. You know his character and if he has to do anything he will devote all his efforts and do it to his best ability. Thank God that at the moment he is well and strong, but I hardly see him at all which makes me unhappy. But what can I do, I have to give in as I can't change anything. I keep hoping just one thing – that when the King sees him working and doing so many useful things he may forgive us.

'At the moment the King is good with Lek but pretends to have no interest in me or Nou. This is his policy, although I know that with other people he enquires about us a lot. I am sure you can understand that until this problem is solved, I will not be truly happy in Siam. It's nothing to do with not being able to go into the Palace or anything like that but I feel threatened. It is as if my child and I do not exist. I am sure you understand me. The Queen is the same as before and very kind and generous to us. But I cannot go and visit the Queen with Nou. Lek takes him there himself and it will be like that until the King changes his policy to us. When Nou goes to the palace all day I miss him very much, but how can I stop his grandmother from seeing her sweet little grandson, especially as he is her only one?'

Finally, it was at Phya Thai in 1910, when Nou was two years old, that he first met his grandfather, who described their meeting thus to the Queen: 'I have seen your grandson today, and he looked so sweet and resembled his father. As soon as I saw him I loved him, for after all he is my own flesh and blood and', he added proudly and thankfully, 'there are no European looks about him at all!'

When the king enquired what he would most like as a present, Nou asked boldly for a horse, a car and a sword. Next day, as though a wand had been waved, there arrived a tiny pony and a red pedal-car, but the request for a sword had been cautiously modified into a replica of an officer's sword and scabbard in the form of a paper-knife.

Unhappily this promising relationship between grandson and grandfather, which Chakrabongse and Katya fervently hoped would also lead to her recognition, was ended by the sudden death of Chulalongkorn, at the age of only fifty-eight, as a result of his chronic kidney complaint, on 23rd October 1910 at Dusit Palace.

As he had reigned so long – forty-two years – no-one could be found who remembered accurately the ceremonial of a royal funeral. In any case nothing could have been prepared, as to have mentioned a monarch's demise beforehand was tantamount to high treason. The whole day of his death was therefore spent in consulting archives and documents, and it was seven in the evening before the ceremonial bathing of the body was concluded by the Queen combing the King's

King Chulalongkorn's funeral urn.

hair with a wooden comb, which was then broken so that it might never be used again.

The body, clad in a red panung and cream-coloured scarf, was first clothed in a silken vest, followed by a gold-embroidered coat, crossed on the breast by a diamond-encrusted baldric. The legs were brought into a sitting position, knees beneath the chin and compactly bound. A cap and gloves of silk and golden shoes were put on, and a gold ring placed in the mouth. The face was hidden by a golden mask, and a high golden crown adorned the head. Thus splendidly arrayed, the body was lifted into a great gold urn with an inner casing of silver, never used except for those of the highest rank. The urn, borne on a gilded palanquin was then ready for its journey to the Grand Palace, where it would lie in state.

By now it was nine o'clock on a dark moonless night, and the procession passing through line upon line of kneeling or prostrate mourners was, as Dr Malcolm Smith described it 'an unforgettable sight … First of all came the master musicians, a piper, a drummer and then two drums so large that each was carried by two men and beaten by a third. They beat upon them softly … and the sound was like the rumblings of distant thunder. Then followed the ancient bodyguard in double file, carrying lighted candles. Between them walked a single file of men, who bore long double-faced drums, some painted silver, others gold. These were the drums of victory, reserved for kings and princes. They herald them into this world, they accompany them in their ceremonial processions through life and they follow them on their last journey. After the drums came the urn set on its palanquin and carried by sixty men. Immediately behind followed the male members of the Royal Family headed by the new King … the only light, the flickering candles of the bodyguard, the only sound the soft throb of the drums and lament of the pipes …'

So died a great king. Dynamic, with remarkable breadth of insight and vision, he possessed also the rare wisdom not to impose too rapidly the modernisation he saw as essential, but to edge Siam towards it gradually while never losing hold of the values, customs, – even superstitions, – that nourish a country's roots in the rich soil of its past. Typical of his instinctive understanding of the age-old traditions of respect in Siam was the occasion at his coronation when, having abolished prostration and crawling, he immediately substituted a 'low bow' to replace them. His achievements were stupendous: the abolition of slavery, the reorganisation of the army, navy and civil service, the foundation of schools, universities and hospitals; the establishment of a respected foreign policy; and the laying-out of Bangkok into a city of tree-lined avenues, parks and palaces. To this day all bear witness to an active mind and heart working together in harmony. As his grandson, Prince Chula, wrote: 'He had a dignified, graceful yet modest personality and will certainly go down in history … as great among kings of any country in the world.'

Katya's more immediate reflections on the King's death, recorded in a letter to her brother, are particularly poignant. At the time, she and Chakrabongse had been planning a trip to Russia en route for the coronation of George V and at

Queen Saowabha, her five sons and grandson in mourning for King Chulalongkorn. Back row: Prince Asdang, King Vajiravudh, Queen Saowabha and Prince Chakrabongse. Front row: Prince Chudhaduj, Prince Chula and Prince Prajadhipok.

recent royal ceremonies it had been intimated that on their return from such a trip, the King would certainly have received her at last.

'I felt as if I was paralysed when I heard the news of this terrible and sudden loss. At first I tried to do my best to help Lek because his grief seemed unending. He was crying like a child because he adored his father. Later I completely lost my appetite and this lasted for a week. I lost weight and became pale. I stayed in bed and tried not to think about anything. I am sure you will understand, as now the fact that the King did not accept me will last forever. This is very hard for me to bear, even though later he had a better opinion of me. However good my life is in the next reign, the thought that the King died without ever knowing me destroys me. He died just at the moment when everything was starting to go well. He had begun to love Nou. I must live just for the present and I have to do it, but I had not anticipated the King's death and how much it would affect me.

'Lek has been appointed Crown Prince for the time being because the King (Vajiravudh) is unmarried and has no heirs. However he has refused to accept any titles saying that if the King has a son he doesn't then want to be stripped of them all again. In addition, he has been appointed general commander of his late Majesty's Royal regiment which previously had been under the command of the Crown Prince. He has a lot of ceremonies, meetings and visits to his mother and I see him even less than I did before.'

*Katya with her sash of the Order of
Chulachomklao Second Class.*

*Certificate from King Rama VI appointing
Katya to the most illustrious Order of
Chulachomklao Second Class.*

VII
A New Reign - Rama VI

As well as making his younger brother, Chakrabongse, heir-apparent, King Vajiravudh, who styled himself Rama VI, promoted him to the rank of Lieutenant-General and Acting-Chief of the General Staff. He was, although holding no ministerial portfolio, required to attend Cabinet meetings, where his opinions and advice were highly regarded. His son was recognised as a Royal Highness, and the King decreed he should be named Chula Chakrabongse.

Katya, who from the first had been known as 'Mom Katerin' – 'Mom' meaning the wife of a prince who is not of royal birth – was now officially recognised as Chakrabongse's consort by the new Sovereign, who also invested her with the order of the Chulachomklao.

Thus the new reign opened auspiciously for Chakrabongse and Katya, and in addition to many official duties, they took an active part in the lively social life of Bangkok, which included keeping open house at Paruskavan, where places were seldom laid at their hospitable table for less than twelve and often for twenty or more.

Two Russian chefs with Chinese assistants, presided in the European kitchen, and a band of women prepared Siamese dishes at a distance from the main house so that odours however appetising, did not offend before the meal was served. The food was particularly delicious for, as well may be imagined, the numerous chefs and cooks vied with one another in the creation of tempting menus. These usually consisted of at least three courses of European dishes followed by delicately spiced Siamese specialities and ended with ices and fresh fruit elaborately carved into imitation miniature fruits, flowers and animals in a manner still common in Thailand today.

Servants at Paruskavan Palace.

Although servants abounded, fulfilling every wish almost before it was uttered, Katya – unlike her lackadaisical mother – took a keen interest in the running of her household. And being like her late father-in-law, Chulalongkorn, a lover of good food and an excellent cook, she soon added many Siamese recipes to her repertoire of traditional Russian dishes.

She also made good use of her professional nursing experience in the Russo-Japanese War, for not a day passed without a visit from her to the staff quarters to advise and care for any of the servants who were ill or ailing. In consequence the staff at Paruskavan grew not only to depend on her for medical attention, but to regard her with grateful affection, and shared her distress when a Russian cook she had earnestly tried to cure of drunkenness reeled into an ornamental lake and drowned among the lotus.

With the assistance of every kind of skilled craftsman, she had also re-arranged and redecorated Paruskavan which was a happy combination of comfortable Western-style sofas and armchairs, covered in flowery chintzes, Chakri family portraits, inlaid mother-of-pearl Siamese tables and red and gold lacquer cabinets filled with curios and shells she had collected on trips to the beach. Similarly Katya would sometimes wear Siamese dress and sometimes fashionable European clothes and, whichever she wears in photographs taken at this time, her attractive generous smile is much in evidence.

The ground-floor drawing-room was blue, while the little sitting-room next door was in pink and was reserved for small tea parties, presumably of a mostly feminine nature. On the floor above, in what was referred to as the green writing-room, she installed her desk, her piano and the only reminder in Paruskavan of her staunch devotion to her faith, an icon where an oil-lamp burned perpetually.

The next door house, previously owned by Vajiravudh, was now taken over by Chakrabongse in an informal swop of land between the two brothers and Katya eagerly planned the items of furniture and lamps she would buy during their forthcoming European trip. In addition to redecorating the interiors of these two houses, she was very active in the redesign and layout of parts of the enor-

Interiors at Paruskavan Palace.

The garden at Paruskavan Palace, designed by Katya.

Chitralada Palace which was given to Chakrabongse by King Rama VI.

The new house at Ta Tien on the bank of the Chao Phraya River.

One of the houseboys carrying food to the main building.

Garden in Paruskavan Palace.

mous grounds, for she truly loved gardening and had the joy of watching flowers and shrubs flourish in the tropical climate.

As if this was not sufficient, Chakrabongse and Katya had also decided to construct a simple villa on a one-acre site on the banks of the Chao Phraya river at Ta Tien. Magnificently sited across the river from Wat Arun, or the Temple of the Dawn, the house backed on to Maharaj Road and Wat Phra Chetuphon, the Temple of the Lying Buddha. The house was envisaged as a simple retreat for boating excursions on the river and for getting changed for state ceremonies at the nearby Grand Palace. As is often the case with building work, all did not proceed as planned and Katya's letter to her brother Ivan are full of complaints about the progress of their house.

Both her garden and the new house were discussed in a letter to Ivan:

> 'I am in the flower and vegetable gardens every morning. I planted them with Thongrod and we have both tried very hard but it is difficult to say what the end result will be. Some of the things are growing now and the cantaloupes and tomatoes are coming up very well. But you have to wait a long time and be patient. I have planted various flowers but they don't do as well as the vegetables. The plants grow too high and I don't really expect any flowers.
>
> 'I have spent such a lot of time on that river house that it is a shame that the building work is going so slowly. In Bangkok there are no independent architects. The man who designed our house is employed by the government and works for us in his spare time so he gives us one drawing at a time. By the time we get the next bit the workers have run out of work to do. But now they have started doing the roof which is quicker than building the house and I hope that within four to five months or sixth months at the latest it will be finished. The garden on the road side I have planted rather nicely but on the river side nothing can be done at the moment. They are building a landing stage and boat house on that side and the whole area is full of building materials.'

As time passed, Chakrabongse, increasingly occupied with his many onerous duties, thankfully delegated most of the supervision, maintenance and running of this vast establishment into the capable hands of his young wife, who at the accession of Rama VI, was still only twenty-two years old.

She was a loving mother, though as was the custom then, with several nurses headed by the beloved Chom, she did not see a great deal of her little son. But when she did, as Chula writes: 'She was perfectly wonderful with toys and cutting out wonderful edifies such as Windsor Castle in cardboard.' Through her, he also became familiar with many Russian and French fairy stories, which she told him in her remarkably fluent Siamese. But when once or twice she attempted to teach him at least a few words in Russian, he either burst out laughing or into tears and, wounded by his reaction, she abandoned the attempt.

Prince Chula with his lead toy soldiers.

Prince Chula with his life guard uniform, a gift from King Rama VI together with a Jor Por Ror medal.

Writing to Ivan, shortly after the King's death she described her two-and-a-half year old son:

> 'He is so amusing now. You can talk to him as if he were a grown-up. He is really very intelligent.
>
> 'Nou's uncle (the King) loves him very much. Nou asked him for a small real car and he promised to give him one. Nou adores him now. When he is naughty or very stubborn the most effective thing is to tell him that his uncle will stop loving him and then he behaves.
>
> 'The King ordered a uniform for him and yesterday the King's tailor, Sompson himself, came to measure him. My "officer" got so frightened of him that at first he refused to be measured but later he agreed and calmed down. He was so excited that very big tears ran down his cheeks... The little boy is afraid of unfamiliar things. When he saw a tape measure he thought it was a doctor's tool... When the uniform is ready I will take photographs of him and send them to you.'

By now the forlorn early days when Katya felt a lonely stranger in Paruskavan were past for, against all odds, she had indeed made it a home, not only for herself but her husband, her son and all who lived there, for as Chula was to write years later: 'I love Paruskavan, the house where I was born more than words can say and, though I have not passed a night within its friendly walls for many years, it is the only place really meaning "home" to me.'

As it happens, he might have spent more time 'within its friendly walls', and with his mother, had his childhood not developed on most unusual lines due to the possessive love of his grandmother.

Saowabha, now Queen-Mother or 'Queen of the Thousand Years', as her title was in Siamese, inconsolable after her husband's death, arrayed perpetually in

Queen Saowabha walking with her grandson.

mourning black, relied on her only grandchild as her chief source of comfort. As Katya acknowledged: 'His grandmother is only healthy thanks to him and he goes to her every day. The doctor says that Nou's visits are the best medicine for the Queen. When he is absent she is very gloomy and she talks a lot about death... I visit her every two and three days and she is always very happy to see me. Now it is clear that I am closer to her than I was before. She has no other grand-children and no other daughter-in-law.'

In her widowhood, as the world held no more pleasure for her, the Queen excluded it – sleeping while it awoke, waking while it slept – and in the seclusion of her palace, reigned unintruded on except by those she wished to see. So it was that Chakrabongse, a most devoted son, noted in his diaries: 'Got up in the middle of the night to see Mother ... ', or 'Went to Phya Thai and stayed till about two a.m.'

As for little Chula, Saowabha could not bear to spend a day – or rather a night – without him. In consequence, from the age of two, his routine would hardly have commended itself to a European nanny! After luncheon at Paruskavan, he rested for an hour and was then awakened, dressed and sent to play with other children in the gardens.

One of these children was Bisdar Chulasewok, son of Chakrabongse's ADC, whose father had brought him when he was three to meet Chula carrying a lighted candle and joss-sticks, symbols of willingness 'to serve the High Prince'. After that, Bisdar came to play at weekends and during holidays, though often he would have preferred to be with his mother, who complained she seldom saw him. Although Chula was always very friendly, Bisdar knew he must never forget their difference in rank. One day when they were enacting a scene from a Western they had seen at the cinema, Chula squaring up to him exclaiming:

'Forget I'm a Prince. Pretend I'm a commoner - then we can really fight!', smiting Bisdar hard on the chin as he spoke. But notwithstanding royal permission and an aching jaw, Bisdar lowered his guard and did not retaliate.

At six o'clock in the evening, Chula was bathed, given another change of clothing and, after supper at seven, his grandmother's car – an enormous red Napier – took him and the faithful Chom to Phya Thai. There the little boy would run to the Great Hall where the children of equerries and other court officials waited to play with him. At nine he was sent for by Chom. He was washed again, made ready for bed and given yet another supper – always the same – cold chicken and ham with a good dash of Worcester sauce.

Then he was taken to his grandmother's room, where she reclined in a great bed enclosed in a high wooden cage, shrouded in a mosquito net. By now, she was herself freshly washed and dressed, ready for her breakfast. Before it was brought in, she chatted with Chula. He was encouraged to bring her news and gossip from Paruskavan, which he knew must include an accurate account of where his parents had been the night before, or who they had entertained if dining at home. He was also expected to describe his mother's evening dress and the jewellery she had worn.

Afterwards, the Queen would enthral him with legends and tales from the rich mythology of Siam, and even a few from Europe. Red Riding Hood was an especial favourite, and often after telling him the story yet again, she would laughingly ask him whether he was quite sure his Grandma was not a wolf in disguise?

Sometimes she would give him an even greater treat and show him some of her wonderful jewellery. This collection had been assembled by Chulalongkorn during his trips to Europe, and included fabulous pieces and parures from Fabergé in St Petersburg, Benson in London and Cartier in Paris. One of Cartier's top designers, Jules Glaezer, recalls receiving a visit from the King, who arrived with his interpreter and asked to see some bracelets. Tray after velvet-lined tray, sparkling with precious gems was laid before the monarch, each dismissed with a negative shake of the head. Finally from a safe the designer's assistant brought out a display of the most rare and costly bracelets in the entire establishment, which was rewarded by an emphatic royal nod and, at last, after a short colloquy with the King, the interpreter spoke: 'His Majesty will take this one.' 'Which one?' 'Why, the whole tray!' Shopping on his scale naturally resulted in a positively Arabian Nights blaze of jewels.

'Grandmother had diamonds in all shapes and sizes,' Chula writes, 'gorgeous rubies like pomegranate seeds, deep green emeralds the colour of creme-de-menthe. Necklaces, rings, brooches and bracelets, all of dark blue sapphires, pale blue turquoise set in beautifully worked enamel, deep rose and pale pink tourmaline and fire opals, shimmering blue, green and gold. There was exquisitely carved jade and, as for pearls, there were cascades of them, every size and colour from pink to smoky-grey, one marvellous necklace in particular which must have been at least six foot long … '.

However, despite ownership of these rare and opulent treasures, his Grandmother would put them all aside and as often as not select merely one

*Queen Saowapha with her ropes of pearls and
diamonds, gifts from King Chulalongkorn.*

bracelet, a ring and a simple brooch – frequently one with Chulalongkorn's
monogram – to wear with her mourning black. When all the cases were closed
and taken away, a mattress was unrolled for Chula behind her bed, and there he
settled till at eleven, the first guests were received and came and went till early
morning.

From then on, lulled by the murmur of conversation and low laughter, almost
awakening at the tone of a familiar voice, listening drowsily for a while then laps-
ing into sleep again, the child slept fitfully. With the serving of the Queen's second meal at two-thirty and the offering of iced coffee and refreshments to the
visitors, the clinking of cutlery and scent of spicy food mingled with their chatter,
flowed and ebbed in and out of his dreams until, at five, the last of them had gone.
Then the shutters were closed on the bright morning, the curtains were drawn,
and all was hushed at Phya Thai until the following night.

Great pains were taken to ensure that nothing disturbed the royal rest. Two
guards diverted traffic to another route on the road outside. In the garden, work
that made the slightest sound was halted, and even birds might not sing, checked
by two men with blow-pipes and clay bullets – both noiseless – who ceaselessly
patrolled the grounds. At eight, little Chula left his Grandmother's room on tip-
toe and, after breakfast, was driven back to Paruskavan with Chom.

Although her beloved husband Chulalongkorn had abolished crawling and
prostration in the presence of persons of high rank, his widowed Queen clung to
the custom, and none might approach her save in this fashion with the exception
of her physician Dr Malcolm Smith. He was permitted to walk into her room for

his daily visit and sit on the floor by her bed while he listened to a long recital of her woes and ailments. Even so, he took good care not to sit with soles of his feet turned towards her – the height of disrespect and bad manners – but from his point of vantage on the floor, noted that it was no easy matter for some of her distinguished callers to exit crawling backwards in full dress uniform and a sword.

The doctor, while he had a great liking and admiration for Saowabha, deriving keen pleasure from her reminiscences of the past with which she often entertained him, nevertheless expressed in his book *A Physician at the Court of Siam* mild disapproval of some of her autocratic ways, particularly that of keeping people waiting so long for an audience.

'Why don't you ask to see her immediately – after all you are her son?' he once asked Chakrabongse.

'Because she is not only my Mother but also the Queen, and that makes all the difference,' Chakrabongse replied cheerfully after kicking his heels for an hour or two.

Dr Smith also noted that one night he saw two elderly princesses wait until daylight hoping to be received, only to be utterly ignored as Saowabha swept past without a word, on her way to a rare morning engagement.

The year after King Chulalongkorn's death, when Chula was three, the Queen had the joy of keeping her grandson entirely to herself for several months at Phya Thai. This was because Chakrabongse was representing Siam at the coronation of George V and Queen Mary in London in June 1911.

Before going to England, Chakrabongse planned to proceed to Russia via the Trans-Siberian railway, taking Katya with him, travelling as his morganatic wife Duchess de Bisnulok. Then after visiting St Petersburg, he would leave for the Coronation while Katya went to stay with her relatives in the Ukraine, where Chakrabongse would join her for a few days before both left on an extended tour of Europe.

Au nom de Sa Majesté le Roi de Siam,

Le Ministre des Affaires Etrangères prie tous les Magistrats ou Officiers, tant civils que militaires, quels qu'ils puissent être, des Princes et Etats Etrangers, de laisser passer librement Madame la Duchesse de Pisnoulok, Epouse morganatique de Son Altesse Royale le Prince Chakrabongs de Siam, Duc de Pisnoulok, avec ses bagages, allant en Europe sans permettre qu'Elle soit opposeé aucune entrave ou empêchement et de donner ou faire donner tout aide et secours, ainsi que les Autorités Siamoises le feraient en étant réquisés.

Le Ministre des Affaires Etrangères.

Donné à Bangkok, le 29 Mars 1911

Katya's passport.

*A*s Chakrabongse wrote in his diary, 'After lighting candles and joss-sticks for my ancestors and the Buddha images, we said good-bye to our son and went by steamboat to Ta Tien.'

Assembled at the landing-stage were members of the Royal Family, prominent army officers, the French Ambassador and the King with a full cavalry escort. Having bidden farewell to each member of this large group and 'respectfully taken leave of the King', Chakrabongse, Katya and Chakrabongse's ADC, Prince Amornthad ('Tapong') continued by boat to their ship the *Donai*. Awaiting them on board were many of the diplomatic corps and their wives and a number of Siamese officials so that it was only after these additional farewells that they finally got away. Even then a few close friends remained for luncheon, going ashore when the ship reached the mouth of the river and finally allowing Chakrabongse and Katya to retire to their cabin.

After two days at sea, their first ports of call were to be French Indo-China – Cambodia and later Vietnam. The journey was recorded by Chakrabongse in his diary and while sometimes disappointingly factual, the reader is able to track their trip in some detail. Of Pnom Penh Chakrabongse commented in a soldierly way that it 'is a city which was attacked in the past by our armies.' Then back on the *Donai* 'on a sea as calm and waveless as a drum-skin', they sailed for Saigon arriving – dead on time – at seven in the morning, where they were welcomed by the Governor's Chef du Cabinet, the Siamese Consul and a representative of the Messageries Maritime.

They found Saigon 'a truly European town with smart shops in the wide main street, shaded by fine trees, with an impressive theatre and pleasant cafés – just as one would find in France.' After an official luncheon and a siesta, they were taken for a drive in the cool of the evening and Chakrabongse noted with surprise that 'what is very strange is that there are graves and burial grounds all over the place, for if the Vietnamese take a fancy to dig a grave, they just go ahead and do so. And for some reason a grave by the roadside is thought especially desirable!' Having dined with the Governor General, one hopes they were early in bed for, around dawn, General Leblois came to conduct Chakrabongse on a tour of army installations.

At the Barracks of the Infanterie Coloniale, after being received by a full fanfare, the Siamese National Anthem and the Marseillaise, they proceeded to the parade-ground, where a company was lined up for inspection in battle-gear. According to Chakrabongse 'company exercises which followed were unimpressive – but the French are often like this'. Nor was he greatly impressed by the next barracks about which his only comment was: 'Not at all clean!'

The next part of their journey was overland by the Chinese Northern Railway, on which their first stop was to be Mukden (scene of the bloodiest battle of the

Russo-Japanese war). Here they were received by the Japanese and French Consuls and officials from the South Manchurian Railway. According to Chakrabongse, 'the station was spacious, clean and tidy, and the hotel, only recently built inside the station, was in European style and extremely comfortable. We had a large bedroom, adjacent bathroom and a sitting-room to receive guests.'

However, hardly had they installed themselves and prepared to relax, than the sitting-room immediately filled with about 20 Japanese officers and officials, who lined up to greet them. As there was no common language, conversation was impossible and Chakrabongse comments: 'They all seemed clumsy and awkward and shook my hand till it was bruised. Even our recently graduated young officers would have coped much better.' These strictures perhaps have a particularly sharp edge due to the ordeal of facing twenty speechless, bowing Japanese, when he and Katya were fatigued and hungry. Fortunately dinner in their private dining-room was 'enjoyable European style food – quite edible.'

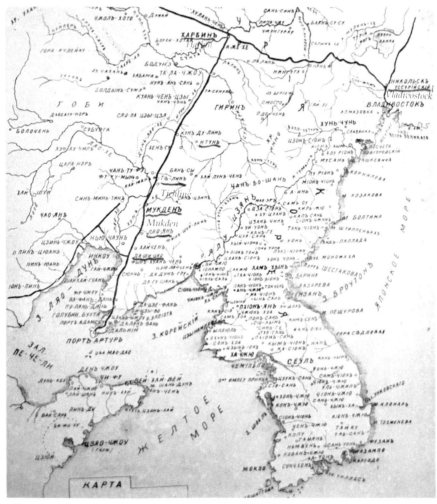

A Russian map showing the route taken by Chakrabongse and Katya on the Chinese Northern Railway.

Early next morning, the Chinese Minister accompanied them on a carriage tour of the town, first with an escort of Japanese cavalry, and on arrival at the Chinese Quarter, by Chinese Mounted Police. In the centre of the walled city was Mukden Palace with a bright yellow and green porcelain roof and scarlet, carved wood supports. Inside the Treasury, they examined rare books and portraits of Chinese Emperors. But what impressed them most was a sumptuous gold-yellow Emperor's coat embroidered with the five-fingered dragon and sewn with seed-pearls, a royal hunting-hat encrusted with precious stones and a lavishly decorated saddle.

From a three-storied pavilion in an inner courtyard, they had a fine view of Mukden and were plied with tea and champagne. After luncheon the Japanese and French Consuls saw them into their train, where they were provided with 'an extremely grand carriage with two beautifully decorated drawing-rooms and a dining-room with the table already laid.'

At Tiehling a General joined them from the Brigade charged with Railway Security. 'He was really of the old school, and much amused us by seizing every chance to bow, salute and click his heels with tremendous verve and precision. These soldiers have no European characteristics whatever.'

Chakrabongse recorded that the train made a short stop at Szepingkai, 'Where the Russian Army made its last stand and where traces of their outposts were still visible.' By eight o'clock that night, they had reached 'Changchun, the last station on the South Manchurian Railway, where the line connects with the Russian Railway.'

Although recorded in his usual laconic manner, this is a moment that must have been emotionally moving for both him and Katya, for it was five years since they had set foot on Russian soil. While to Katya it was naturally dear, as being her native land, it must also have been of great significance to Chakrabongse as the country where his most formative years had been spent – where he had worked so hard and so successfully – where he had fallen in love so madly, and participated in the glories of Imperial splendour, now inexorably in decline.

Chakrabongse continues:

> 'At this station there were not only Chinese and Japanese Guards of Honour and the Mayor of Changchun in uniform, but also a representative bearing greetings from the Emperor and an official from the Russian Railways. Thus there were three nations vying with one another to pay us the greatest attention!
>
> 'After dividing conversation between them as best I could, but naturally chatting a little longer with the Tsar's Emissary, we were just about to board the train in which we had been given a coach from the Imperial Palace, when I was grabbed by a Chinese Official, who announced we could not possible go before he entertained us. So we were hurried into a minute room – not big

enough to swing a cat – and also dirty and smelly, where after drinking even more tea and champagne, we were at last allowed to leave!'

On the train, to his great surprise, was his old batman Alfred whom he had not seen since his days in St Petersburg. At Harbin reached at 9 am the next day, Chakrabongse donned his Russian uniform brought by Alfred, noting that 'although all was in order, my sword had inexplicably been sent to Japan, so I had to borrow Baron Mayendorff's. (The latter presumably being the Tsar's emissary sent to accompany the Prince's party.)

> *'To greet us at Harbin were four Russian Generals including General Mardunoff, whom I was particularly pleased to meet: a most excellent soldier, who made a great name for himself in the recent war. In addition to these top-brass, there was a hundred-man strong Guard of Honour and not one, but a whole line of buglers.*
>
> *'After descending from the train, I inspected the Guard of Honour, followed by two soldiers in the Russian manner. The troops did a march past actually in the station. They have to be battle-ready at all times as their main task – railway security involves many hazards including contending with armed bandits.'*

These formalities completed Chakrabongse introduced the bevy of Generals to Katya and they were then taken on a tour of Old and New Harbin. As it was cold with a chill wind and a sky dark with rain, they were glad to return to their train for luncheon to entertain all who had welcomed them. But although due to leave almost immediately, there was an inordinate delay spent in strolling round the station, of which they must have become heartily tired as the Russian Express came in six hours late!

Continuing their journey, the train passed first through flat cultivated country then twisted and turned among wild hills, where each halt was the centre of an entirely Russian-style village. When Chakrabongse awoke about 8 am they had reached the Bay of Armur, its shores covered by thick dark forest. Shortly afterwards Vladivostock – meaning 'possession of the East' – came in sight.

'Waiting to receive us were the Governor General and a number of notabilities including General Iramen – who fought at Port Arthur – and of course the Mayor.' After presentation of the traditional bread and salt and a bouquet for Katya, there was the usual inspection of the Guard of Honour, followed by luncheon in a restaurant-car that had been joined to their train. At three, they stepped into a motor-car for a tour of the city with the mayor. While ascending a steep hill, the gear-box broke down and, to pass the time before a horse-drawn carriage arrived, they visited what Chakrabongse described as 'a massive store selling everything under the sun.' Thus while the Mayor may have been discomfited by the performance of his motor-car, it must have been delightful for Katya to indulge in a little feminine shopping as a break from the repeated displays of military protocol, bugling and fanfaring that punctuated their long and exhausting journey.

Prince Chakrabongse at Harbin.

Prince Chakrabongse at Vladivostock.

Postcard of St Petersburg.

Indeed, reception committees and guards of honour were on hand at all the various stops made by the train on the way to St Petersburg, where they arrived on 4th June to be installed in the Europe Hotel, just off the Nevsky Prospekt and at that time the finest hotel in the city. The rooms were large and spacious with much walnut panelling, mirrors and even pretty marquetry pianos in the best rooms. Unfortunately, Chakrabongse's diary preserves its factual tone and one can only imagine the excitement they both felt at being back in the city where they had met and fallen in love. In addition, the timing of their visit was most opportune as June in St Petersburg is the time of the famous 'white nights' when dusk does not come till two o' clock in the morning and the Nevsky prospect and banks of the river are thronged with strolling couples into the early hours.

Next day they were up early to devote the morning to Chakrabongse's wardrobe – a Russian tailor measured him for a new white general's tunic, followed by an English tailor charged with equipping him with English court dress: black satin knee-breeches and silk stockings for the Coronation. Later a cobbler attended to take instructions for making buckled shoes. These vital sartorial matters dealt with, after luncheon he and Katya visited Deguy, Chakrabongse's personal tutor in the Corps des Pages, who was in hospital, and they 'discussed certain matters in full'. Perhaps Poum was the subject of this talk as he had been advised to quit St Petersburg during Chakrabongse's visit, as a result of his refusal to return to Siam in 1906 when commanded by King Chulalongkorn and thereby becoming 'persona non grata' with the Siamese royal family. However despite the two old friends being unable to meet, Chakrabongse and Katya would have had all the latest news of him from Madame Chrapovitzkaya, to whom Poum remained devotedly attached.

In late afternoon Chakrabongse was delighted by his visit to the Siamese Embassy for 'all was exactly the same – even every chair and table in the same place as I remembered it, and my bedroom also completely unaltered.'

On 6th June, wearing 'full dress Summer uniform – grey tunic, holster belt and sash', Chakrabongse left by special train accompanied by the Head of the Protocol Department to call on the Emperor at Tsarskoe Selo. After a short 40 minute trip he arrived at the pretty cream-painted station to be greeted by Grand Duke Cyril and a guard of honour, together with some old friends, with whom he had been in the Hussars. After inspecting the Guard and presenting his own suite, the whole company bowled off in open carriages to the Alexandrovsky Palace, which he writes 'was surrounded by flower-beds, some filled with wallflowers, which not only looked beautiful but smelled wonderful.'

At the Palace, he was received by dignitaries of the Imperial Household, then a page conducted him to a reception room adjoining the Tsar's Audience Chamber where, shortly afterwards, he was shown into the imperial presence. The Emperor was 'wearing Hussar uniform and the Chakri sash and chain, and received me in the most charming manner and showed he was really pleased to

Chakrabongse and Katya visiting the Siamese embassy at St Petersburg together with his aide-de-camp Prince Amornthad Krisdakorn (generally referred to by his nickname Tapong).

see me again.' The Tsar talked of the long journey from Siam to Russia, and enquired after King Vajiravudh and the Queen Mother before saying how much he regretted the death of his old friend Chulalongkorn. He also asked after Katya and, as there is something sad and almost cruel in the manner in which a morganatic wife is generally completely ignored by royal personages, this pleased Chakrabongse immensely. (This incident draws attention to the fact that Chakrabongse himself, while mentioning every detail of protocol, dress and deportment of the procession of personalities that stream through his voluminous diaries, also hardly ever mentions the appearance or reactions of his pretty young wife.)

After Chakrabongse had presented the Emperor with a richly chased gold and enamel box which was received with every mark of pleasure, they returned to the reception room, where tables were set out with an enticing assortment of 'zakuska' before luncheon was served, and 26 guests sat down at a long table glittering with silver and a profusion of pale pink roses; Chakrabongse sitting on the right of his host and next to Prince Dolgourouky.

Afterwards Chakrabongse and the Tsar moved to a terrace where the Tsarina Alexandra Feodorovna reclined on a chaise-longue, suffering from a 'nervous disorder', that effectively sequestered her at Tsarskoe Selo and exempted her from her public duties. Her state of health often retained her husband by her side to the detriment of his role of Emperor, and also laid him open to the evil influence of Rasputin, whose star had been in the ascendant since 1908, the year of his introduction to royal circles. Also present grouped around their mother's couch, were the four young Grand Duchesses and the Tsarevitch.

'The young girls', wrote Chakrabongse 'were much grown – the two eldest are now young ladies, and the Tsarevitch, now seven, looks very sweet. The Empress

The Imperial family. From left: Maria, Anastasia, Tsar Nicholas II, the Empress, Tatiana, the Tsarevitch and Olga.

was extremely gracious – much more so than the last time we met, and she enquired most kindly after all my relatives – except my wife.' He presented the Empress with a gold fan encrusted with diamonds before he rose to go and then, accompanied by the Emperor as far as the library, he took leave and left.

He was now whisked off by car to the mess hall at the Hussars HQ where he 'met everyone' – he names them all – and of which 'half were from his time and half were new'. They sat on the balcony used for dining in the summer and, on this particular occasion, for drinking champagne. Chakrabongse drank to the Regiment and the Regiment drank to him; trumpeters played the regimental song; military songs were sung by a band of singers; the commanding officer drank his health; he was toasted by officers of the First Company in which he had served; the trumpeters sounded the First Company song. They all drank together …

Then amidst roars of laughter, an old receipt for horses' hay, which Chakrabongse had never signed, was produced – perhaps it had been fed to Ramushka – and, having signed it some five years late, he finally said good-bye and returned to St Petersburg.

After dining, just as he and Katya were setting out for the theatre, a Minister of the Imperial Household called with a decoration – the Order of St Andrew – a gift from the Tsar. In addition, before leaving, the dignitary asked to meet Katya, which Chakrabongse commented 'was very gracious'. Due to this undoubtedly welcome delay, by the time they reached the Palace Theatre for an operetta 'The Emperor's Guard', the curtain had risen on the second act. Chakrabongse was surprised and discomforted to recognise the theatre as the former palace of the Grand Duke Nicholas Nicholaievitch, where, although the auditorium was new, the entrance and rest of the building were as he well remembered them. 'It felt strange and odd' he wrote and might well have added 'ominous'.

On 7th June, pleased to have no engagements, he and Katya had planned to sleep late, but instead were disturbed quite early with the startling news that Chakrabongse was dead! This report had reached the Siamese Embassy from the Danish, and the Siamese Embassy, thrown into utter confusion, had immediately dispatched a messenger to check the story from Chakrabongse himself, who sent back a reassuring note stating 'I'm not dead yet!' After this unnerving beginning to the day and having concluded the boring task of leaving cards on members of the Imperial Household Staff, Chakrabongse was driven to the Velagin Palace to visit Stolypin, the Prime Minister. One might have hoped for some fascinating insight into Stolypin's character but all that was noted is that they discussed China and the Duma (Russian Parliament), and that Stolypin looked thinner than in his photographs.'

A more descriptive account of the ill-fated premier may be gleaned from Sir Harold Nicholson's book on the life of his father, also Sir Harold Nicholson, later the first Lord Carnock, the British Ambassador, where he describes Stolypin as: 'A tall still man with a dead white face and dead white beard. He spoke in a cold even voice, as cold as the clasp of his white hand. He left an impression only of cold gentleness, of icy compassion, of saddened self-control.' And the Ambassador says further that he considered Stolypin 'A great man - the most notable figure in Europe.' There is no doubt he was an ardent patriot, responsible for far-reaching agrarian reforms, but implacable against the rising tide of terrorism and statesman-like in his manoeuvrings in the Duma in his resolute struggle against revolution. He was also courageous enough to warn the Tsar of the disastrous influence of Rasputin. At the time that Chakrabongse met him, this remarkable man had only three months to live for in September he was assassinated in the presence of the Emperor during a gala performance in memory of Alexander III at the Kiev Opera House.

On 8th June Chakrabongse was again at Tsarskoe Selo where, outside headquarters, he found the Commanding Officer already on horseback with a mount

Postcards sent to Prince Chula from Prince Chakrabongse.

for him, and together they rode to where the Regiment was assembled, where-upon the band again gave a stirring rendering of the Regimental song. The usual inspection and march past followed and after luncheon a special train took him to Gatchina, where he was met by the Commanding Officer of the Cuirassiers attached to the Tsar's mother, the Dowager Empress Marie Feodorovna, who now lived at Gatchina for fear of terrorists.

He was conducted to her presence by General Prince Obolensky, and members of her suite and two of her grand-daughters were present. Chakrabongse recalls that 'like her daughter-in-law, the Tsarina, she was extremely cordial, much more so than on previous occasions. She asked after the King and my mother, which was most unusual as she had never troubled before.' They chatted for twenty minutes and whether this extra veneer of 'cordiality' had been laid on for a specific reason or was merely due to the chance coincidental good humour of the two imperial ladies, he does not speculate or offer any explanation. Possibly they desired to have better relations with an Asian power since Russia's humiliating defeat in the Russo-Japanese War, or maybe both were beginning to appreciate the vulnerability of their own positions.

On 10th June, Chakrabongse and Katya paid a visit to the Empress Marie Hospital, where she had trained and where, with the enthralled student nurses, she had watched the almost daily arrival of her ardent lover in a dashing Imperial carriage.

After this nostalgic visit, he records – perhaps rather too casually - 'I went on to see Tina, an old friend, and chatted about this and that and so I forgot the time and didn't pick Katya up until 8.30.' At this point one really feels for Katya, debarred from entry into the imperial and aristocratic society in which her husband moved so freely and then being keep waiting while he dallied with the mys-

The Summer Palace, Tsarskoe Selo.

terious Tina who, one suspects, must have been more of an old flame than an 'old friend', particularly as unlike everyone else he mentions, he only refers to her by her christian name. It is impossible to know how Katya felt about being back in her native land, or whether she had reunions with old friends and relatives in St Petersburg. Unlike her time in Siam, where extended news bulletins were sent by letter to her brother Ivan, now there was no need and her thoughts and views remain frustratingly hidden.

Next day Chakrabongse went to Tsarskoe Selo for the third time but this time with Katya, as General and Madame Wyekoff, old friends of both of them, had asked them to dine. Having rung and waited for the door to be answered, it suddenly sprang open – and there was Petrof – who had taught Chakrabongse and Poum the rudiments of Russian long ago! It turned out that Petrof, who now tutored the Emperor's children, lived in the same house as the Wyekoffs and had planned this surprise for his old pupil.

The dinner-party which followed with music from a band of spirited balalaika players was lively and amusing. Chakrabongse was also most intrigued by something quite new to him: a very fashionable game – pieces of thin wood, each a fragment of an image which when fitted together formed a complete picture! It was his first sight of – but certainly not his last, for it indeed became all the rage, the jigsaw puzzle!

The next day he went to see the melancholy Resurrection Church built on the site of Alexander II's assassination in 1881 The exact spot where the Emperor fell, mortally wounded by the second bomb, is marked by the inclusion of part of the actual road and railings inside the building.

On 15th June, the day before their departure, they made a point of dining at Ernest's on the Islands, which must have recalled to Chakrabongse the joyful dinner there – their first in a public restaurant – shared by all the promoted Pages at the end of their studies in the Corps des Pages.

On 16th June at 8.30 in the evening, Chakrabongse was at the Warsaw Station to put Katya and her maid Cham on the train to Kiev to stay with Uncle Vanya with whom she was now back in favour. (Being a morganatic wife she was not expected to share in the Coronation ceremonies.) When farewells had been said and she had been waved good-bye, he again went to see Tina at her house, 'because she had asked me to', he adds rather defensively, blanketing any account of their rendezvous with his habitually non-committal phrase: 'We chatted of this and that'. One would have enjoyed hearing more even about this triviality, and how much more one would like to have known his innermost feelings and reflections on what he must have recognised as the precarious and ominous state of affairs in Russia.

But now the hour of his departure had come, and the Mayor of St Petersburg, Major General Wyekoff, Madame Chrapovitzkaya and three or four friends including Tina, saw him off at 11.15pm on the first leg of his journey to England for the Coronation. He and his suite 'travelled by an ordinary train, but the Royal

Household had laid on a special carriage, which was very comfortable.' On 19th June they reached Ostend, and at 10.30 in the morning went by car to the port where the channel steamer 'Princess Elizabeth' awaited them.

Dover was reached at two after a calm crossing and before the ship docked Chakrabongse had changed into a frock-coat in readiness for his reception. The Siamese Ambassador and First Secretary in London, together with the Advisor were there to met him, as well as a Mr Lampson from the Foreign Office. At 3 pm precisely a special train, entirely filled with notabilities invited to the Coronation, left Dover and en route he was handed a list of British and foreign representatives in order of precedence, all to be present at this great event. From this he gathered that 'they are coming from every corner of the earth'.

Sharp at five, the train drew into Victoria, which was splendidly decorated with swagged scarlet curtains, a profusion of banked hydrangeas and geraniums and acres of red carpet. The Duke of Connaught, the King's Uncle, was there to receive him, but surrounded by such a press of relatives and people he already knew, that Chakrabongse remarked ruefully: 'Being rather short and dark, as well as unknown, I was at a disadvantage, but finally got to speak to him.' Even so, as he was still not told how and when he should leave, he and his suite stood around until nearly everyone else had gone.

Eventually however his car was found and before Chakrabongse left, the Duke came up and introduced him to Colonel Sartorius, who revealed that he

Prince Chakrabongse with Phraya Akarajvorathorn, the Siamese Ambassador, arriving at Dover.

had looked after Chakrabongse's father on the occasion of Queen Victoria's Diamond Jubilee and that it was in his residence, Old Swan House in Old Church Street, Chelsea, that Chakrabongse was to stay during the Coronation.

Mr Beale, British Ambassador in Bangkok, Colonel Hume in charge of Siamese students in London and one or two others were waiting to meet him and remained for tea. The house was staffed by members of the Royal Household, there were two cars at his disposal and, having looked over the house, which incidentally had been designed by Norman Shaw in 1876, he pronounced it 'really very nice', and went upstairs to change for the evening. Hardly had he done so when, in a manner reminiscent of the Tsar's emissary arriving precipitately in St Petersburg with the Order of St Andrew, he was told that George V's equerry had called to present him with the Royal Victorian Order, First Class.

Having got dressed again rather hurriedly, he descended and after the exchange of courtesies and expressions of gratitude for the honour, he remounted the stairs to change into court dress, confessing that although he knew his attire was correct, the knee breeches and black silk stockings made him 'feel like a footman', despite wearing the Chakri Star and the newly-acquired order.

Upon arrival at Buckingham Palace he was conducted to a first-floor reception room, where at least eighty people were assembled. He greeted the few he knew but remarked that, though the majority were polite and pretended they remembered him, he could see they did not. Fortunately there were others such as Grand Duke Boris, Prince George of Greece and the Crown Prince of Serbia, who welcomed him warmly and teased him about his 'death' in St Petersburg. He also talked to the Crown Prince Boris of Bulgaria – only eighteen and apparently much nicer than his father 'Foxy Ferdinand'.

A Turkish potentate – short and fat – a Chinese Prince and the Desjamatach Kasa of Ethiopia, none of whom could speak a word of English, made him thankful for his command of the language, though even with this great advantage, he comments:

> 'It is difficult for us to get in with these European royalties as, being all related, they know each other well, whereas I who meet them only rarely, find it hard to know what to say. It's different for the Japanese, because they are powerful and everyone wants to know them, even if they're boorish. But the Siamese are not important enough for anyone really to bother with. It's lucky for me that my relationship with Grand Duke Boris shows I shouldn't be completely ignored. I do notice however that when I'm chatting to someone like him, some of the European royals look quite shocked! In addition, which is rather unpleasant, when some of them are speaking to me, they never look me in the face but stare over my head as though I am not really there!
>
> 'If I were a European royal, I'd be told whom to take into dinner and where I should sit, whereas I have to find it all out for myself. However I made the best of it and discovered I was to take in one of the King's aunts, the Duchess

of Albany, so as I'd never met her, I got the Duke of Saxe-Coburg to introduce us and she was perfectly pleasant.

'When all the guests were assembled, the King and Queen appeared and shook hands with everyone. The King is much more informal than the Tsar. He's got a large bald patch, bulging eyes and a red face, but has an agreeable smiling manner. The Queen looks much better than her photos. She's not all that fat, is quite attractive, smiles a lot and is very polite.'

At dinner, served at small round tables as was the new fashion in Europe, Chakrabongse was seated between the Duchess of Albany and Princess Charles Friedrich of Hesse, and he later noted more happily: 'I talked to both very successfully'.

After dinner the King and all the gentlemen retreated to the smoking-room where he met 'a lot of new people including the Crown Prince of Germany, who was most agreeable.' Later, all the foreign nobles presented their accompanying staff to both the King and Queen, who shook hands with each one of them, which Chakrabongse found most impressive, particularly as he thought the King looked very tired. He was concerned about this, as he had promised to give King George a letter from his brother, King Vajiravudh, and had asked a member of the Household to tell him when to do so. As this had obviously been forgotten, he told a senior official of his problem who, after a word with the King, said he should give it to him right away. It was graciously received by George V, who 'thanked him for it most warmly'.

When they left Buckingham Palace, although it was already 11 o'clock, the evening was not over for all were invited by the Duke and Duchess of Sutherland to a ball at Stafford House.

'Getting there was a nightmare. Everyone had to fight for their cars, and total confusion resulted. Even when our car was found and we got into it, we sat in the vast traffic jam for half an hour. Then it took another half hour to struggle into the house and up the stairs to a reception room, where we were received by the Duke and Duchess. They'd invited the whole world – about 1,500 people – and, as it was impossible to see who anyone was or even move around the rooms, it was no fun at all, so I simply vanished into the crowd',

he adds despairingly.

'Stafford House is massive and very grand, covered in gilding and much nicer than Buckingham Palace, which is very dark and not really suitable as a King's main residence. I longed to leave but couldn't as I knew I was meant to take someone into supper – I thought it was Princess Charles Friedrich so I looked around trying to find her. But when I did get hold of her, she said Prince George of Greece was taking her in. I did my best to look sad, but was really thankful, longing as I did to get away. I began assembling my party, but the minute I'd got them all together, I was spotted by a member of the Royal

Household, who insisted I must have supper and was most concerned that I lacked a partner. He fussed around and found some Englishwoman or other – quite charming and not bad-looking – but I shall never know who she was'.

Nor does he indicate whether her conversation was dull or lively, but merely stated in his usual laconic manner: 'We chatted of this and that.'

Rising with relief from the enforced session at the supper table, he tried once more to organise escape. But though first hopefully and then despondently he searched one gilded drawing-room after another, his party seemed to have vanished without trace. At last by dint of perseverance born of desperation, he succeeded in rounding them up. Triumphant as a shepherd with a recovered flock, he herded them to the hall where a seething crowd of distinguished persons, all with fraying tempers, also waited fretfully for their cars. It was another hour before Chakrabongse's car appeared, and only a wry consolation for him to learn next day that the Crown Prince and Princess of Germany had waited three hours before they got away!

After a boring morning leaving cards and signing visitors' books in embassies and stately homes, there was a horse-show at Olympia. This proved more enjoyable for as Chakrabongse writes 'It was well organised, the hall was lavishly decorated with flowers, a band played and the head of the judges was Lord Lonsdale, whose every breath is devoted to horses, boxing and other sports.' Events were competed in by cavalry from all over the world including the Russian Hussars and there was even a troika in the carriage races.

The evening began with a banquet at Buckingham Palace which was enlivened for Chakrabongse by the congenial company of Crown Prince Boris of Bulgaria, who afterwards remained a lifelong friend. As Chakrabongse noted: 'He had no airs and graces and we laughed and joked a lot until he made such fun of the Turkish Prince that I had to tell him to stop!' At 10.30 the round of gruelling pleasure continued with a fancy-dress ball at the Albert Hall, where all the guests except the royalties were in Elizabethan costume, to raise funds for the new Shakespeare Memorial Theatre at Stratford. Chakrabongse was impressed by the dance floor built over the stalls, the ceiling painted like the sky and the picturesque effect of the dancers in period costume. All the royals left early, thankful to reach home by one o'clock.

He slept late, and, rested and refreshed, attended a great review of 60,000 troops in Hyde Park under the command of General Lord Kitchener. Dinner at St James Palace, requiring knee-breeches once again, was hosted by the Duke of Connaught and Chakrabongse took in Princess Alice of Teck, daughter of the Duchess of Albany, who must have been a delightful woman for there was no talking of 'this and that' but, for him, quite a lengthy description: 'She has a very pleasant manner and isn't arrogant. She was fun to talk to, like a young girl, and was also attractive with a good figure.'

On 22nd June – Coronation day – he was up at seven and reached Buckingham Palace in full General's uniform at 8.30, where all the processional carriages waited in line. In his carriage were the Crown Prince and Princess of Sweden and, to his great pleasure, Crown Prince Boris of Bulgaria. 'The Princess wore a very grand décolleté dress with train, and being an English Princess, the daughter of the Duke of Connaught, she carried her coronet, which would not be assumed until the crowning of the Queen. The carriage was closed owing to the typical English summer weather: strong wind and squally showers.'

By 9.30 the carriage was on the move, and he mentions that 'in front of the Palace was the Memorial to Queen Victoria, just finished and in place this year, which looks very fine', while at the end of the Mall was 'a newly constructed triple arch. Our carriages go through the two side arches, while the King's will proceed through the centre.'

Arriving at Westminster Abbey via Trafalgar Square, they left their carriages and formed a procession to enter the Abbey in order of rank. Chakrabongse then gives a detailed account of the entire ceremony, which, rather surprisingly, he criticises as being 'though impressive, a bit lax and not formal enough'. This was because he had noted one or two furtive nibblings at chocolate and biscuits and cases of 'nodding off' among the aristocratic congregation, though he did hope that when the newly-crowned King and Queen retired behind St Edward's Altar, 'they maybe had something to eat as by then it was two o'clock.'

Back at the Palace 'It was a muddle, no one knowing where to find their cars though eventually everyone got away and probably, like me, after lunch at four felt pretty done in.'

Prince Chakrabongse dressed in the uniform of Commander-in-Chief of the Siamese army for the coronation of King George V.

On 23rd June, Chakrabongse took a brisk walk through the gardens of Buckingham Palace to reach Constitution Hill in order to see the Royal Progress through the City. 'Unfortunately the weather was still terrible … rainy and cold. The police were well in charge of the crowds, but of course got complained about purely for that reason!'

That evening there was a reception at the Foreign Office given by Sir Edward Grey, the Foreign Secretary, who only three years later, would pronounce in grave and memorable words his valediction to a world which still seemed secure at this time.

The next morning, yet again windy and cold, saw the King and Queen leave with all the visiting royalties in a special train for a Review of the Fleet. After the Mayor of Portsmouth had welcomed the new Monarch, the King and Queen and some of their distinguished guests boarded the royal yacht 'Victoria and Albert', while Chakrabongse and others were assigned to the 'Alexandra', where luncheon was served on board. At Spithead, 164 warships ranging from dreadnoughts to torpedo-boats and submarines were assembled in four lines, the last entirely composed of foreign vessels.

As the 'Victoria and Albert', followed by the 'Alexandra' steamed slowly between the second and third lines, a simultaneous gun-salute was fired from every ship, while each sailor at his station, cap off and waved in the air, gave three rousing cheers and the band struck-up 'God Save the King'. 'It was', Chakrabongse noted, 'most moving and memorable.' The royal yacht then turned and, passing between lanes three and four, cast anchor so that both English and foreign admirals could come aboard and be received by George V. 'This was indeed a tricky business, involving boarding numbers of small craft bouncing and tossing in the choppy seas, and then scaling a ladder into the 'Victoria and Albert.' Meanwhile a sedate tea was served in the 'Alexandra' to Chakrabongse and other royals, thankful – one imagines – to be spared so perilous a proceeding and possibly an undignified ducking!

Although the King and Queen were to stay the night and would see the Fleet dressed overall and illuminated, there was insufficient accommodation for everyone so Chakrabongse and many others returned to London that afternoon.

After a week-end with no particular engagements, there was a garden party at Buckingham Palace but, as it was pouring, Chakrabongse decided not to attend as he thought it 'unappetising weather to wander round a garden', regretting his decision later when he heard that, owing to the rain, the party had been transferred inside the Palace and was entertained by Russian dancers and singers, which he knew he would have enjoyed. However he did attend a Gala performance at Covent Garden. 'My seat was right behind the King and Queen in the large new royal box opposite the stage. All boxes, stalls and circle seats were crammed with ambassadors, foreign ministers, Indian Rajahs, government officials and their wives. Men were in full dress and the women covered in jewellery … all very grand and glittering in the magnificent auditorium.'

The first act of 'Aida' opened the proceedings followed by the balcony scene from 'Romeo and Juliet', with Melba in fine voice; then 'The Barber of Seville' and, to make up for Chakrabongse's disappointment of the afternoon, a ballet in which the leading dancers were Nijinsky and Karsavina. A supper party and ball followed given by the Duke and Duchess of Manchester. 'Although the King and Queen were not present, it was the usual awful crush', and, as the evening wore on, Chakrabongse became nervously on the alert, fearing a repetition of 'the ordeal of Stafford House'. However, by leaving as soon as he decently could, he escaped this dreadful fate and got away in comfort, arising in good spirits the next morning for a tour of the magnificent new Automobile Club, where he much admired the huge swimming-pool, fencing-room and shooting gallery.

As there was yet another garden party at Buckingham Palace on, for once, a fine afternoon, he went to it and commented: 'The only good thing about this palace – which is so dark – is the garden which is really lovely; much bigger than Dusit Park in Bangkok, so that even though 6,000 people had been invited, it did not seem overcrowded.'

After dining at home, he went in full dress uniform to His Majesty's Theatre for a Gala Performance with Forbes Robertson speaking a specially written prologue and scenes enacted from Shakespeare. During the interval, as some of the foreign envoys took leave of the King and Queen, Chakrabongse followed their example, thankfully returning home instead of proceeding to a 'grand party given by the Earl of Derby' where he was certain to suffer in another 'awful crush'.

The festivities over, Chakrabongse left for Dover next day in company with the Crown Prince of Montenegro and his wife, two Coburg Princes, Crown Prince

Prince Chakrabongse together with guests at the coronation.

Prince Chakrabongse with King Gustav V of Sweden.

Boris of Bulgaria, and the Archduke Franz Ferdinand of Austria with his morganatic wife the Duchess of Hohenburg, whose assassination only three years later would alter forever their enclosed world of royal rank and privilege.

Boarding the channel steamer about 10.30 am, some of the party retired to their cabins while Chakrabongse, the Coburg Princes and Boris remained in the saloon, 'chatting in a friendly and pleasant manner'.

Chakrabongse in fact, was feeling so relaxed that he only just caught his Berlin train by 'running and jumping on it', anxiously watched by Tapong, his aide-de-camp, 'while the Crown Prince of Bulgaria waved farewell and seemed very sad to see me go.' After a brief stop in Berlin, he went in an ordinary train through Prussia where he and Tapong changed to a Polish train at Alexandrow on their way to Warsaw.

Evidently having had enough for the time being of receptions, guards of honour and finding something appropriate to say to perfect strangers, he had informed no-one of his journey and in consequence, upon descending from the train at Alexandrow 'in my plain civilian clothes, I passed for an ordinary person. A lowly customs official asked me to bring my luggage for inspection, but I stopped the porter, who seemed puzzled, from complying. Then, on seeing my passport, the police were shocked and began to rush around and wouldn't even let me get a glass of tea.' Finally he managed to obtain this, and returned to the train, which reach Warsaw about midnight. Here, despite being incognito, the Head of Police was on hand with a car to take him to the Hotel Bristol where, because accommodation had been booked in Tapong's name, they were given 'very ordinary rooms'.

However, once the police had revealed his identity, he was begged to accept one of the hotel's best suites. Angered at being deprived for a few hours of being 'ordinary', he 'vehemently refused', and after supper retired in high dudgeon to his 'ordinary' rooms! Nevertheless, in the morning he admitted in his diary that having travelled by 'ordinary train, not wagons-lits, I was very tired and yawned and dozed all day'.

The following day, Chakrabongse and Tapong started on the last leg of their journey to Kiev. Having not much enjoyed his brief excursion into the 'ordinary' world, the prince remarked with satisfaction that 'a comfortable special waiting-room had been put at our disposal, and when the train came in at four, wagons-lits had been reserved.' Although only a fortnight had passed since he and Katya parted in St Petersburg, it must have seemed to him far longer. With so much magnificent entertainment and sumptuous ceremonial compressed into this period, each day must have seemed prolonged beyond its actual span.

Meanwhile for Katya, having returned to the easy-going simplicity of a Russian country house full of relations and old servants who had known her from childhood, her life in Siam must have begun to seem unreal and the dark Asian faces and sounds and scents of the Orient, figments of a singular exotic dream. Furthermore, the lengthy letters she received from her husband, describing the

Kings, Queens, Princes, Princesses, Dukes and Duchesses who had attended the crowning of a monarch of a great and powerful empire must have increased her awareness that, despite their marriage, their lives to some extent would always be divided by her being a commoner. Even in Russia – her native land – she had scarcely been acknowledged, and must have noticed, rather ruefully, Chakrabongse's gratification when she was asked after or even mentioned by august personages who would never have condescended to meet her.

When Chakrabongse's train drew into Kiev on the morning of 1st July, he saw as if for the first time the pretty girl who had so enchanted him, not in isolation, as in St Petersburg and Bangkok, but among her own people: uncles, aunts, cousins and friends in the environment where she had spent her earliest years.

After the joyful welcome and introductions, everyone accompanied Chakrabongse and Katya to the church of St Vladimir, which on a previous visit had so impressed him that it had been arranged for him to go and revisit it on arrival. They were received by a venerable priest and a Reserve General in charge of security and when, having admired the building and its fine mosaics, they emerged from its dark interior into dazzling sunshine they were taken aback by the sizeable crowd which had assembled to inspect the Siamese Prince, who had married a girl from Kiev.

After a festive luncheon, they set out in two cars for Uncle Ivan's country estate Krasnaya Sloboda. The journey in the intense summer heat took two hours on roads thick with dust that rose in suffocating clouds, choking their nostrils, powdering their hair and almost completely obscuring the landscape. As usual there was a puncture and a tyre change before they transferred to horse-carriages for the last stage of their drive, over an unmade road.

They were therefore thankful to reach the house, which Chakrabongse described as 'large and well built of wood, set in a charming garden filled with fragrant shrubs and roses, and also a vegetable garden, while beyond was a rambling tree-shaded park.' Here they encountered another contingent of relatives, so that there were more greetings, handshakes, embracing, low-bowing from the numerous servants and unconcealed curiosity about Katya's princely husband.

'Next day', wrote Chakrabongse, 'was spent in doing nothing in particular except the usual country-house pursuits: eating, sleeping, wandering about, playing tennis and playing bridge.' The day had been extremely hot and in the cool of the evening they played cards and sat or strolled in the garden, all of which was so pleasant that they did not retire until one o'clock in the morning.

On 4th July, in true Russian tradition there was to be a picnic in the woods, and from early on there was great preparation with much running back and forth, and animated chatter and laughter before they finally set out. As the old days of going to picnics in creaking wagonettes were no more, they went in cars and paid the penalty of progress by once again being smothered in dust. But walking with hampers, baskets of provisions and wine into the depths of the shadowy forest, they were almost instantly cooled and refreshed by shade and silence. After the

Katya's uncle's house in Krasnaya Sloboda, outside Kiev.

Uncle Vanya and Katya.

Katya playing tennis.

picnic a light wind sprang up foretelling rain which, fortunately, was delayed until nightfall, bringing with it a scent of clean delicious freshness.

On 5th July, as it was so much cooler, there were many games of energetic tennis, and although Chakrabongse was out of practice and dissatisfied with the way he played, 'after a number of sets, my game began to take shape'. As the following day was their last at Krasnaya Sloboda, the morning was occupied with taking photographs. Although in all of them Chakrabongse is arrayed in Russian Hussar uniform, he still strikes an unmistakably exotic note among the country gentry, the hatted ladies and formally dressed gentlemen, seated on sunny verandas or grouped beneath leafy trees.

About seven in the evening, they proceeded to the main road in carriages and then left by car for Kiev. The rain had freshened the air and laid the dust, allowing the rolling pastures, the forests – mostly royal property – and rustic villages to be clearly seen and admired. Back in Kiev, after stopping at Uncle Ivan's house to wash, change and rest, they went to a park called 'The Merchants' Meeting Place' situated high above the River Dnieper with a distant view on the other side of a statue of Saint Vladimir. Here they dined in an open-air summer restaurant, where the food was excellent, and later sauntered along the flower-bordered paths of the park, listening to the band and the splash of many fountains, which proved so agreeable that they lingered there till three in the morning.

'Khijniakoff was my guest to-night', Chakrabongse records with evident pleasure 'and everybody from Sloboda came. I had a good chat with them all and felt I got to know Katya's relatives really well.' It will be remembered that the Khijniakoffs were Katya's relatives on her mother's side and occupied various professional posts such as Uncle Vanya the Director of the Regional Railway, or other cousins becoming doctors, or lawyers.

On 6th July after luncheon, Chakrabongse and Katya bought flowers and went to lay them on her mother's grave. The cemetery was a long walk away at the summit of a steep hill and they found it melancholy and depressing, not only because death presided there, but because it was sadly neglected and overgrown, the grandiose monuments standing stark and forlorn among weeds and uncut grasses. 'Besides', noted Chakrabongse 'it is an unpleasant neighbourhood where prostitutes are on the prowl.'

After dining very early all the relations came in full force to see them off, and it was just as well that Katya did not know, as she leaned from their carriage, waving good-bye after so happy a visit, that she would never see any of them or her childhood home of Kiev ever again.

Before returning to Siam, Chakrabongse and Katya decided to take a short European tour together. Their first day was in Warsaw where, after a sightseeing tour by car, they had in the evening the rather unnerving experience of seeing a performance of 'The Mikado' in Polish. Unable to comprehend a word of it, they were baffled by the plot – and no wonder! They did however enjoy 'buying a few trifles next morning, in the excellent shops, and found it good fun to walk around

Katya and Prince Chakrabongse with cousins and friends in Kiev.

Katya mother's grave in Kiev.

without anyone knowing who we were!' By eleven that night they were on their way to Budapest and were given a corner suite at the Hungarian Hotel, where they had not only a fine view of the city, but also a fine full-length portrait of King Chulalongkorn, with a caption stating the date that he had occupied the same suite long ago.

Then on to Vienna where the high point of their stay was a visit to the Old Palace to admire a magnificent display of royal regalia: crowns, maces and sceptres encrusted with diamonds, the Emperor's resplendent Order of the Golden Fleece, jewellery from the reign of Marie Theresa and parures of rubies, emeralds and sapphires. Also on view was the cradle of the King of Rome, the crown of the Holy Roman Empire and the Royal Hungarian crown. They visited the Royal Riding School where Chakrabongse described 'teams of eight black and eight white horses with noses like Roman emperors'.

Next stop was Berlin, where they stayed in the new Adlon Hotel, completed three years earlier in 1908, and replete with all up-to-date equipment: messages via pneumatic tube, bells worked by a flashing light system, a vast cold store and a pool for live fish. In Berlin they also saw an operetta concerning a Siamese King called Chulinglong with twelve sons who followed him around from one act to another. The Siamese consul had told Chakrabongse that the operetta was no longer on, no doubt fearing he would be angered by such a frivolous treatment of his country and revered father. In fact, he was heartily amused. On a more serious note, the avid tourists sat through Lohengrin and Tannhauser, Chakrabongse finding the latter 'a Wagner opera which is quite bearable'.

The next day in his capacity as Commander of the First Regiment, Chakrabongse had made an appointment with Lieutenant Englehart, Agent for the Wright Flying Machine, who duly took him to an airstrip east of Berlin, where he saw much of interest, particularly a plane designed for military purposes. He was informed that the price of 22,000 marks included pilot training and a full explanation to mechanics for repairs etc. Other companies were also accommodated on this site, and had hoped to charge onlookers for watching the flight and descent of the still novel flying machine, but as spectators could see these without entering a payment area, the scheme was hardly remunerative!

Another day was spent pleasantly in the 'Western Shop', one of the large new emporia which were beginning to spring up everywhere at this period. They were especially interested in this particular store as, when he was last in Berlin, King Chulalongkorn had spent three consecutive days there. As Chakrabongse had inherited an indefatigable zest for shopping, not only from his father but from most of the Siamese Royal Family, they 'went to practically every department and bought many things in the enormous Renaissance-style building which sold food, clothes, hardware, toys, theatre and train tickets and even land, as well as including a restaurant and coffee-shop.'

From Berlin they went to Paris, where naturally they did much feminine shopping: dresses, millinery, gloves and two diamond brooches. They lunched at

Armoneville in the Bois and dined at Durand (*Canaton la Presse*) and Chateau de Madrid. They enjoyed 'Mariage de Figaro' at the Comedie Française They spent a whole day at Chantilly, and visited the Sèvres Factory near St Cloud, while at the Louvre they 'walked until our legs were stiff and our eyes glazed and, at the Luxembourg, admired many fine painting apart from some ugly modern ones in shades of mauve and green'.

At this point several days are omitted from Chakrabongse's copious diary, and it would seem likely that he was becoming jaded after four months of continual travel. For, apart from the visit to St Petersburg and his attendance at the British Coronation when he knew his presence was of service to his country, as a professional soldier devoted to his calling, he may have often found days filled only with sightseeing and even more trivial pleasures more onerous than the hard-working organised life to which he was accustomed.

Their next stop Hamburg which they found unremarkable and rather repellent with its massive Town Hall and huge monument to Bismarck – typically German. They stayed at the Hotel Atlantic, where the restaurant was run by Forte, 'a well known restaurateur' – could it have been an ancestor? Their train left for Flushing in the afternoon, from whence they crossed to Folkestone and, on reaching Charing Cross, drove to the Ritz which disappointed them. It did not live up to its worldwide elegant reputation for although their suite was pleasant, 'the curtains were shabby and quite grubby. This bad impression was increased when they dined in the restaurant where there were few people as, being August, 'all the smart set is out of town', nor did the food make up for this as it was pronounced 'poor and in fact down right not tasty!'

However, London had compensations such as an amusing supper at the Savoy, shopping at Asprey's and Liberty's, the theatre ('Kismet' at the Garrick), the Zoo, the Wallace Collection and the National Gallery.

On Sunday as the weather was pleasantly warm and fine, they decided to leave town, and caught a train from Paddington with an acquaintance only referred to as Dickson, with the intention of going on the river. At Taplow they hired a fly and clopped past Taplow Court which Chakrabongse was anxious to see again, as it was there he had stayed with his brother the Crown Prince in 1900. From Skindles Hotel at Maidenhead, having ordered a picnic meal to take with them, they hired a motorboat and joined the throngs of bustling or slow-moving craft – some graceful under sail – that animated the sparkling river. The verdant fields and shady trees, the charming coquettish villas, with their trim lawns and brimming flower-beds sloping to the water's edge, enchanted them, leading Chakrabongse to exclaim: 'It seemed like being in a lovely park. I've never seen a river like this before – indeed there is nowhere so pleasant for an excursion as boating on the Thames.'

Refreshed after their day out, Monday saw them shopping again. First at Tooth's in Bond Street where Chakrabongse bought 'two oil paintings, five coloured engravings after Fragonard and three engravings of dogs', while at

*Katya in two of the fashionable outfits
purchased during their European trip.*

Katya in her room at the hotel.

Agnew's he added 'a snow scene with a flock of sheep and two cottages, whose lighted windows were reflected on the snow.' The afternoon was devoted to a fitting for Katya's riding-habit in Hanover Square where she had to mount a model horse leading her husband to comment: 'This was a serious business taking a full hour and was no laughing matter.' A brief stop at Atkinsons the perfumer and a hat shop followed, and then a move was made to Waring & Gillow, the decorators of the ballroom at Paruskavan, who were also much patronised by other members of the Siamese royal family. Here they bought 'a lot of good stuff' from the five floors of this emporium.

The next morning, they left England en route for Siam, and Chakrabongse's diary entries become brief and hurried as his thoughts began to turn homeward.

King Vajravudh in coronation regalia.

IX
Life under King Rama VI

*B*ack in Bangkok in late October, Chakrabongse and Katya were precipitated immediately into the elaborate preparations for the coronation of his elder brother, King Vajiravudh, who had elected to assume the title of Rama VI. This was to be celebrated with traditional splendour on 2nd December 1911 and would be attended by a great concourse of foreign royalties invited by Chakrabongse during the recent British coronation, including Prince Alexander of Teck, younger brother of Queen Mary, with his wife Princess Alice; Grand Duke Boris who had been in the Corps des Pages with Chakrabongse, and who would stay at Chitraladda Palace, put at Chakrabongse's disposal during the Coronation; Prince William of Sweden with his wife Grand Duchess Marie of Russia, also known to Chakrabongse since his days in St Petersburg; Prince Waldemar, brother of King Frederick VIII of Denmark; and Prince Fushimi of Japan.

Among the many items reaching the capital for the events were no less than seven hundred and fifty tons of furniture, shipped from England – most probably from Waring and Gillow – to refurbish some of the many palaces chosen to house these distinguished guests, and thousands of lamps for street illumination.

Queen Saowabha, a connoisseur of cars since the early days of motoring and a regular subscriber to the *Autocar*, was also awaiting delivery of 26 assorted motors, which she proposed to distribute among favoured members of her family as mementoes of her son's accession. At the same time, the *Bangkok Times* of 3rd November 1911 announced: 'Mr Carl Fabergé has the honour to announce that during Coronation Week, he will hold an exhibition of his famous objets d'art from 2-4 p.m. at the Oriental Hotel.' The visit of the great Russian craftsman and jeweller had been arranged by Chakrabongse, an admirer of his work since the first days of his ardent love for Katya, when Fabergé had designed an enchanting blue enamel handbag initialled K.D. as his first gift to her. The Bangkok exhibition proved an immense success and was to be the beginning of a long-lasting connection with the Siamese Royal Family. A miniature model of the mighty Emerald Buddha carved in jade was given to the newly-crowned King by Chakrabongse, and over the years, exquisite jewellery and elegant and costly trifles flowed into the royal palaces from the same source.

On 28th and 29th November, the Royal representatives with their extensive suites arrived by State Barge on Chulalongkorn's yacht 'Maha Chakri', to be officially welcomed and conveyed in state carriages with cavalry escort to an immediate audience with the King and the Queen Mother, before dining with their royal hosts that same evening. On such an occasion, waiting at table was in the hands of the royal pages wearing blue tailcoats and cream-coloured knee-breeches, and the complete service of gold plate consisting of at least one thousand pieces, brought back by Chulalongkorn from Europe, would be used.

Prince Chula aged three (bottom left) at the coronation parade of King Rama VI.

King Rama VI at the coronation ceremony.

Foreign royal guests attending the coronation of King Vajiravudh. Front row (left to right):- HSH Prince Alexander of Teck, HIH Grand Duke Boris Vladimirovitch of Russia, HI and RH Princess Marie of Sweden, Duchess of Södermanland (formerly HIH Grand Duchess Marie Pavlovna of Russia), HRH Princess Alexander of Teck (later HRH Princess Alice, Countes of Athlone), HRH Prince Waldemar of Denmark and HRH Prince William of Sweden, Duke of Södermanland. Back row (left to right):- HRH Prince Axel of Denmark, HRIH Prince Fushimi-no-Miya of Japan, HRH Prince Aage and HRH Prince Erik of Denmark.

Protocol, seating of guests, choice of menus and wines, was given painstaking care and thought by one or two of the many Siamese princes who had been educated in Europe. In fact one of them would often remain in the kitchen quarters during a dinner or banquet to ensure that all was served in the right order, particularly the wines.

Religious ceremonies, luncheons, dinners, banquets, illuminations and fireworks followed each other in rapid succession. No guests however were expected to be present on the morning of 30th November when, according to the *Bangkok Times*: 'His Majesty gave a feast and distributed robes to the eighty High Priests of the Kingdom at Amarindra Hall'. However, on 1st December – the day before the Coronation – there was a luncheon and, in the afternoon at the Emerald Buddha Temple, consecration of the holy water for the Coronation, when Royal representatives were expected to attend in full dress.

The splendid ritual of the King's crowning was duly celebrated, culminating in the presentation to the King, dressed in robes of silk and gold brocade, of the Regalia: swords, gold slippers, a gold water-vessel and spittoon, and finally the high tapering diamond-studded crown, which the King placed on his own head as monks chanted a blessing and the artillery fired a royal salute.

Little Chula, aged three, permitted by the monarch to wear the full dress uniform of a subaltern in the First Foot guards, attended some of the festivities that followed by the side of his grandmother. Much photographed in this martial outfit, one picture shows the tiny officer, overcome by fatigue, asleep in a chair during the review of troops.

Before they returned to England, Chakrabongse took Prince Alexander and Princess Alice to Ayudhya, the former capital of Siam. There the Governor introduced his brother to the distinguished visitors in their own tongue. Unfortunately, in Thai more emphasis is placed on whether the sibling is older or younger rather than the specific sex, and Princess Alice recounted that, when an impressive figure in military uniform with a luxuriant black moustache was presented to them as 'My Sister', she was hard pressed not to break into helpless laughter.

As Prince William of Sweden was a keen sportsman, Chakrabongse, though a sincere Buddhist who abhorred killing any living creature, felt it his duty as a good host, to organise a tiger shoot for him. His wife, Grand Duchess Marie, accompanied the hunting-party, and a delightful place was chosen on the west coast of the Gulf of Siam, where a luxurious camp was pitched.

Many year later Prince Chula was to recall in one of his books of memoirs: 'My mother was deeply impressed by the beauty of the place. The beach was so wide and the sand was so white and soft as snow. Beyond the plain by the sea there was a range of wooded hills, so that between the hills on one side and the bright blue sea on the other, it was destined to be an ideal seaside resort.'

The Grand Duchess later wrote about her trip in *L'Education d'une Princesse*:

> *'The fêtes which began directly we arrived were so splendid, so varied, so sumptuous and of such fantastic beauty, that they seemed unreal – fairy-like…*
>
> *'After the Coronation, all the other guests departed, but we stayed to see more of the country and take part in the hunting-parties organised in honour of my husband … We went up the river in sampans, arranged most comfortably. At each stopping-place, a meal awaited us, served beneath an arbour of bamboos covered with palm leaves. Native musicians played softly while we ate … travelling thus, we reached the sea where vast tents filled with every possible comfort awaited us. Here we passed several days, we bathed delighting in the freshness while the men hunted every day … Never in my life have I known a whole period so luxurious as the time I spent in Siam.'*

The place of their encampment where 'the sand was as white and soft as snow', was called Hua Hin, meaning head of stone, so-called because of the large granite boulders bordering the deep blue sea. So enchanted were Chakrabongse and Katya with the place that they decided to build a small white wooden house there, which from 1913 became a favourite retreat during the hottest months. Here dispensing with formality, they enjoyed rustic seclusion as had Chulalongkorn and Saowabha at Phya Thai. Just as in Bangkok, Katya developed a beautiful garden, despite the water shortages of the area and eventually a larger more solid house was built, designed by the British architect Edward Healey, who became a close family friend. This second house was built of teak very close to the sea, leading Chakrabongse to write in his diary: 'Being in the new house is like being in a ship … the balcony resembles a deck and the various rooms are like cabins, and one hears all the time the sound of the waves and wind …' Soon a tennis-court was added and the house was filled with guests every weekend. Chakrabongse records more than once that he went out rowing before daybreak,

The house at Hua Hin c. 1917.

Katya and Chula on the rocks at Hua Hin.

walked with friends along the beach in full moonlight, went swimming and sometimes gathered oysters near Tortoise Hill.

Even before a fast train linked it to the capital, Hua Hin had blossomed into a fashionable and popular seaside resort which had become so, like Brighton, due to royal patronage.

During these last few years before the First World War eroded and destroyed so much that seemed stable and immutable, Katya and Chakrabongse's life seemed set on a course of happy equilibrium combining rewarding hard work, formality and relaxed carefree pleasures.

The promise of Chakrabongse's youth, his devotion to duty and great mental abilities were fully and increasingly recognised, while Katya's wonderfully quick and lively personality, the full part she played both in her home and the wider social sphere, had earned her general regard. Both the King and one of her husband's half-brothers, Prince Mahidol, had great affection for her, while Queen Saowabha's heart she had won from the first, not least because she so admirably accepted the Queen's claims upon her son. In addition, the interest she took in every detail of the running of Paruskavan, the personal work she put into replanning some of the gardens, her swift acquisition of their difficult language, knowledge of their cuisine, and above all her care for their health and welfare, had endeared her to all her staff, while her personal maid Cham had become her deeply attached and devoted shadow.

Formal rites and religious ceremonies played an almost daily part in their life, and a typical entry in Chakrabongse's diary read: 'Today, apart from going to the office, I went to three funerals – all military people.' Besides these melancholy events, there were birthdays, commemorative services of many kinds – and plays – these last, although they would seem to offer only entertainment, sometimes required a high degree both of stamina and sheer endurance. Particularly was this the case when they were produced, not at a theatre, but at the Palace, where they were frequently written and performed by the King himself, so that attendance was obligatory. For instance, Chakrabongse noted in his diary: 'Tonight there's another play. One of the King's new ones from an Indian story – started at twelve and finished at four a.m.' And the next night: 'Play at the Palace again which went on for ages!'

On the other hand, there was the cooling refreshment always to be found at Hua Hin, while back in town new entertainments were springing up. There might be spur-of-the-moment visits to the still novel cinema where films shown included such enticing titles such as 'Million Dollar Mystery', 'The Devils Eye', 'Madame Sans-Gene', and the 'Red Circle', a series in fourteen episodes. Occasionally, there was the circus, where alas one year 'the best performing bear died from sunstroke'. Among other annual events, the Dusit Park Fair was always well attended as royalty and nobility ran stalls or charged for amusement. One year Katya was an exhibitor when she was congratulated on her 'charming pale

blue stall, featuring a fountain and a fishing-pond which produced many agreeable sur-
prises for fortunate anglers.'

After their return from Europe, Katya developed a passion for racing at the fashionable Royal Bangkok Sports Club, owning several racehorses herself. Over the years she
owned, 'Sally', 'Nancy', 'Why Not', 'Flirt' and 'Aminda', and according to the *Bangkok
Times*, 'Sally' and 'Aminda', each in their turn, delighted their proud owner by coming
first.

An interest which engaged Chakrabongse's serious attention was aviation, for he
had long recognised the future importance of the aeroplane for civil and military purposes. Therefore when a French pilot gave a flying demonstration in Bangkok,
Chakrabongse and one of his brothers – uniformed, booted and spurred – were each
taken up for a flight. As a result, Chakrabongse was even more convinced of the aeroplane's strategic value and, subsequently, despatched three of his young officers
to France to be trained as pilots.

Although he worked at the War Office from ten to five, Chakrabongse often rose at
five a.m. to watch the training of military cadets. As Heir Apparent he also had to attend

*The three Thai airmen sent to France by Prince Chakrabongse, seated with
their fellow officers.*

Prince Chakrabongse and Katya at an Air Show.

Queen Saowabha in her car before picking up Prince Chula.

Chakrabongse, Katya and Chula.

weekly cabinet meetings and yet, like many highly organised people, he had the ability to stretch time to include social and family duties and pleasures, as well. His son recounts in one of his books: 'However busy my parents were, if they were alone in the house, I could see them anytime, and they were invariably pleased to see me ... Even when fully occupied in his library, my father would be ready to put down his work to translate for me some passages in an English children's book.'

Looking at his photographs, one is not surprised that his parents were 'invariably pleased' to see him, for he was a most appealing child. Surrounded as he was by care and affection, not only from his father and mother, but his grandmother and his Nurse Chom, whom he loved very dearly, he took his place within the frame of a charming picture of a happy family. A picture often held up in Bangkok, in those last years before the First World War, as representing a rare and ideal marriage.

Meanwhile, Chakrabongse's brother, King Rama VI, remained an obstinate bachelor, filling posts at his court with personable young men and remaining quite impervious to the charms of the many eligible pretty young princesses, whom his mother Queen Saowabha summoned to engage his attention when he came to see her. All was in vain. For through the ante-room where they displayed themselves in a variety of becoming poses, the King always strode, looking distant and preoccupied, as though hastening to an urgent appointment elsewhere. This behaviour sorely vexed his mother, who, according to her physician Dr Malcolm Smith, protested loudly that 'celibacy was for the priests and no man outside a monastery should remain celibate'. The doctor rightly observed that the King's seemingly obstinate refusal to marry 'was the beginning of a rift between them that widened as time went on.'

In fact, the Queen Mother was not alone in her disapprobation, for it was shared – though still so early in his reign – by society in general, which, despite the reverence in which the throne was held, looked to the King to follow the example of his ancestors in marrying and fathering many children to perpetuate the Chakri Dynasty. The monarch was also considered too retiring, hardly showing himself to his people except at state and religious ceremonies. The fact that he spoke and wrote English perfectly, translating nearly a hundred plays in both these languages, including three by Shakespeare – pronounced by admirers to be 'exact and poetical' – meant less than nothing to his critics. Indeed his talent for writing plays himself, in which he often took the leading role, was merely deplored as being unseemly.

In person, he was rounder in face than his brothers, with a more diffident air and, even in his early thirties, inclined to be stout. He was said to be extremely shy – a shyness which took the unfortunate form of shunning the company of his princely brothers, ministers, and advisors, and despite his declared affection for Chakrabongse, seldom seeking occasion to see him, preferring to communicate with him by letter. This behaviour caused considerable bitterness among the educated inhabitants of Bangkok, particularly as it was combined with exorbitant demands made on the Treasury by his lavish style of life, and a prodigal generosity to his close circle of courtiers. Two of these, the brothers Feua and Fuen Puenbun, who were special favourites, even had authority to draw cheque in the King's name, and as Prince Chula writes: 'were completely devoted to the Sovereign, looking after his every mood, wish or whim, and almost knowing what he wanted before he asked for it, so that in return for their selfless service, honours and riches were showered on them'. Eventually it became almost impossible to approach to King without their mediation and assistance.

They were particularly active in the promotion of the ill-fated Wild Tiger Corps. This volunteer corps was modelled on the British Territorial Army, greatly admired by Vajiravudh during his military training at Sandhurst, and was intended to supplement the regular army and be maintained by the King's Privy Purse. In addition to provincial regiments in which honorary colonelships were accepted by various royal princes including Chakrabongse, a Wild Tiger Brigade of Guards was raised and commanded by the King. The Brigade was issued with particularly splendid uniforms – an immediate cause of envy – and had a well-appointed clubhouse in Bangkok, open to all ranks. Here the King often lectured and mixed informally with its members. Civil servants and business men therefore hurried to join the Brigade, so as to benefit from such comparatively easy-going contact with their King.

At first, service in the Brigade was not open to the Regular Army – a restriction so unpopular that is was later rescinded – nor did commissions in the Regulars entitle officers to commissions in the Wild Tigers, leading to senior army and navy officers being frequently seen about the club dressed as privates in the Corps. The resulting confusion, which might well have been foreseen, led to jealousy, resent-

King Rama VI and fellow officers in Wild Tiger Corps uniform.

ment and dissension, so that the club became a fertile breeding ground for dissatisfaction and intrigue.

So much was this the case that Chakrabongse in 1912, his suspicions aroused, and therefore on the alert for signs of disaffection in the forces, obtained the confession of a repentant army officer, and uncovered a plot to depose the King that involved not only the army and navy, but a group of civilians. Their aims, however, seem to have been lacking in co-ordination, for while some favoured a constitutional monarchy governed by another prince – the most likely candidate being Chakrabongse himself – others would have preferred an outright republic with a president. In the event, so swiftly and secretly did Chakrabongse move, that on 27th February 1912, all those implicated were rounded up and arrested. After trial, some were actually condemned to death for treason, though later their sentences were commuted to life imprisonment.

In the course of the same year, in spite of the growing number of doctors trained in European medicine – a trend initiated since the reign of Chulalongkorn – a severe outbreak of smallpox found people still turning to traditional remedies instead of availing themselves of vaccination. However the King, by contributing a large sum from the Privy Purse to combat the disease, and by wisely insisting that his subjects must be persuaded and not compelled to be vaccinated, caused vaccination to become more popular, and smallpox was controlled, and eventually almost eliminated.

Vajiravudh also supported the foundation of the Pasteur Institute in Bangkok, where a snake farm produced serum against snake-bite. Inoculation against rabies was also perfected at the instigation of one of the King's brothers, Prince

Damrong, one of whose daughters had died from it. The Institute was staffed initially by a team of French doctors under the direction of a Dr Leopold Robert, of whom more will be heard later.

Events continued to be tense throughout the year and a letter to her brother from Katya in September gives a good idea of their life at this time:

'Dear Vanya

'I have been waiting for your letter for a long time. I have received your third postcard but your letter still does not arrive. You write that I am not interested in you. But on the contrary, I think it is you who are not interested in me… I have only written a little. Firstly, so many things have been happening here that I haven't wanted to write letters and, more importantly, latterly I haven't been feeling very well. I have been feeling weak. It is because this year there has been no cool season and at the moment it is extremely hot.

'The matter that has made us extremely worried is as follows. It was discovered that there was a large group of people who were planning secretly to carry out a coup d'état and to kill the King. In the group were some officers, although not many. But Lek was fortunate in finding out the names of all the officers and now they have all been arrested and are in custody pending trial. However the civilians have not yet been arrested as there is insufficient evidence. There were three different approaches to changing the government as there were many groups. The first group was that which would carry out the coup d'état. They also intended to kill Lek as they said that if he was still alive they would not be able to make the country into a republic. The second group wanted to make him King but with a constitutional government. The third group wanted to make Prince Boripatra King. Now the danger is definitely over because all the leaders have been arrested, but dissatisfaction with the King has not declined and confusion and chaos can still arise at any time. In this situation we are just waiting to see what new event might occur or what news comes in from Lek's secret sources, of which he has a great deal. To sum up, our life is not calm but it is not dangerous for us in any way. At the moment the King consults Lek all the time and Lek tells him everything quite straight including those things which he thinks that the King has done wrong. In many things the King has agreed with him and there will have to be many changes in our country. I beg that God will help everything to go smoothly. The reason I am telling you all this is that everyone is sending news about it and you will no doubt have read about it in the newspapers.

'Usually in the evening I am alone because for the last two weeks the Queen has requested that Nou should spend the night with her. She is unwell and misses him. Her requests are in fact commands and so a car comes to pick him up every day at 5 o'clock and then returns him at 9 o'clock the following morning. I feel lonely but as I have had disagreements with the Queen before about Nou, this time I haven't argued and given in with good grace.'

Katya also mentions the problems suffered by Thongrod, Chakrabongse's former ADC, who as a result of studying in Russia had also fallen in love and marred a Russian girl, Ludmilla. Katya's reflections on their life indicate the pressures that she herself still suffered:

> *'Thongrod has been working particularly hard at the moment because he is on the examining board for the officer school and the regiment. His mood is not very cheerful, but he knew how difficult it would be to have a European wife. He torments himself as what he should do for the best ... The husband being European is one thing, but the European wife of a Siamese man is even worse and more difficult. Apart from the weather, which is very enervating, there is the attitude of Siamese people towards such people and small actions which are not done with any malicious intent whatsoever. They are quick to pick on things and see them in the wrong light so that they can say "You think she's great because she's a European, but actually she did such and such wrong."*
>
> *'I have felt like this for six years now and it has only reduced slightly recently because I have been here for a long time now. In addition, I can get on with them and I can help the poor people. I am not doing this because it is a good thing to do but to really help and people love me because I am kind hearted. But if I didn't have money, I wouldn't be able to show my kindness. Money is really full of significance.*

Prince Chakrabongse with Prince Thongrod who also studied in Russia.

Mom Ludmilla, the Russian wife of Prince Thongrod.

'Can you believe it that many old Siamese ladies thought that I would not return to Siam, imagining that I was heartily sick of this country. They were very pleased that I came back. This shows you that they love me, but at the same time they don't trust me. And it will be like this for ever and there is no one who I can talk to who understands me. So that is how it goes on.

'I am playing the piano a lot recently and I have taken up English lessons with Mr Young again. I look after my chickens and take and develop my photographs as well as reading books. To sum up I try not to waste time. Amoratat comes every Saturday and we all go off to see a film, or something like that. Saturday nights he stays with us and on Sundays we stay with our close friends. Every Thursday he and his three younger brothers come to dinner at our house and after dinner we play billiards in the new house. On other days he is not free, nor is he in Bangkok. Apart from that others who come are Phraya Boriboon Mahibal, although his wife doesn't come much as she is always coughing. Other officers also come, but not many people come as this isn't a time for much entertaining.

'Write to me dearest. What are you up to? And how are you? Are you happy? Now that you know why I have been quiet for so long you shouldn't be cross with me any more. I get depressed when I don't receive a letter for a long time. Next year in the spring I am desperate to come to Russia. It is time for me to have a rest. I have been working for six months now and the weather has been hot all the time. It is not surprising that my heart is not quite normal.'

As a result of all the pressures experienced by Katya, in mid-1913 she left for an extended trip to Europe. At first Chakrabongse had hoped to accompany her, but owing to his heavy commitments, she travelled on ahead and they arranged to meet in Naples. From the letters to her brother it would seem that at this time, she had began to suffer from a succession of illnesses which it was thought a trip to Europe would put to rights. Symptoms ranged from coughing blood to feeling faint, but no exact diagnosis has been ever obtained. One of her stays was in Celerina near St Moritz which suggests that her doctors might have suspected tuberculosis.

During her absence, Chakrabongse did his best to see more of his son, and often came back to Paruskavan earlier in the evening so as to have a chat with him. This was much appreciated by the little boy, who later wrote in his memoirs: 'I admired and worshipped my father like a god, and in the scarlet full dress of the Footguards or the blue of the Horseguards, sitting so splendidly on dear old Ramushka, he was a picture never to be forgotten.'

At that time, Chakrabongse also took Chula on an expedition in quite a fleet of little boats, including a cook-boat for both Siamese and 'farang' food, to Kanchanaburi, on the River Kwai (later scene of the infamous Bridge) where he had to inspect a local barracks. Like a good father, he saw to it that Chula was in bed by nine, although he regretted he would miss the resounding martial fanfare

A postcard sent to Prince Chakrabongse by Katya from near St. Moritz in 1913.

A postcard sent to Prince Chakrabongse by Katya on board ship showing the steamship 'Yorck'.

A postcard sent to Prince Chula from Prince Chakrabongse, 1913.

and drumming that welcomed their arrival. After the barracks inspection next morning, he planned to take Chula to see a temple and a cave, but in a fit of childish obstinacy, his son refused to leave the boat until coaxed ashore to buy a basket of orchids for his granny.

In Bangkok, his father took him to a temple, where the priests were most happy to meet him, and where Chakrabongse notes proudly, 'He behaved very well'.

During one of his nocturnal visits to his mother, Chakrabongse showed her some photographs sent to him by Katya, but was disconsolate when Saowabha – whose slightest word was law – kept for her collection the one he himself liked the best.

On September 25th, he set out for Naples, sad to leave Chula in tears, but certain he would soon be consoled by Chom. His ship the 'Deli' was, he says, 'most comfortable', but Tapong's wife, included in the party for the first time, 'was very boring and made me feel alone when in her company. 'After an uneventful journey, he found Katya awaiting him in Naples, though the pleasure of reunion was marred by his discovery that she has put on weight and 'looks very fat'. Via Rome and Turin, they reach Paris on 1st October and stayed at the Majestic, where they had been allotted 'a very grand room because they know who I am and it will be very expensive', he wrote, adding: 'tomorrow we'll change to something smaller.'

Next day he ordered a smoking-suit, took Katya up the Eiffel Tower, and visited some Siamese friends. However by 2nd October, Katya had a bad cold, and left to dine by himself Chakrabongse grumbled, 'She's often unwell these days, and it's most annoying as there are so many things I wanted to do.' Sadly, it seemed that the much-needed holiday, looked forward to with happy anticipation, was not working out quite as he had hoped.

In the morning he strolled down the Rue de la Paix all by himself to try on his suit, noting that 'Katya is still unwell. They seem to think she may have tuberculosis or appendicitis ... the doctor will do some tests ... what a commotion – and it will mean putting off our departure.' To add to the disorganisation of their stay, they choose to acquire a dog. Not a small tractable creature, but a large and doubtless lively and energetic German-Shepherd called L'Or. However, when the doctor finally materialised, he announced that his distinguished patient had neither tuberculosis nor appendicitis, so that next day Chakrabongse, greatly relieved, was able to go off on his own to London for a night at the Savoy, to see one of his younger brothers.

Back in Paris, he bought Katya 'an unusual diamond ring surrounded by square-cut sapphires' and received another visit from the doctors merely to announce that she was better. Two days later, she was having consultations with two further doctors, a dermatologist about a skin problem on her neck, and a lung-specialist. We are not told what the first of these had to say, but the second pronounced her lungs 'all right, but she must be careful'.

The visit to Paris ended with Chakrabongse developing a cold and by 27th October, when they took the night-train to Naples, Chakrabongse was still feeling most unwell while Katya had stomach-ache for three days. Fortunately by the time they had reached Penang, she had begun to recover. A faint cloud of disillusion, a sense that their previous pleasure in each other's company had faded somewhat, hovers over these days in Paris, as though after seven years of marriage, the accord of these two widely different personalities was faltering to the detriment of their relationship. While Katya may genuinely have been ill, her seemingly capricious consultation of three doctors in as many days does suggest a search for the excuse of ill-health to keep her husband at arm's length, behaviour which after a long absence he would have found most upsetting, and he may well have begun to reflect that a Siamese wife would not have treated him thus. In fact, Katya's ability to tolerate an Eastern way of life may have been wearing thin and she may perhaps have begun to reassert the extremely dissimilar values in which she had been brought up.

Grand manoeuvres, 1916. Queen Saowabha watched from the specially constructed pavilion.

Prince Chakrabongse leading a parade.

X
War & Revolution

*T*he assassination of the Archduke Franz Ferdinand of Austria and his morganatic wife on 28th June 1914 at Sarajevo, followed by the Great Powers' declaration of war on Germany in August the same year, were events that had repercussions even in far-distant Siam. Although the King sided with the Allies in spirit, he could do little more at first, as public feeling ran strongly against the French for their high-handed annexation of Siamese territory in the past. In comparison, the Germans were relatively popular, being regarded only as friendly traders.

Rama VI however sought to ameliorate this antagonism by writing articles and translations of war news for various newspapers. These, although printed under a number of different pseudonyms, were known to be from the royal pen, and doubtless in consequence had the advantage of certain publication. Chakrabongse, now a full General and Chief of the General Staff, was also ardently pro-Allies, and followed every move of the belligerents on huge maps set up in his study. He also eagerly gathered all available information about tactics and new weaponry for use in army training.

Katya's reactions were naturally more personal, in which fears for her native land, her relations and friends, predominated and she suffered much from being so far away from the country she had so immediately volunteered to serve in the Russo-Japanese War. These particular concerns were shared to a large extent by her husband, because of his long association with Russia, and his high rank and standing in the Imperial Army. They both therefore looked forward impatiently to their next visit to Russia, due to take place in the course of 1917, during which Chakrabongse had been invited by the Tsar to accompany him to the Front.

In the meantime, Chakrabongse's duties continued unabated. As well as work in Bangkok, he also made inspection tours in the provinces and in 1915 he, Katya and Chula made an extended trip up country to Nan, Prae, Chieng Mai and Chieng Rai.

In 1916, instead of the customary regional exercises, Chakrabongse organised Grand Manoeuvres lasting four days, in which 20,000 to 30,000 troops participated. Under canvas himself and fulfilling the role of Chief Umpire, he was able to put into practice much that he had learned from his intensive study of the European War; and to make use of machine-guns, field-telephones and seven aeroplanes! Great enthusiasm was engendered by the scale and scope of these exercises. Even Queen Saowabha temporarily forsook her nocturnal routine and, travelling by boat, landed at a series of designated places, where she was carried on a chair by her sailors to pavilions especially constructed for her reception. From these she had an excellent view of the proceedings and gratifying glimpses of four of her sons – the King, Chakrabongse, and two younger sons, respectively a battalion commander and a staff officer.

Prince Chakrabongse watching the Bung Fai rocket festival during a trip to Prae.

Prince Chakrabongse dining at Pak Pan station in Den Chai district, Prae province.

Her grandson accompanied her on these expeditions and wrote: 'I shall never forget the sign of my father's slight figure sitting on his white horse (more than likely this was the Russian veteran, Ramushka), when at the flash of his sword and word of command, twenty thousand men presented arms as one man.'

On 11th January 1917, *The Siam Observer*, notable for its remarkably full coverage of news from Russia, carried a report of the murder of Rasputin by Prince Yussoupoff, Grand Duke Dmitri and Captain Sukhotin on 29th December 1916, and commented on the monk's 'sinister and magnetic influence especially on the weaker sex', a veiled reference to the unhealthy control he had exercised over the Russian Empress.

In February, Chakrabongse records in his diary that he went to see the newly-arrived Russian Ambassador, Loris Malikov: 'He seems quite a nice chap, direct and to the point. He told me what had gone on in Petrograd before he came to Siam. He's certain there's going to be trouble. It seems the root cause was the meddling of the Empress and her monk, Rasputin. She listened only to him and forced the Emperor to do what he said. Everyone was and is dissatisfied.' The 'trouble', of course, was the imminence of revolution, and events now moved rapidly and inexorably toward the downfall of Imperial Russia with the abdication of the Emperor on 14th March at Pskov, and the establishment of the first Provisional Government headed by Prince Lvov, with Kerensky as Minister of Justice.

Naturally long before this, any hope of Chakrabongse and Katya's journey to St Petersburg had been abandoned. Perhaps the gloom and heartbreak they felt may have lightened for an instant, when they learned that poor Chulasewok, now Chakrabongse's ADC, balked of his first trip to Europe for which he had assembled a splendid wardrobe, had had himself, as some compensation for his disappointment, photographed in a number of striking poses, in costumes varying from an elegant lounge suit to white tie and tails, and full dress uniform!

In April Chakrabongse records in his diary that 'we went to see Loris Malikov again, and remembering the importance of Easter to Russians, took him an Easter egg.' He then continued: 'This Ambassador is very active and wants to make a name for himself'. (Not surprising when it is recalled that Malikov was the grandson of the General and powerful Minister who, among his many distinctions and achievements, was particularly responsible for persuading Alexander II to agree to a form of constitutional government, and in February 1881, had laid the draft before him. But only nine days later, this plan, which might have had incalculable consequences for the good of Russia, came to naught with the assassination of the Emperor, whose successor Alexander III preferred to return to the principles of autocratic power.)

Chakrabongse further noted: 'Malikov wants Siam to join the Allies'. And, as Chakrabongse heartily endorsed this opinion, he went to discuss it with one of his Uncles, Prince Svasti, who was Foreign Minister, only to find to his disappointment that the Prince still wished to sit on the fence. Siam's equivocal standing was finally resolved when America, after circularising all remaining neutral states, declared war on Germany and Austria in April 1917. This powerful addition to the Allied cause enabled Rama VI to sweep away remaining opposition, and Siam entered the war in July that same year. This led Robert Martignan to write in his book *La Monarchie Absolue Siamoise* that: 'Chakrabongse, Prince of Bisnulok, principal and prime mover of the alliance, showed clairvoyant good sense'.

Under Chakrabongse's direction, German and Austrians were interned, and about forty merchant ships were successfully taken over by the Siamese Navy, after an abortive attempt at blowing them up on the part of the Germans in order to foil their capture. A great extra burden of work was now laid on Chakrabongse's willing shoulders, and he dreamed of commanding a mixed brigade in France if sufficient modern equipment could be supplied by the Allies. They, however, only agreed to accept a motor transport corps and about one hundred pilots. This reluctance, rightly or wrongly, was interpreted in Siam as being due to racial discrimination. In the event, the Motor Transport Corps saw some service, but the Siamese pilots were still being acclimatised and trained in France when the fighting ended with the declaration of the Armistice in November 1918.

One minor result of Siamese involvement in the war, was the redesigning of her flag. Until then, this had shown a white elephant on a scarlet ground. But as the representation of this revered animal, when flown on Allied occasions, appeared to Western eyes to resemble that more homely creature, the pig, Rama VI decided that five horizontal stripes in red, white, dark blue, white and red, would be more seemly and render further misapprehension impossible.

Working longer and later than even he had done before, Chakrabongse was probably unaware of how profoundly Katya suffered, not only from the known disastrous facts about her country, but from an ever-darkening cloud of uncertainty and apprehension that worse was to come. In the past, she would have been able to share her anxieties and grief with him, but swept along and away from her by a heavy programme of duties, he could not realise how isolated she felt. In addition, her health had not improved, and she was considerably debilitated by two distressing miscarriages.

Her Slav temperament, prone to extremes of ebullient joy or black despair, hindered her from rising above her deep depression and, although complying with the demands made on her by her position, she felt them as 'demands' and did not undertake them wholeheartedly. For underlying all she did was a nostalgia for Russia – the snow, the bubbling samovar, and voices speaking her native tongue, voices that for all she knew might now be stilled in death or only faintly heard in echoing vaults of prisons.

During October 1917 there had been serious flooding, causing hardship and grave damage to city and countryside. The carefree young in Bangkok, paddling boats along the drowning avenues and boulevards laid out by Chulalongkorn, took thoughtless pleasure in the disaster. But Katya's beautiful gardens at Paruskavan as they slipped and gradually disappeared beneath the rising flood, washed away her remaining equilibrium and she underwent a severe nervous breakdown.

She was so unwell and so unlike herself, and her 'lovely smile', that her mother-in-law had remarked on long ago, became so marked by its absence that Chakrabongse, during his rare hours of leisure, many of which were spent at Hua Hin, grew to rely on the more active companionship of a group of young people, one of whom was his niece Princess Bimrambai, daughter of his half-brother, Prince Rabi. Here, while Katya worked alone in the garden she loved and had created, he played tennis, swam and went for strenuous climbing expeditions with this pretty lively girl and her light-hearted friends, finding in their undemanding company, relaxation from the exhausting days of driving work in Bangkok. At length he suggested that Katya might benefit from a complete change. He was far too busy to take a holiday himself, and in any case it seems that at this stage of their marriage, both welcomed the prospect of being apart for a while.

In April 1918 therefore, Katya set off on an extended tour of China, Japan and Canada, travelling with her faithful Cham. By this time, her brother Vanya was living in Peking, as were many escaping Russian refugees. No doubt, if she could not go to Russia, the thought of seeing her brother again and meeting other Russians must have seemed better than nothing. She was also accompanied by Edward Healey, architect of their house at Hua Hin, who had become something of a family friend and in this instance was to act as a sort of courier, responsible for smoothing out the irritations and difficulties of foreign travel. Well known later for his design of the Siam Society building on Asoke Road, photographs show him to

Edward Healey who accompanied Katya on her
trip to Japan and Canada in 1918.

Postcard from Katya to Chula in 1918 showing the hotel where she stayed
in Canada.

Postcard to Chakrabongse from Hong Kong en route to Japan 1918.

Katya and Cham on their trip to Japan in 1918.

have been good-looking and moustached with a genial expression and a certain
rakish tilt to his panama – an odd choice as an escort, one would have thought, for
a young married woman on her own.

On Katya's side it would seem, nevertheless, that she still loved her husband
deeply as no sooner had she got on the train than she was writing to him:

> *'I hope that everyone is well. You mustn't be lonely when I'm away – go to
> the cinema, play tennis. Of course, you will be lonely but how happy you'll be
> to see me fit and well again. I felt I had to get away as the last few months I've
> been getting by on will power alone and I wouldn't be able to go on like this
> much longer.*
>
> *I am worried about all the dogs, my friends. You will play with them, won't
> you? I'm sure they will miss me a lot. I'll send them postcards even though they*

can't read so you can tell them that I haven't forgotten them. Please tell Nou that I am no longer afraid of thunderstorms. Today when it rained and we were in the train I was quite calm so it shows what will power can do. Sitting in the train is very boring particularly between 11 and 4 pm when the weather is very hot. I felt sticky and dirty but I saw many new places and I didn't feel sick.'

By May she was writing from Peking where she met with her brother Vanya and various Russian émigrés:

'The next day at 9.20 am we left for Peking. Vanya had sent some telegram or other to the minister of transport and he ordered a special wagon for me. The trip took three hours and, apart from the four rooms with beds, there was a large salon with comfortable upholstery. Our wagon was at the back and had a good view. The railway line is very wide, only slightly narrower than in Russia and so there is very little vibration. We reached Peking at about 12.30 and Mitrofanov brought the Duke's car to meet us. Vanya took Healey to the Wagon Lits hotel and from there we all had lunch with Mitrofanov.

On Sunday I went by car to visit the Summer Palace. I looked at everything and had tea in the pavilion shaped like a boat. I think that you had a meal there on your previous visit. We were just four. Veriga Darevsky accompanied us. He escaped from Russia and is now going to join the resistance in France. When the war first broke out he was in the Hussar regiment and met with Osten-Sakien [one of Chakrabongse's old comrades], *but he was in the general staff. He says that few of your hussars are left, mostly they are young men. At the river Don he changed regiments to be with Kaledin and, when he was surrounded, he escaped by disguising himself as an ordinary soldier.*

On Monday morning Vanya, Healey and I went to the bank. I took out £300. To change it into Hongkong dollars is very expensive. £300 gets only 1800 dollars. I gave 1,000 to Vanya in case he gets an opportunity to send it to Alla and Mathilda and my other relatives who have nothing to eat.'

It was still only May and Katya would not return home for another eight months – not until January 1919. Although she and Chakrabongse corresponded

*Katya during her trip in China.
In the centre is Ivan Desnitsky
and on his left, Mr Healey.*

Postcard of the Temple of Heaven from Katya to Prince Chakrabongse during her 1918 trip. Unusually the postcard is written in formal royal Thai, not Russian.

Postcard to Prince Chula from Katya

Postcard from Katya to Prince Chakrabongse.

regularly, Katya in particular showering him with letters and picture-postcards (the latter also for Nou and the dogs), this long break in their relationship – as unshared experiences multiplied – distanced them from one another . . . .

After her departure, Chakrabongse's life continued much as usual as, due to her breakdown, she had already slipped into the background of his rare leisure time. He was hurt and rather offended when all his invitations to Hua Hin were refused by Bimrambai, who felt it was wrong for her to stay there in Katya's absence, despite his insistence that the married ladies always among his guests were more than adequate as chaperones. So, rather disconsolately, he asked her younger sister Princess Chavalit to stay instead. Chavalit did not share Bimrambai's scruples and arrived with a devoted maid, who slept under her bed!

In 1918 Chavalit was only fifteen and, even prettier than her sister, she was as irresponsible as a playful kitten, tireless in pursuit of the pleasures of the moment. Her high spirits, her still childlike voice and a way she had of rocking on her little heels when she laughed, endeared her not only to Chakrabongse, but also to his son who, at ten years old, was not all that much younger than she was. The first summer days they spent together at Hua Hin – playing tennis, riding and swimming – with numbers of young relatives and friends, were so light-hearted and cheerful that Chakrabongse, forgetting his cares, felt young again, while Chula felt he had grown up.

On their return to Bangkok, Paruskavan without her quick darting presence, seemed so staid and dreary that Chakrabongse persuaded her to come there more often. In fact little persuasion was needed, with Chavalit's mother eagerly encouraging what she saw as a very advantageous liaison. Soon Chavalit's band of youthful friends began arriving with her, coming, as she airily explained, as company for Chula, who now openly adored her and wrote her many little notes to tell her so. These she pasted into an album together with his photo, and greatly daring, one of his father on the opposite page! Bisdar, Chula's playmate recalled in his seventies that: 'We were all in love with Chavalit in our boyish way . . . she was so full of fun, very pretty, not dark but with a complexion described in Siam as being 'pale, like coffee with milk'.

Gradually the atmosphere of the house and gardens altered, alive with chattering voices and easy-going laughter, until a kind of frivolous anarchy prevailed. The ballroom with Katya's favourite hyacinth blue curtains had become an indoor tennis court, bicycle races were won and lost along the well-swept gravel paths, and the latest dance tunes picked out on her piano. Chakrabongse smiled indulgently at the transformation of his home, telling himself it made life more cheerful for his sometimes lonely son, but beneath this assumption of a quasi-paternal role, other feelings – the stronger for being unadmitted – grew and flourished.

Princess Chavalit.

Soon their love affair became an open secret and, although on the surface decorum prevailed, not a glance, covert clasp of hands or whispered word, would have been missed by the respectfully lowered eyes of the retinues of servants. Everyone who was anyone in Bangkok knew of it, and speculated about what would happen when Mom Katerin returned. Most of the gossips were convinced that the affair was temporary – a husband on his own without a wife – it was surely nothing serious, it would all blow over.

Poor Chula became jealous not because Chavalit changed her attitude to him at all, but because without understanding it, he sensed the alteration in her relationship with his father, and began to long for his mother's return, who would surely set everything to rights again.

Meanwhile in the cool of the evening, Chakrabongse would sometimes embark with Chavalit in a little boat and, as the moon rose, take her down the quiet river to see her mother. This filial duty was often combined with a delicious picnic, and perhaps a halt at Chakrabongse House, Ta Tien, where shuttered rooms away from prying eyes offered the setting for a very different kind of rendezvous.

Many of Katya's letters from this period survive, together with the hundred or more picture postcards she sent to her husband and son as she and Healey travelled around first Japan and later Canada. In the final stages of her trip in Canada, an increasingly wistful tone may be discerned. 'Why haven't you written?' 'Lovely place but not so nice as home.' 'Down all day as Cham got a card from you but not me.'

This altered key may also have been due to the fact that she had received several anonymous letters referring to her husband's interest in Chavalit, from the sort of 'well wishers' who hastened to draw attention to their 'friendship' in such circumstances. On the other hand, a most affectionate letter reached her from Prince Mahidol, one of her husband's many half-brothers, which concluded: 'May the feeling that your life is precious to so many of us give you the health and happiness you need to cheer up those who are far away, waiting for your return. A happy voyage and au revoir from your very faithful Mahidol.' These words may well have been prompted by the Prince's knowledge of what awaited her in Bangkok and his desire to assure her of his support.

The letters written to Katya by Chakrabongse, with their factual and slightly chilly tone may not have encouraged her to discount the 'well wishers' innuendoes. But instead of hastening back earlier than intended, a feminine perversity or perhaps a dread of facing an unhappy situation impelled her to postpone her homecoming to a later date.

Eventually she returned in January 1919, and was met at Singapore by Chakrabongse in the royal yacht, while Chula, bursting with joyful excitement, awaited them at the landing-stage in Bangkok.

A few days afterwards, there was an important function at the Military College, where Chula was a junior cadet, and a play written by the King himself was to be performed by the senior boys, while a number of their juniors, including Chula, were to appear in the interval singing patriotic songs in costume. Before the show there was a banquet which the King attended, and where Chakrabongse and Katya were host and hostess. All went off perfectly, yet when Chula from the platform proudly identified his mother in the audience, he was struck to the heart by the sadness of her expression.

The shock of this revelation – of something being very wrong – haunted him and clouded his pleasure in the many gifts she brought him from abroad. As day followed uneasy day he found that, far from his mother's return lightning the disturbing atmosphere, it now became sombre in the extreme. From now on, he existed in the baneful climate engendered by married people when hidden discord instead of harmony prevails. What he hated most were the false smiles, the sudden silences or changes of conversation when timidly, unsure now of his reception, he entered a room. His mother's face was always strained, sometimes marked by tears hastily wiped away, while talk between her and his father was increasingly in Russian which he did not understand.

Although after a time, Chavalit's visits were discontinued, her presence still seemed to permeate the house, though no-one now played tennis in the deserted ballroom, and the gardens no longer rang with the joyous voices and heedless laughter of her friends. Everyone, including the servants, became specially kind to him, but he felt it was a mournful kindness, quite unlike the spontaneous yet disciplined indulgence to which he was accustomed. His grandmother, too, seemed unlike herself, given to sighing when she looked at him, and proposing little treats more often than before, which he obediently accepted but with a very heavy heart. For one or two nights running, he slept at Paruskavan instead of at his grandmother's, as Chom told him the Queen had business affairs to discuss with his parents.

The Winter Fair attended by his parents came and went, and their normal life of many engagements punctiliously fulfilled continued as before, but with a quality of underlying disquietude, felt most of all by their uncomprehending little son. He was told that soon Uncle Vanya would be coming from Peking but, first, in April, his mother retreated as usual to Hua Hin and here, where once she had been so happy, the last stages of the drama between her and her husband were conducted by means of long and tormented letters. At first it is clear that Katya struggled to come to terms with the new situation. She was accompanied by Mila, the Russian wife of Lek's cousin, Thongrod, and no doubt her pragmatic countrywoman, only too aware that return to Russia was out of the question, would have counselled caution and reconciliation. Sometime in April Katya wrote to her husband:

> '*As to your letter which greeted me on my arrival here, I have already told you how much your suggestion that you should meet Princess Chavalit secretly without my knowledge has hurt me. Your words to the effect that if I didn't care so much I wouldn't know when you visited her, have cut me to the quick. I can hardly bear to think about this idea. Apart from that, in your letter are*

several things which totally contradict the attitude expressed in all the letters I received in Japan and Canada. In those letters you described her as a young girl who was full of chatter and laughter, but in this recent letter you have described her as a young woman for whom you care deeply. Lek, please admit that what you write now is very different to what you wrote before.

'Since being here my state of mind has returned to normal and I feel more like myself again and I don't want to reopen the wound before Vanya arrives. All I want to say is that however hard I try I can't understand your feelings both towards the princess and me. What is the truth? What you wrote to me when I was abroad, or what you have written to me now? The letters were written by the same person but the meaning is different. I no longer know what to believe and my heart is heavy. I can no longer understand human beings or their feelings however hard I try.

'However, I promise that when I return to Bangkok I will not be as I was before I left. Being here alone I have had a chance to think everything over. At night under the beautiful moon I sit by the sea and calm my spirit. I reflect on my life since childhood. I have suffered before, but have always recovered and surely this time it will also pass. Thinking this way makes me feel better.'

A subsequent letter again saw her attempting to comprehend her husband's changed feelings.

'Dearest Lek

'Yesterday I wrote you a long letter and today I want to add some things that I forgot to say. I feel that if we can't come to an understanding, we may no longer be able to live together. I would come home in an unstable state and we would be together like two people living in hell. I beg you to listen to me one more time. You write that you cannot give her up. I agree but not because it would be unfair to her, but in order to protect both your good names, in order to stop all the gossiping and above all for the sake of your happiness. I understand that if you can't meet her, you will suffer greatly. That's why yesterday I begged you to ask her to the house, to take her to the cinema with us and go riding together. As I also said I will be kind to her and today I reiterate that I will behave well towards her.

'I think that when you say that she has done nothing wrong, you are exaggerating somewhat. Everyone has said that she was encouraging you. Some people have even said that she seduced you and if she behaved in front of me as if she was your wife, then of course that is very wrong. But let's not dwell on this matter. You say that you want to be yourself but over the past 12 years, have I made you feel so uncomfortable? It is true that I have tortured you over this last few months, but you must understand how I feel. In the past we were truly one, sharing all our thoughts and feelings together. Of course, I am heartbroken to learn that you want to live in a different way, but I have never stopped you doing anything, because I have no right to stop you. But I do ask you one thing – for some compassion. Think of me as a sick person whose only medicine is you. I will try to ensure that your life is calm and happy. I won't make a scene any more when you say you want to work or read the newspaper. I will not beg you to leave your work to come and have lunch or tea with me. All I ask is for you to be true and faithful to me as you were in past. After we had talked and you decided to continue seeing her, you saw how your decision destroyed me. How could I act as normal when I realised that you attached no importance to our happiness and that of our son, as well as my health, all so that she could have a good time. The rumours have increased and what will Prince Rajburi say when he hears that you have gone to her house because she can't come to ours. By visiting her in this way you have encouraged the view that you want to leave me. I can't bear it and will leave with no money at all if you don't wish to give me any. It would be much better for me to go and work anywhere, rather than endure such a life with you carrying on in this fashion. You want to try and make me seem jealous by not allowing her to come to the house.

'Lek, you haven't thought things through carefully enough. If you had, you would never have suggested such a course of action. And, as I wrote yesterday, I must repeat, if I stay with you I will love you and help you as before on one condition. You must promise me that you won't conduct a secret affair. If you have to hide something from me, there must be a reason. Your argument that it is to protect me and stop me getting upset, does not seem logical to me. Such secrecy is like a poison and I can't support it for very long. That she didn't like coming to our house when I was there for the first time, I can understand. But what about me? And Lek, how did you feel? Why do you only think of her? Can it be possible that all you think of is her happiness?

'Lek, you are really torturing me with this. If you have fun with her, then keep her as a friend and let her come to the house. Secret visits between you will kill me. The chauffeurs will talk and if you forbid them it will only make things worse.

'I don't understand why you want me to stay with you. You have never said that if I left you would suffer. You say you don't want a divorce but you don't say why not. Do you still love me as you did before I went away? Before we make any decisions, which affect not only us two but also our son, we must agree on certain matters. You write that you want your freedom in a way that won't destroy my peace of mind. But you might as well know that your new plan will certainly destroy me. You must make up your own mind. If you will suffer when I have gone and will regret your decision, then think carefully about all that I have said. But if on the other hand, you will feel happy that you have made the right decision, then so be it.

'I will not come home before receiving an answer from you. Everything depends on whether you can accept my conditions or not. I do not object to your being friends, but I do object to a secret liaison and I cannot remain here any longer.

'Have you ever concealed anyone's visits before? No. Or if you have ever disliked anything I have done, why did you not say so?

'You always think that I am going to be angry. Is my behaviour so difficult?

'If you agree to live as I have suggested, then answer me. If not, what shall we do?

'To part would be better than torturing each other. Is such a life worth living? If we do divorce I can promise that I won't embarrass you. Your reputation will not suffer at my hands. You can rest assured on that point. I have my pride. It's not your fault that you're bored with me. If you can't make up your own mind we can go and see Prince Svasti and maybe he can help us come to an understanding if we can no longer work things out between us.

'I am staying at the old white house with the maids. The main house makes me feel sad because I decorated it so lovingly and now I feel that I am about to leave it for ever.

'I still love you.

'From Dusya, whom you don't understand or don't wish to understand.'

Chakrabongse's reply no longer exists. The visit of Vanya came and went but nothing could reconcile the feelings of these two strong-willed, determined people. Then in June, to Chula's astonishment, his mother moved into the so-called Guest House at Paruskavan 'because she was unwell'. Yet when he saw her there, she was not in bed or attended by their doctor, and he noticed almost unconsciously that she had brought with her none of her favourite ornaments, cushions and photos with which she liked to surround herself, but only her icon, so that her rooms had an oddly temporary air. One day she gave him a beautiful box of Russian crackers, printed with a captivating picture of the little Tsarevitch wearing a fur cap. As she looked at it she suddenly sobbed, 'Russia is no more!', and while he felt for her, Chula's heart lightened as he eagerly seized the chance to think it was the Revolution that distressed her and not anything personal and nearer home.

Rising early a few days later, he was wandering aimlessly in the garden where the paths were being raked and the lawns watered, lending a scent of freshness to the already hot June morning, when he saw his mother's dog, the German Shepherd L'Or, looking dejected and purposeless. This surprised him as at this time of day, L'Or was usually wherever his mistress was. He turned and followed the dog, who made disconsolately for the Guest House, where they entered his mother's sitting-room. There, all was neat and orderly and, as he had noted previously, impersonal. The whole place was quiet and he imagined she still slept; something however was missing, he could not at first think what. But as he turned to go it struck him – the icon with its flickering lamp was there no longer.

This indeed was ominous, and followed by the despondent dog, he went slowly back to Paruskavan. Here too, a hush subdued the usual active bustle of the household, and full of foreboding he went in search of his old nurse Chom. He found her in his playroom, not setting things to rights in her customary cheerful

Katya and two of her dogs, including the German Shepherd L'Or on the steps of Paruskavan Palace.

fashion, but staring out of the window, her plump cheeks wet with tears. He threw himself into the shelter of her kindly arms, his refuge since early childhood, and very gently she told him that his parents had been divorced and that his mother had left his father, him, and Paruskavan for ever. As he was later to write: 'I was too dazed to take it in for weeks'.

For the rest of that long wretched day, a day that seemed to prolong itself into eternity, Chakrabongse remained invisible in his study, while his son roamed miserably about the gardens his mother had designed. He visited her little zoo, where he felt even her baby elephant knew that never again would she bring him the ripe bananas to which he was so partial. It was a relief when at last the sun went down, and moving more briskly, he made towards the house, only to be suddenly met by Chom who guided him firmly toward the back of Paruskavan and up to the back stairs, instead of the front, to his room.

It was only long afterwards that he learned that poor Cham, so devoted to his mother and in dark despair at her departure without her, had flung herself from a top floor window, to lie broken and dying in the garden, from whence she was rushed to hospital, not only vainly to try and save her life, but because according to Siamese belief, she would forever have haunted the house, had she died there.

His mother's disappearance without a word to him, seemed at the time the most cruel desertion to Chula, although he tried to understand, when older, that she had left him thus because she could not bear to say goodbye. She also felt she would have wronged him greatly if she had tried to remove him from the security of his father's affection, his home and his future as a royal prince of Siam. In addition, she knew that had she proposed to take him with her, she would have had to fight a battle – lost before begun – not only with his father, but with his formidable grandmother, Queen Saowabha, who would have been determined to keep her one and only grandson at her side.

From what can be gathered from the letters and diaries after so many years, it appears that the marriage of Chakrabongse and Katya, begun in so high a blaze of romantic ardour in 1906, had by 1918 run into trouble, though it was trouble that might well have been lived through had it not been for the advent of Chavalit. But, as so often is the case in matrimonial tangles, Chakrabongse's passionate love affair with her in all her youth and freshness highlighted his difficulties with Katya and vitiated his will to deal with them. It must also be remembered that, to a man of his temperament, once set afire by a woman – as had been proved by his early love for Katya – neither the Russian Emperor, royal father or religion could divert him from pursuit of his desire.

Excerpts from a letter to her brother dated 9th April 1919, in which she refers to Chakrabongse as the General, give another picture of Katya's feelings at this troubled time:

> 'Our relationship is that of a husband and wife leading entirely separate lives. Not only is he not going "there" [a reference to Chavalit's house] less, but he goes more often … he goes there first before going to the palace … None of this would matter if he only acted towards me as a friend. But believe me there is nothing left for me but to sit at my desk and read the newspapers. And I am sorry, Dearest, but I will not be able to stand such an existence for long in order to give those who love me a certain satisfaction …
>
> 'Now I will tell you a little about my life as I used to do in the past: I still wake up early and go downstairs to instruct the servants and gardeners. Then I get dressed and Lek and I have lunch together. At 1.30 he goes out and generally goes "there" … at 4pm I take a bath, get dressed and have some tea.
>
> 'If the General is out, I go to see relations or friends. After that I listen to records on the gramophone. After that I have dinner and then read the papers or go for a drive. At 11 pm I go to bed. The General goes to bed about 1 am …
>
> 'Last Friday I went to see Mahibal and she asked me why I did not go to see Prince Rajburi (Chavalit's father) anymore, as he loved me so much and was distressed that I thought he was the cause of all this, to which I, of course, replied that I had never thought such a thing.'

A further thirteen years later in 1932, no longer in the heat of the moment, she wrote thus to her son in English:

> 'I had a great sorrow in my life when Chakrabongse preferred Chavalit to me … I tried many months explaining to him that he will lose me. If instead of speaking like a lawyer discussing the points, he put his arms round me and asked me to stand by him to fight that infatuation, I would never leave him and maybe today, he would be alive. But he thought that I can stand everything, even the biggest wound in my heart …
>
> 'No-one can say they saw me crying or miserable. I left Siam with a smile on my lips when my heart was perfectly broken: it cost me a lot to keep myself in hand. But the suffering made my will very strong and Chakrabongse was, for me dead, the day I left Paruskavan.

'It was awful to leave then. I did not care about position, money, love of Chakrabongse; the most painful thing was leaving you ... I knew I can't give you all your Father could ...'

These fierce yet touching words, matured in her heart for so long, speak for themselves. Clearly she was not an easy-tempered woman, but one perhaps with more than her fair share of the faults that make marriage, particularly romantic marriage, so traumatic. For when the rapture of passionate love inevitably subsides and the personality with its many failings emerges from the rosy clouds of euphoria, it is hard for both the lover and the beloved to submit so sublime an experience to the routines of daily life, blessed no longer by the magic ardour that brought them first together.

Katya, however, proved herself a realist, more so than the King and Queen Saowabha, who tried to intervene, and her brother who came from Peking to entreat her not to leave. For to Katya, it was clear that, had she accepted Chavalit in a triangular relationship as perhaps a Siamese woman might have done, her position would have been untenable. She was after all a foreigner, while Chavalit was not only Siamese but a Royal Princess. Moreover, she knew that in a society where rank counted so enormously, their difference in status would be entirely to her disadvantage and an open wound to her pride. For she was extremely proud: it was pride that made her refuse a handsome settlement and accept only twelve hundred pounds a year - and it was pride again that impelled her to fling in the face of the King's emissary the gift of jewellery that he brought from the monarch.

As to Chakrabongse's attitude, there is one long passage in his largely factual diary in which he gives a frank version of his feelings, with an eye to posterity.

'Monday 14th July 1919. In the evening I signed the divorce agreement between myself and Katya. This has been a matter of great difficulty for a long time, but I haven't recorded it in my diary, because in this diary I have not written down my innermost thoughts ... Here I am just giving the brief facts so that later readers can understand the situation. The causes go back many years and stem from Katya's dissatisfaction with a multitude of matters. If she is dissatisfied with anything it is always my fault. It is very difficult to make her happy because one has to judge it absolutely right. If she realises that one is agreeing to something, merely to humour her or in an attempt to please her, again she becomes angry. She says she doesn't want anyone to make sacrifices and won't accept them. Thus not only does she want everyone to do what she wants, but also she wants them to think what she wants - an extremely tall order. Recently whenever she's been dissatisfied, she's immediately asked for a divorce. Before, she went for a change of scene and holiday; this time, she was determined to get one. I persuaded her that her health was poor and she should go for a holiday and she calmed down. I've been very unhappy. My house is no longer somewhere where I can relax and unwind. I am someone who has a fair amount of work and commitments. I need support and a restful atmosphere at home. This

time, when Katya went away, I felt a great sense of release and was able to relax. I also became closer to Chavalit. Both of us have become increasingly fond of each other. However, I had no intention of divorcing my wife and taking a new one, feeling that that would not be a proper course of action. I thought that possibly when Katya came back she might take Chavalit under her wing as part of the household, so that I could have some one at least who gives me some pleasure and makes me feel calm and relaxed.

'Everyone tried to plead my case, right up to the Queen Mother and the King. However, the only thing that would satisfy Katya would be if I were to break with Chavalit completely and were never to see her again. If I were to do this, I feel it would be unfair to Chavalit and also it would mean I would never be able to hold my head high again. I would have to carry my wife constantly on my back. If I give in to her on this point I would have to give in to her forever… Actually, divorce will cause Katya a lot more suffering than me and I've told her this repeatedly and advised her long and hard on this matter. Other people have also tried to influence her but to no avail. She just wants to get the better of me in this and there is no other solution. The whole discussion has been raging for six months, and I haven't had a moment's peace, arguing all the time. Those who are aware of the situation, feel it is intolerable and shouldn't continue.

'Katya has appointed Mr Wright to be her lawyer and, on my side, Sadet (Prince Svasti) is organising things for me. I have given her 40,000 baht as a first payment and thereafter will give her £1,200 per annum. She is going to leave the country.'

Letter from Mr Wright to Katya.

Queen Saowabha's urn in the Dusit Throne Hall.

The lying-in-state of Prince Chakrabongse at Paruskavan Palace.

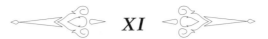

XI

Death of a Queen and a Prince

$\mathcal{S}$o in melancholy fashion ended this romantic love, strong enough to have brought two such disparate people together, but perhaps too strong, too temperamental, to evolve into the loving friendship a long happy marriage requires. From Chakrabongse's diary it can be seen that his first thought was now for Chavalit and that, drained by months of dissension, emotional exhaustion had set in leaving him numb and devoid of any feeling except a yearning for peace – peace and quiet at almost any price.

For 13 years, in a polygamous society, Chakrabongse and Katya's marriage had presented a picture of a couple secure in their happiness and contented with one another. The news of their divorce broke like a thunderclap. All the more because 12 years earlier they had successfully weathered the initial royal displeasure at the union of the Heir Presumptive with a foreigner. Even his love affair with Chavalit, by no means known to everyone, had not been regarded as a serious threat to so long-standing and well-tried a relationship.

At Paruskavan, once Katya had gone she was sadly missed because of the active interest she had taken in the house, the garden, the medical problems of everyone, from a servant to her son, and the welfare of the birds and animals in her little zoo.

Chula, fortunately, still had his beloved nurse Chom, his home and a father who did all he could to make up for the absence of his mother. Although he went to school every day, he continued to spend weekends with his grandmother, now growing ever more frail as her sedentary life began to tell on her. In fact, his attendance at school did not inconvenience the autocratic old Queen in the least as, if she suddenly wished to see him, she thought nothing of despatching her car to whisk him from his classroom to her palace. In addition, she also sent him in a hot luncheon daily from her own kitchens, which could have hardly have made him popular with his fellow pupils.

Chavalit was often at Paruskavan, where she was well liked for she interfered in no way with the running of the house but, like the charming child she was, enlivened its rather sombre atmosphere after Katya had departed. In due time, Chakrabongse, as he was bound to do, applied to the King for the royal assent to his marriage to Chavalit. To his amazement, he met with a peremptory refusal based on the grounds that Chavalit was his niece. As such near relationships in royal circles had always been of small importance, Chakrabongse persisted in his demand and, on its being again refused, enlisted his mother's help to plead his cause. Unsympathetic at first, she later supported him, but the monarch remained obdurate.

Unused as she was to being thwarted, the Queen was very angry and as a mark of her displeasure, for several days refused to take the numerous pills and potions prescribed for her, but still to no avail. This situation led to an almost open breach between the two brothers and the Queen was so incensed that the next time the King called to see her, she turned her back and would not speak to him. Vajiravudh sat patiently in unbroken silence in her room for one hour, till he rose and with due ceremony took his leave, little knowing that it would be for the last time.

It is difficult to believe that his attitude towards his brother's remarriage was only governed by a rather sudden disapproval of the close blood relationship between Chavalit and Chakrabongse. Apart from the many consanguineous royal marriages, their own grandmother, Princess Ramperi, was their grandfather King Mongkut's great niece.

Surely it is more likely that the unmarried childless King feared the ascendancy of his more popular brother, whom he may have secretly thought better suited for kingship than himself. Such being the case, it would not have been unnatural that now Chakrabongse's position as Heir Presumptive had been enhanced by his no longer having a foreign wife, the King was unwilling to improve his stature further by sanctioning his marriage to a highly eligible princess of his own race. Whether this is so or not, his brother's behaviour wounded Chakrabongse deeply and injured their relationship irreparably.

As for Chavalit, she came to live at Paruskavan and was soon generally regarded as Chakrabongse's common law wife. She fitted gracefully and unobtrusively into this role and continued her affectionate teasing, slightly flirtatious, relationship with the eleven year old Chula. The latter still spent part of every weekend with his grandmother, who now seldom left her bed and was becoming disinclined for news of the outside world.

Nevertheless, when her doctor was summoned to her bedside on 20th October 1919, he was not unduly alarmed suspecting it was due to 'one of the usual attacks of nephritis brought on by her artificial way of life'. However, this time the attack was of increased severity and, because there was no resistance left in her debilitated body, within a few hours she was dead.

Chula, summoned home from school, had no premonition of what had happened until he arrived at Paruskavan, when seeing that the servants assembled in the hall all wore black mourning armbands and black pasin skirts, he guessed at once that his grandmother had died.

Later when his father returned from Phya Thai, his son, until then numbed with shock, ran to meet him at the top of the stairs, where Chakrabongse holding him close, broke into bitter weeping. Chula's tears were also now released and it is touching to imagine them, locked in each other's arms, racked with sobs, comforting one another. 'The first and only time I ever saw my father cry.'

The elaborate funeral ceremonies, beginning with the bathing of the body before it was lifted into the ornate royal urn, proceeded according to time honoured ritual, the urn being carried in procession to the Dusit Maha Prasad Hall of the Grand Palace, reserved solely for the Coronation and lying-in-state of Sovereigns. There, surrounded by her regalia and beneath the seven white

Prince Chakrabongse seated on a palanquin during the funeral procession of Queen Saowabha.

The royal urn and meru of Queen Saowabhu 1919.

The lying-in-state of Queen Saowabha.

umbrellas, symbolising her Queenly rank, the urn would rest for seven months, during which time, a weekly memorial service was attended by the King, Royal Family and various dignitaries. Then in June 1920, the urn borne in the huge golden funeral coach, was cremated in the specially constructed royal crematorium on the Pramane ground in front of the Grand Palace.

Although she had virtually withdrawn from the world since Chulalongkorn died in 1910, the death of this lively, volatile and dictatorial, lady removed the focal point of existence from her sons, grandson and relations, as she had exerted a power akin to that of a revered image in a temple, always to be found and bowed down to in the same place.

In addition to the prolonged strain of the funeral rites, other tensions made themselves felt among the royal mourners. For as well as relations being at a low ebb between the King and Chakrabongse, there were also rumours of plots against the King, whose unpopularity had been growing.

Together with three other generals, Chakrabongse, at this time, had become president of a committee established to work on a scheme for retiring a number of inefficient senior officers. Even before the committee had published its findings he had received an anonymous letter stating that as his loyalty to the King was unquestioned, he himself was to be removed before the King was also put out of the way. The letter obligingly named the officer entrusted with poisoning him.

Convinced that this letter was an angry response to his retirement scheme, Chakrabongse boldly sent a copy of it to the officer in question with his compliments! However, despite this stylish gesture, the atmosphere of hatred and suspicion engendered by such sinister threats, his profound grief at his mother's death, combined with his usual load of work and responsibilities, began to overwhelm him. Eventually he was driven to request leave from the King to take an extended holiday.

This being granted, he set about organising a leisurely trip by boat to Singapore, to be followed by a return train journey up the Malay Peninsular to end in the peace of familiar surroundings at Hua Hin. With respite from his arduous life in sight, he dealt with a lighter heart with his remaining commitments and engagements before he departed. One of these was a military dinner in honour of a visiting British General at the Ministry of Defence, an elegant colonial style building just opposite the Grand Palace. Not only Chakrabongse, but the three other Generals concerned with him in the officers' retirement plan were present. The evening seems to have been routine and unmemorable, although later it would be recalled that there was a brief failure of electricity, which plunged the room in darkness for a few minutes.

On 4th June, Chakrabongse and his aide-de-camp, Chavalit and his son, set out for Singapore on the *Katong*, owned by the Straits Steamship Company. Despite torrential rain, the little party was in holiday mood, and Chakrabongse, in particular, although he got a soaking walking from his car to the ship, stood about chatting cheerfully to relations and friends who had come to see him off.

However, by the next afternoon, he had developed a feverish cold and decided to stay in his bunk. Chula was much perturbed, for his father had a soldierly disregard for physical ills, and the boy feared he must be really unwell to retire in this way. Unfortunately, Chavalit, in her heedless manner, did not share his concern. Only seventeen, and extremely immature, she repeatedly urged Chakrabongse to get up and come on deck, saying the fresh air would do him good. This he eventually did on the day before the ship reached Singapore, though by then he had a painful cough. No one could gainsay him, however, certainly not his anxious son. Not only was he unaccustomed to giving in to illness, but, as the lover of a young girl twenty years his junior, was probably determined to appear strong and youthful in her eyes.

Even so, when they reached their hotel in Singapore on 8th June, he felt so exhausted that he sent Chula and Chavalit for a drive around the town, saying that he hoped to feel better by lunch time. When they returned he felt, if anything, worse and kept to his bed. It so happened that a millionaire Chinese merchant, a resident of Singapore who knew Chakrabongse through business dealings in Bangkok, called to see him. Finding him so unwell, he instantly proposed that he and his party would be more comfortable at his house, whence they gratefully removed.

An English doctor was summoned, who diagnosed Spanish influenza. This was a particularly virulent form of the complaint that swept the world after the First World War, and was responsible for many deaths. Unfortunately it was complicated by double pneumonia in Chakrabongse's case. On hearing this, the aide-de-camp, now thoroughly alarmed, sent telegrams to the King and Ministry of War while poor Chakrabongse, only 37, dictated a farewell letter to his brother Vajiravudh and a new will, both of which he managed to sign, albeit barely legibly. Having thus tacitly recognised his serious condition, he appeared relieved and joked and laughed almost naturally, but by the following day he was completely delirious.

On 13th June, his unhappy son was awakened early and led to his dying father's bedside. He later described the scene with words that convey in stark simplicity the anguish he felt:

> 'I was then twelve years old. I helped to join his hands together in prayer and tried to make him repeat the name of the Buddha, which I had been taught was the best thing one could do at the approach of death. He was able to do so, but would occasionally relapse into delirious mutterings. He was thirsty but could only take water in small spoonfuls. He fought magnificently. Then he could no longer drink even a spoonful of water. At 1.50 pm he died. As the English doctor bent down to close his eyes, I think I must have aged about ten years. After making the profoundest obeisance to my father's corpse, I then left the room and asked the aide-de-camp to send a cable to my mother.
>
> 'More vividly than when my grandmother died, I realised that the life I had known or expected to have, was quite at an end, and henceforth I would stand completely alone.'

That same evening Prince Prajadhipok, Chakrabongse's youngest brother, arrived with his wife Princess Rambai Barni and the long drawn-out tragic return to Siam was set in motion. Along a road lined with British troops, on a Royal Garrison Artillery gun carriage, the coffin, covered with the Siamese flag and accompanied by a full military band, wound its way slowly to the railway station while the guns at Canning Fort fired a thirty-seven gun salute – one salute for each year of Chakrabongse's life.

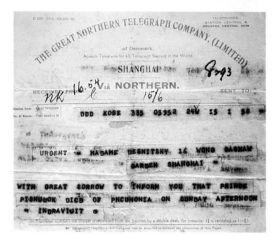

A copy of Prince Chakrabongse's revised will made while very ill leaving everthing to Princess Chavalit including the guardianship of Prince Chula.

Telegrams to Katya informing her of Prince Chakrabongse's illness and death.-

The train which brought Prince Chakrabongse's body from Singapore.

A halt on this last journey before reaching the capital, was made at Hua Hin, scene of much simple happiness which had ended so suddenly and unexpectedly. Virtually the entire village turned out to show respect and to mourn not only a prince but a friendly and well-liked neighbour. On arrival at Bangkok, when the cortege was met by the King and all the Royal Family, the officer in charge of a battalion of King Chulalongkorn's Own Bodyguard was so distressed by the occasion, that he was barely able to utter the words of command.

There followed the lengthy lying-in-state in what had been the ballroom at Paruskavan. As with his mother just eight months before, Chakrabongse's body was encased in a metal urn which in turn was housed in an elaborately carved wooden urn decorated with gold leaf and precious stones. Before the fateful trip and following the death of his mother, Chakrabongse had mused out loud to his son, 'When I die you will have to arrange for the ceiling to be pierced to accommodate the urn', little thinking that his prophecy would come true so soon and that an octagonal hole would indeed have to be cut, a task organised by another of Chakrabongse's brothers, the architect Prince Asdang. In the room amidst a profusion of flowers and candles, were displayed not only the deceased's regalia, but all his uniforms and many foreign decorations, including the splendid scarlet of the last Russian Emperor's Own Hussar Guards – a poignant reminder of the forever vanished past.

Everyone was kind to Chula, bereft of his mother, grandmother and above all his revered father, in the space of a few short months. During the customary 100 days before his cremation, the Prince was sincerely mourned, not only by his family as they gathered for the customary weekly services in his memory, but by the nation as a whole.

Phra Sarasas, formerly Chula's tutor and headmaster of the Military College wrote in his book *My Country Siam*: 'It was a misfortune that Prince Chakrabongse, heir to the throne, should have died before he was crowned. He epitomised all the desirable characteristics of a King. His character was a compound of earnestness, deference, pleading and dignity, with a profound sense of patriotism and democracy.' Although in fact only Heir Presumptive, a position he would have lost should Vajiravudh have produced an heir, at the time of his death, there is little doubt that he was widely regarded as probably the next king of Siam.

Robert Martignan in *La Monarchie Absolue Siamoise* stated:

> 'His death deprived Siam of one of her best sons. His intelligence, his military worth, the loyalty of his character and the clarity of his spirit, the Sovereign and the nation would lack at a time when they were most needed.'

To add to the profound sadness at the death of so young and able a man, who might well have had another 30 years of life still before him, disquieting rumours were circulating about the sinister coincidence that the three generals, colleagues of Chakrabongse, who had also attended the dinner at the Ministry of Defence, had all been stricken with Spanish influenza at about the same time, two having died and the third just managing to shake it off and survive. The failure of electricity during the dinner, combined with the known fact that Chakrabongse had received an anonymous letter warning he would be poisoned, led some to surmise that in the dark while the lights were out, germ-laden knives and forks had been substituted for those used by the victims.

Even the name of the French director of the Pasteur Institute, Dr Leopold Robert, was bandied about as having supplied the poison. The motive for his cooperation in so deadly a design was, it was said, Chakrabongse's well-known antagonism towards the French for their annexation of Laos and Cambodia in the reign of Chulalongkorn. Is it possible that an Heir Presumptive, who might well one day have become King, was thought sufficiently detrimental to French interests to necessitate his removal along with others known to be his close associates? Whether the technology of the time could have cultured and prepared such germs is not known and whatever the truth may be about Chakrabongse's mysterious and tragic end, no investigation or enquiry was ever made. Today over 70 years later it is impossible to arrive at any definite conclusions.

The portrait of Prince Chakrabongse displayed during his lying-in-state.

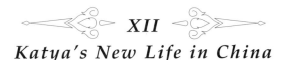

XII
Katya's New Life in China

atya's heart and mind were in an agonising turmoil of wounded affections and utter loneliness as she left her cherished home, having parted not only with her husband and son, but an assured way of life in a country and among people she had grown to understand and love.

Her bitter anger and mortification at having been rejected in favour of Chavalit, blinded her completely to the undoubted fact that her own somewhat demanding nature and year-long absence had paved the way for the advent of her rival.

It must be remembered, however, that since 1917, she had been living beneath the dark shadow of the Russian Revolution: the murder or disappearance of the Tzar and all his family in 1918, the Civil War, the precarious situation of the counter-revolutionary forces, and the German occupation of the Ukraine where her Desnitsky relatives lived – or did they?

Her decision to join her brother Ivan in Peking was not because she felt she could rely on his feeling and concern for her, but for the bleak reason that there was no-one else to whom she could turn. Now no longer well-married to a wealthy prince, but a divorcee who, from impetuous pride had refused a generous settlement and accepted only a small allowance, she doubted she would be welcomed.

Her relationship with her brother had indeed never been close, and one has the impression that even when, as a girl of sixteen she had come to St Petersburg to train as a nurse, he had troubled himself very little about her welfare. It is true that, when apart, they corresponded in a most affectionate terms, but had only to meet for there to be a possibility of a fiery wrangle.

A hard-headed, hard-working career diplomat with no private fortune, he had achieved great success in his profession and spoke fourteen languages, including many Eastern dialects. And, even after his diplomatic career was terminated by the Revolution, he had soon obtained an excellent position as a Director of the Chinese Eastern Railway.

During their last meeting in Bangkok when he had attempted to dissuade his sister from leaving her husband, he had also informed her of his own marriage and that he was the proud father of an infant son, also named Ivan. Not unnaturally under the circumstances, Katya had been too distracted to learn more about her sister-in-law except that her name was Olga and that, but for the upheaval of the Revolution, she and Ivan would never have met.

This was because, like many of her fellow countrymen, Olga had fled before the Bolshevik menace, walking from Kazan to Ufa with her friend Marussia. At Ufa quite by chance they met one of Olga's uncles, who generously gave them a red blanket, beneath which they shivered a little less than they would have done, jolting for one month across the Siberian Plain in a cattle truck to reach their destination, Omsk. This was where Admiral Kolchak had based the headquarters of one of the White anti-revolutionary forces in an heroic but doomed endeavour to weld their many factions together. Here Olga and Marussia joined a settlement of about sixty refugees, sheltered in a dilapidated abandoned mansion.

Also at Omsk was General Sir Alfred Knox, Chief of the British Military Mission to Siberia, who was more comfortably accommodated in a special train. Sir Alfred had not only spent many years in Russia as Military Attaché at the British Embassy, but was evidently a man of feeling with great sympathy for the dispossessed refugees. He hired a cook and found a stove for them, though there was precious little food to prepare, and milk when available was sold by the frozen plateful. And on discovering that Olga slept on a table under the stairs, covered only by her trusty red blanket, he somehow tracked down a camp-bed and bedding, which made her staircase nook comparatively homely. Despite the discomfort and disadvantages of living in this makeshift fashion, after their meagre evening meal the refugees sang and played folk and gypsy music, though far from homes they might never see again, and facing a harsh future – if indeed they had one.

In addition to his great knowledge of Russia, Sir Alfred loved music and therefore delighted in Olga's glorious voice and doubtless in her great good looks, for she was a tall statuesque beauty with magnificent eloquent eyes. Also to Omsk eventually came Katya's brother, Ivan Desnitsky, sent by the Russian Minster in Peking under the purposely vague title of 'Advisor', to report on Kolchak and the situation at Omsk. Besides his official duties, this plain hitherto unromantic man fell in despairing undeclared love with the captivating Olga, who remained serenely unaware of the havoc she had wrought in his troubled heart. It was the observant Sir Alfred, by now unhappily convinced that the days of the Kolchak regime were numbered, who drew her attention to this fact.

Taking her aside one day, he advised her in no uncertain terms to get out of Omsk. 'But where to?' 'To Peking.' 'Peking?' 'Yes, don't you realise that the Advisor is madly in love with you? Marry him and leave – the sooner the better!' So on 29th September, Olga became Madame Desnitsky and the bridal couple left the same evening for China. In this manner, though it could hardly be called a love-match on her part, Ivan acquired a beautiful charming wife, and Katya a sister-in-law.

No mention exists in a diary, letter or even a postcard, of Katya's arrival in Peking, but one imagines she must have stayed awhile with her brother and Olga before moving to Shanghai and renting a small house for herself in Wankashaw Gardens.

As Katya found herself in a city teeming with refugees, some in a deplorable state of destitution, others resolutely taking almost any employment however grand their previous status might have been, she energetically set about joining the Russian Benevolent Society. And being an excellent organiser, with practical nursing experience, she was welcomed with open arms, and soon found her days

Katya in China in the early 1920s.

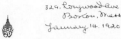

324. Longwood Ave
Boston. Mass.
January 14. 1920

My dear Catherine.

To my great disappoint-
ment to day the Telegram
I sent to you to express to
you my hearty thanks for
your greeting, has been
returned to me by the Company. They told me that
the line has been interrupted
and will not be restored for
quite a while.

I hope you have received

my letter I have written on
the same day I sent you
the Telegram.

How are you now? I
do look forward to meet
you and tell you all about
what has happened to me.

It is such a pity that
Sangwan and I cannot
travel together, because
the King wants us to marry
at home. And without
having married we can
hardly travel together.

Sangwan will take the next
boat and hopes to be able
to meet you at Shanghai
too.

Don't forget to drop a line
telling me where to meet
you. Address your letter
to the Siamese Legation
in Tokyo.

I am looking forward
to my visit at home.
Things will have changed
so much. The only thing
I hope is that they will not

me come back again to Ame-
ria to finish up my studies.
Why don't you come and
visit me here? Would not
it be a pleasant surprise
to see you turn up unex-
pectedly!

With hearty greetings from
your old faithful friend
Mahidol.

*Letter from Prince Mahidol to
Katya, 1920.*

*Katya during her trip back to Bangkok to attend the funeral of
Prince Chakrabongse. Standing from left: Prince Traitip and
Prince Priddhitepong Devakul and Prince Mahidol. Seated from
left: Princess Pichitchirapa Devakul and Katya.*

*Katya and her brother Ivan in Peking,
circa 1921.*

well-filled with committee and welfare work. She reverted to her maiden name, calling herself Madame Desnitsky, but the contrast in this existence of earnest endeavour, living in a small house on a small income, with the opulent ease and aura of royalty surrounding her at Paruskavan, must have seemed very great.

Katya's duties took her sometimes far afield, and although the hours passed rapidly enough while she was absorbed in work, on return to her dull empty house, the bitter regretful memories that surged into her heart made the evenings seem longer and more lonely. Partly because of this and partly because her brother had represented to her that it was unwise, even unsafe, for her to be so completely isolated, she decided to let her top floor and quite soon succeeeded in finding two lodgers, a Swedish businessman and an American engineer employed by the American General Electric Company. Although it was true she seldom saw them except when they came to pay their rent, she could hear them moving overhead, and the sound of their footsteps on the stairs, a door slamming or their muted voices, relieved to some extent her utter solitude.

But suddenly one night, the electric light failed, and groping about in pitch darkness, she realised she had no idea where the fuse-box was or how to mend a fuse even if she found it. After some hesitation, she therefore brought herself to call for help from the engineer, who promptly came to her aid and soon put all to rights. And afterwards in the restored illumination, on getting a closer look at his pretty landlady, he stayed to chat and to her great surprise, but not entirely to her displeasure, before leaving he drew her to him and kissed her good-night.

He followed this bold move a few days later by asking her to dine and Katya, finding him congenial, also took pleasure in shaking out and wearing some of her elegant dresses again, and being escorted by an attractive man. She came to look forward to seeing him and, although he was not at all the type to appeal to the cosmopolitan Europeans clustered around her sister-in-law, the latest report on 'Katya and her American' was looked forward to.

Harry Clinton Stone was from Portland, Oregon and had served with the American forces in the War. Although good-looking in a tall rangy way with rather cold grey eyes and pale complexion, his personality was irredeemably provincial and the unexceptional sentiments and high-toned judgements he pronounced in a chilly nasal voice seemed so unimbued with genuine feeling as to sound insincere. He also possessed an apparently inexhaustible store of set 'funny stories', none of which were 'risqué' – a daring Continental word to which he was addicted – but all dull. These set-pieces and chunks of accurate information on a wide variety of subjects made up his conversation, which was therefore stilted and somewhat lacking in spontaneity. Such drawbacks to enjoyment of his society would, however, not have been apparent to Katya who, although she spoke good careful English and understood it well enough for ordinary purposes, would be unlikely to recognise the banality of his opinions.

If she had searched the whole world over, she could hardly have met anyone more different from Chakrabongse and, perhaps to her bruised ego, this was part of Harry Stone's attraction. In addition, his attentions slowly restored her faith in herself as a desirable woman, and she began to rely on him to add a dash of colour to her days.

Slowly the sharp pain of loss and thorny stabs of fierce jealousy caused by Chavalit lessened, and she began to dream of visiting America to meet Harry's parents, referred to in special sanctified tones as 'Dad and Mother', to whom he had confided his happiness at meeting Katya in his weekly letters. He had a good position in the GEC and prospects seemed set fair and to be moving towards another phase in Katya's strange life, perhaps to be lived in as different a clime as Siam had been from Russia. Even so, although she continued to feel she was right to leave Chula with his father instead of exposing him to the hazards of whatever fate had in store for her, she often yearned for him and relived in memory their mutual happiness as mother and son.

Sometimes haunting fears for her relatives in the Ukraine, natural preoccupations which Katya shared with other refugees, plunged her into Slavonic gloom but the telegram she received on 13th June must have driven all other considerations from her mind. For in that telegram, the king told her that Chakrabongse was dead. She could not believe it, and at first experienced that sensation of uncomprehending stupefaction that postpones immediate acceptance of tragedy till the mind feels more able to support it.

So it was that, only eleven months after they had parted, Katya returned to Bangkok where the King had placed a fully-staffed house at her disposal so that she might attend Chakrabongse's cremation in September. She was treated with every mark of consideration and respect but, though Chula spent much time with her, he continued to live at Paruskavan in the affectionate care of his nurse Chom, and where Chavalit remained discreetly in residence.

Notwithstanding her joy at seeing him again and the pleasure she derived from the companionship of her dog, L'Or, who seldom left her side, this period before the cremation when she could see the elaborate royal funeral pyre rise higher every day against the summer sky was a traumatic ordeal. Warring emotions – memories of shared happiness within the gates of Paruskavan, closed forever against her now – and vain remorse for sharp words and bitter wrangles that seemed at present so trivial before death's irrevocable finality, tormented her. In addition, from what Chula told her of Chakrabongse's last days, she felt he had been hurried towards his end by the childish irresponsibility of Chavalit. And years later, as quoted before, this still provoked an anguished cry of regret in a letter to her son: 'If we had not parted, he might still be alive!' She meant, of course, that being medically trained, she would have realised how gravely ill he was and, unlike Chavalit, would not have urged him to leave his cabin for the deck on that last fatal voyage to Singapore.

While she was in Bangkok, Katya had several audiences with the King, during which Chula was naturally the main topic of discussion. The monarch, now Chula's official guardian, had created his nephew a Royal Highness, and had decreed he should go to England, first to private tutors and then to Sandhurst, as he himself had done. Katya's suggestion that she should live in England to be near him and look after him was agreeably but firmly turned down. Vajiravudh believed that Chula should 'rough it on his own' as he and other princes had, adding graciously that Katya might see him during his long summer holidays.

As all had been decided without reference to her, she knew she had been relegated, courteously but definitely set aside, so that whatever part she eventually played in Chula's life would be within limits set by the King, which would effectively remove her son from her influence. And while she perceived that, under the circumstances, this was only to be expected she began to feel alienated from the country and people she had once made her own. This in its turn made her realise there was no going back and that she must make a new life for herself elsewhere.

She also learned that the King, being an absolute monarch, had suspended Chakrabongse's will in which he had left his entire fortune to Chavalit, and to Chula on her death. The King decreed instead that Chula, Katya and Chavalit should each receive income from Chakrabongse's estate, but could not touch the capital. Furthermore, Paruskavan was to be returned to the Crown, and Chavalit was ordered to move to the much smaller house at Ta Tien, scene of many a romantic rendezvous with Chakrabongse when they were first in love.

As it happened, this frivolous light-hearted girl who, if she had not caused, had precipitated the break-up of his marriage to Katya, quite soon forgot him for she married one of her cousins, Prince Amorn, only a year after Chakrabongse's death, in 1921. As Prince Amorn was well-connected and wealthy, he presumably had no objection to Chavalit giving up her income from Chakrabongse's estate, a condition imposed by the King before he would grant her permission to marry.

The day of the Cremation – a day dreaded by Katya for months – arrived and was conducted with the impressive formality and moving ceremony she knew so well. However, she again suffered from a now familiar feeling of alienation, as though it was not she who walked so slowly and solemnly in the lengthy procession but someone else – a former self. And that evening her thoughts turned as though just liberated, to Peking and Harry Stone, who had proposed to her before she left. Being then uncertain what awaited her in Bangkok she had neither answered 'yes' nor 'no' but begged him to wait until her position was clear. Now she began to wonder whether during her lengthy absence he had begun to waver and perhaps to change his mind. She felt her life was in suspension: she neither belonged in Siam nor knew for certain what awaited her in China.

As for her relationship with her son, while she accepted she must play a minor part in his life while he pursued a course laid out for him by the King, this was not accomplished without resentment. In later years, Chula would accuse her of 'desertion' and remain unconvinced by her explanation of the complicated web of circumstances that had led to her departure. Thus the remembered pain of the boy of eleven, as he wandered in the gardens of Paruskavan after she left, was never really healed and remained an open wound in their relationship.

By the beginning of December, Katya was longing to be gone. Bangkok for her was only filled with sad recollection and regret. Therefore on the 10th, all farewells said and last visits paid, she went on her way, taking with her the dog, L'Or, the gift of Chakrabongse in happier days in Paris. This time the severance from Siam, where she had once been so happy and, despite prejudice, had been held in affection by so many, was final. Gradually the memory of 'Mom Katerin' faded, though the consternation and affront her marriage to Prince Chakrabongse had caused in the Royal Family, was longer remembered as the first intrusion of a 'farang' and commoner into their near sacred circles.

King Rama VI and Princess Laksami Lawan.

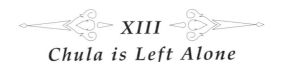

XIII
Chula is Left Alone

*T*he unexpected demise of Chakrabongse at such an early age, combined with the fact that he was, childless, began to cause the King deep concern on account of the succession; a concern which, in October 1920, led him to invite a number of his cousins to attend his court at Phya Thai. As these cousins were not princes but princesses, the royal gesture, not surprisingly, proved unpopular among his coterie of predominantly male favourites and courtiers. Undeterred, Vajiravudh encouraged the presence of these ladies and, as a particular mark of his favour, included roles for them in several plays he wrote and had performed at his palace.

One of these princesses, Vallabha Devi was, according to Chula, not only charming and dignified but, as a daughter of Prince Naradhip and, like Vajiravudh himself, a grandchild of King Mongkut, eminently eligible. At the age of twenty-eight, she was also not too young for a bridegroom of thirty-nine.

The announcement of her engagement to the King on 9th November was therefore welcomed by all except, quoting Chula again, 'by some well-known personages at court who tended to feel left out in the cold'. Many in the Royal Family must have wished that Queen Saowabha, Vajiravudh's Mother, who had so deplored her son's unmarried state, might have lived to share their rejoicing. A round of festivities was soon in full swing in honour of the engagement, the King's betrothed was installed in the comparatively newly-built Chitraladda Palace, and all concerned began to plan and look forward to the splendour and ceremony of a royal wedding.

As Vajiravudh had announced that their marriage would be monogamous, Vallabha Devi must have anticipated a position of undisputed importance in her married life, and had already gathered around her a little court of her own, which included several of her pretty younger sisters, including one who was particularly charming, Princess Laksami, her junior by seven years. Meanwhile, the King visited his affianced every day at teatime and telephoned her every evening which, while formally correct, does not suggest an ardent courtship.

A great distraction at Phya Thai, particularly for his nephew, the bereaved twelve-year-old Chula, was a miniature city laid out by his Uncle in the palace grounds, complete with exact copies of the Grand Palace, temples, theatres, hotels and private houses, some with entrancing gardens shaded by tiny Japanese dwarf trees. A water tank concealed within a 'mountain', fed a river flowing to a lake, and when lit up at night, the whole scene was one of magical enchantment. Courtiers were encouraged to own property and elect a mayor and councillors, the King announcing – perhaps to justify the extravagance of such a costly toy – that he wished them to comprehend municipal administration which he intended to introduce into Bangkok.

However, Chula was not to enjoy this for very long as, in February 1921, accompanied by his youngest uncle, Prince Prajadhipok, he left for England where he would be privately tutored prior to entering Harrow in 1923. For Prajadhipok, the trip was primarily to seek medical advice, but subsequently his health being much restored, he entered the French Staff College at St. Cloud, and did not return to Siam until 1924 when he was promoted Major-General.

Meanwhile in Bangkok, despite their bright beginnings, Vajiravudh's matrimonial plans clouded with uncertainty and ended with a bleak statement in March 1921 that ' owing to incompatibility' his engagement to Vallabha Devi was at an end. Later that same year the King made it known that he would now wed Vallabha Devi's sister, Laksami, which he actually did in August 1922, raising her to the rank of junior Queen. What heartache and unhappiness lay behind these curt announcements can only be imagined, for neither of the two sisters revealed their feelings, and Vajiravudh's journals have never been made public. Even now, sad to say, things did not go well even for the lovely Laksami, for she bore no children and eventually the royal pair decided to live apart, though continuing in the time-worn words 'to be good friends'.

These unfortunate experiences eventually terminated the King's preference for monogamy, for in October 1921 and January 1922, he suddenly took to wife two well-born sisters Prueng and Prabal Sucharitakul. The younger of the two, after suffering several miscarriages, was demoted from the title of Supreme Queen to being a mere queen and, to add to her pain and humiliation, heard that yet another lady – Suvadhana – was expecting His Majesty's child. One cannot but feel for the unhappy monarch, so belatedly anxious to do his duty and provide an heir to his throne, whilst also sparing a sympathetic thought for the unfortunate ladies involved in this frantic quest.

To add to Vajiravudh's tribulations, during these five years the deaths of his two full brothers, Chutadhuj in 1923 and Asdang in 1925, left only the Monarch himself and his younger brother Prajadhipok – whose health had never been good – as sole remaining representatives in the line of succession from Chulalongkorn and Saowabha. As by an act of 1924, the King had reserved to himself the traditional right to name his successor, it was generally assumed that unless a son was born to Vajiravudh, Prajadhipok would succeed him.

In the same act, the King had also decreed that if he remained childless, Chula's father, Chakrabongse, would have been next in line and Chula after him. But as the act went on to lay it down that any prince married to a foreigner forfeited the right to the throne, this posthumously disqualified Chakrabongse and therefore Chula.

Long afterwards, looking back on the Act of 1924, Chula has this to say in his book *Brought up in England*: 'This act had a nuisance value for me. Up till then, no-one had connected me with the throne or bothered their heads about me, but the act made people conscious that I was the nearest heir to Vajiravudh by ties of blood and should have succeeded him had my mother not been Russian. After

King Rama VI and Princess Suvadhana Devi.

Prince Chula shortly before leaving for England.

The royal urn of Prince Asdang Dejavudh, 1925.

The royal urn of Prince Chutadhuj Dharadilok in the same room as where that of his elder brother Prince Chakrabongse had been, 1923.

that everything I said or did was suspect; either I was scheming to get the throne or I was resentful at being disqualified.'

Towards the end of 1925, Vajiravudh in poor health, distressed by the failure of his matrimonial ventures and burdened with heavy debt mostly due to his personal over-generosity, fell very ill, and the news that Queen Suvadhana had given birth to his child was brought to him only on his death-bed. Gently caressing the baby girl, whose sex debarred her from succeeding him, he murmured resignedly, 'Perhaps it is just as well'. Then knowing that death was near, he requested he should be moved to the Grand Palace where he sent for his brother Prajadhipok, whom he had indeed named as his successor and, after lingering on a few days, he died on 26th November.

During these years Chula was embarking on the struggles of an English education. At first he was tutored in a small semi-detached house in Brighton by a clergyman. For him and his wife he has nothing but praise, saying, 'he was a splendid teacher', who took infinite pains to teach the young Prince colloquial English and the rudiments of French. 'It was a far cry from Paruskavan', he says cheerfully, describing how he tucked in to his first supper of tinned tomato soup and tinned salmon. When taken to church by the worthy pair, though dismayed by the plainness of the simple brick building compared with the glittering splendour of Siamese temples, he managed to explain in his rapidly improving English that, as he could hear no difference between the teaching of Jesus and the Buddha, he saw no reason to change his religion. His reasoning was clearly effective for, following his explanation, neither the tutor nor his wife discussed the matter with him again.

Pleasant though they were, a dispute between them and Phraya Buri, Siamese Minister in London, caused Chula's removal in 1921 to the household of a vicar, this time in a country parish about 40 miles from London. Here there were twelve other boys, and all of them were obliged to attend church twice every Sunday.

His summer holidays were spent at the Legation in London with his uncle Prince Prajadhipok who, his nephew recounts, was 'a fanatic shopper, hard at it from ten am until the shops closed, with only a short interval for luncheon!' As a change from this strenuous programme, in the remarkably hot August of 1922, he welcomed a motor-tour with his uncle in Switzerland during which they attended a session of the recently formed League of Nations under the presidency of Dr Wellington Koo. The three Siamese delegates, however, could not have been particularly effective, as one was deaf, one had a bad throat and could hardly be heard when he spoke, and the third was incapacitated by chronic headache.

It was during this trip that Chula first heard that his Mother had remarried and was now Mrs. Clinton Stone. Though hurt at first at not having been informed of it sooner, he was overjoyed when, at the end of August, she paid her first visit to England to see him. Katya had previously been to stay with her new in-laws, 'Dad and Mother', and had not concealed from Chula in her letters that she disliked America and was 'bored by the dreadful middle-class people' she had had to mix with in her husband's home town of Portland, Oregon. Doubtless in a wise wish to spend some time with her son before introducing him to his stepfather, Harry Stone did not join them until September when, according to Chula, 'they had a lot of fun together'. And it may well have been Chula who nicknamed him 'Hin' which means 'stone' in Siamese. However that may be, Hin he became and remained thereafter to everyone.

Queen Rambai Barni and King Prajadhipok.

Katya and Mr Harry Clinton Stone.

A postcard from Chula to his mother in Shanghai showing him and fellow students at Ashington Rectory.

It was in 1925 – three years later – before Chula saw his Mother again, by which time he had been two years at Harrow. On this occasion she took him, during the summer holidays, to the South of France and afterwards to stay with friends of hers in Rome. In 1926, Katya and Hin left China for good as the climate no longer suited him. They decided to settle in Paris, where Chula could spend his holidays, and where Katya had many relatives and friends who had fled there during the Revolution.

At first they rented a furnished flat at Neuilly and Katya was soon in touch with her Desnitsky relations. There were comings and goings from the Siamese

Katya and Prince Chula in France.

Legation. The Rahm family kept open house in the old Russian style and Shura Rahm became great friends with Chula. Olga, widow of Katya's brother Ivan, had remarried, her new husband being Paul Petithuegenin, a charming Frenchman, whom she deeply loved. Her two sons by Ivan Desnitsky, Ivan and Michael, often stayed with them, Ivan later becoming well-known in films as Ivan Desney.

Amid the babble and chatter of French, Russian and Siamese, Hin, who had given up his job on leaving China and now devoted himself completely to his wife, felt like a fish out of water. Like any man without definite occupation or great inner resources, especially one at the mercy of a demanding wife, he felt bound to assert himself in other ways, but his sententious pronouncements on world affairs and tedious repertoire of 'droll' stories fell equally flat and he felt isolated and alone.

Chula, having hitherto spent holidays at the Siamese Legation in London or with one or other of his royal uncles when they visited Europe, was very happy to 'have a home to go to', and sometimes Prince Abhas, one of his many cousins who was also a Harrovian, came with him and Katya enjoyed their company, and made them feel at home by cooking their favourite Siamese dishes for them. She was also always pleased to welcome Henry Maxwell (son of the distinguished Edwardian novelist W B Maxwell) a great friend of Chula's both at Harrow, Cambridge and afterwards, who describes her on their first meeting in 1924 as 'very animated, full of fun, amused by people and surroundings, excellent company – a glowing relaxed personality'. Later on, he found entertaining the dogmatic opinions she held on almost any subject, trivial or serious – describing how, when involved in argument, she would light yet another Russian cigarette, then, forcefully stubbing it out, half-smoked, demand: 'True – yes?' Thus challenged, it would be indeed a brave man or woman who would dare retort – 'No!'

This domineering side of her character may well have come to the fore in her second marriage as, being no longer surrounded by high-ranking royalty in Siam, to whom deference was obligatory, she may have felt that though uncrowned, she was now queen and her word was law. Whether or not this was so, she ruled Hin with an iron rod and, though outwardly her devoted subject, referring to her lightest wish as though it was an 'ukase', he was at times driven to subterfuge and evasion by her tyranny. He literally crouched behind her when a scene blew up, which was not infrequent, since Katya had come to believe it her duty to tell the truth as she saw it – regardless of consequences which socially, understandably, were often dire.

Hin always referred to her as 'mother', with the rolled American 'R', and sometimes was heard to wail despairingly: 'No one can stop motherrr doing whatever she likes'. His attitude to their finances was penny-pinching, and he often resorted to petty meanness, as when Chula bought first-class tickets for him and Katya to go on holiday, and he exchanged them for second-class and pocketed the difference. On another occasion, when Katya was given a generous cheque by Chula to buy a brand-new car, Hin adopted similar tactics, bought a car not only second- but third-hand, which became clearly evident when on a first outing, one of the doors fell off.

In 1927 Chula went up to Trinity College, Cambridge, where Abhas followed him a year later, Chula reading History and Abhas, Architecture. At Cambridge, Chula made many friends, from time to time coxed the First Trinity Boat, and was elected a member of the Leander Club. He sat for the Historical Tripos Examination, parts one and two, in 1929 and 1930, achieving second-class honours in both. Afterwards he stayed on at Cambridge till 1932 to do research on eighteenth century history.

In 1929 Abhas's younger brother, Prince Birabongse, who was also Chula's cousin, entered Eton where Chula and Abhas often visited him, and where they

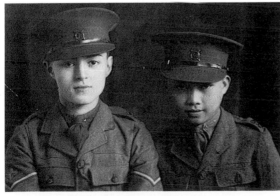

Prince Chula and his cousin Prince Abhas.

Prince Birabongse in his Eton top hat.

taught him to drive on Chula's Voisin – Bira proving an apt pupil. Spending his Christmas holiday that year with the Siamese Minister in Paris, the friendship and driving lessons continued, and he and Abhas were often dropping in to see Katya and Hin. Chula indeed came to regard Bira as a younger brother and later on, as is well known, under his management and guidance Bira blossomed into the famous racing driver B. Bira.

To begin with, Katya was well disposed towards Bira and Abhas, but occasionally she could be extremely jealous of her son's attachment to them, and the flat to which she and Hin had moved in the Rue Parmentier was often the scene of hot dispute and hurt feelings, echoes of which sound in Katya's lengthy letters: 'I am used to the idea that you make your life where there is no place for me', and begging Chula 'not to come and see me for just a few days, it will only upset me', and telling him 'unless you come at least for a fortnight, don't come at all'.

'I wish I could write a short letter', she exclaims on the twelfth page of one of these missives. 'And I'm too tired to write to you in English or French'. This is touching and reminds one that the set phrases she sometimes employed were due to difficulties in using a foreign tongue.

She was a very knowledgeable cook, and when she prepared food herself it was delicious. She had a large repertoire of dishes, being particularly partial to those she had learned in Siam. 'I like Siamese food best in the world' she wrote to Chula. But she also delighted her Russian relatives and friends by making traditional Russian specialities for them at Easter and other festivals. She would, for instance, go to infinite pains at the Russian New Year to prepare dish after Russian dish starting with 'zakuska'. All day she would labour, supervising whatever servant she employed at that time.

By early evening, the table would be beautifully arranged, the hostess impeccably dressed, her hair freshly set; drinks, including excellent vodka, perfectly presented and well iced, candles lit, all in readiness, and then the murmur of voices, the gradual entry of a large concourse of guests, happy to be invited, delighted with the display of delicacies, all prepared in true Russian style. Greetings, hand-kissing, presentation of flowers in crisp paper cornets, drawn-up chairs, the atmosphere every party-giver hopes for – genial, relaxed, in anticipation of a convivial evening. Often, alas, somehow, someone inadvertently would strike a wrong note and shatter the harmonious ambience, and the hostess, exhausted by her preparations for the feast, would declare the evening at an end.

In 1931, Chula returned to Siam, where he had not been for six years and where, to Katya's joy, he was very well received by his uncle, now King Prajadhipok and his royal relatives. She had feared that, as he would have been heir-apparent to the throne had she not been Russian, they might have regarded him with misgiving, afraid that motives of advancement and ambition might lie beneath his natural wish to keep in touch with his father's people and royal relations. On the contrary, her mind was set at rest on hearing his detailed account of the kind and royal reception he had received on his return, when he had been invested by the King with a personal royal order, the Ratanaporn First-Class, and met many people she had known, not least his old nurse Chom.

Chula, however, kept to himself that his stay in Bangkok 'was, in part, spoiled by an undercurrent of political anxiety and unrest'. This led him to warn the King that he thought revolution of some kind was imminent, also going as far as to suggest that, as the following year, 1932, would be the celebration of 150 years of the Chakri Dynasty, it would be an ideal occasion to announce the creation of a constitutional instead of an Absolute Monarchy. In this he showed great perspicacity for, when staying with his mother in Paris, on the evening of 24th June 1932, on return from the cinema accompanied by Shura Rahm and Sophia – one of Katya's friends – they found a note by the telephone that 'Mr. Pila had rung from the Siamese Legation but left no message.'According to Katya's diary, 'Chula became very worried as he said when Mr. Pila calls so late, it's always bad news and he's sure someone died in Bangkok. I tried my best to calm him, but I felt worried too as he's right, Mr. Pila never calls me so late for nothing'.

Morning brought confirmation of their presentiment, for when the maid brought Katya's morning tea and the newspapers, she announced 'that a very bad news are in the papers that revolution broke out in Siam'.

'My heart nearly stopped', Katya continues, 'but I waited till ten then I went to waken Chula and tell him this awful news. I drew the curtains and spoke to him quite calmly, telling him he mustn't worry as it may turn out very good yet, as I trust no Siamese would harm anyone of the royal family.'

All that morning friends telephoned Katya incessantly, either to find out if she knew more than they had learned from the newspapers or to express sympathy for the concern they were sure she must be feeling. 'It was such a relief to hear so many friendly attentions', as Katya puts it. The following day passed in the same atmosphere of apprehension as no-one at the Legation had heard any more except that 'King Prajadhipok did not yet give no answer to the demand for a constitution, but had asked time to read and study it'. In the afternoon Chula and Shura went to the Legation to see if anything more had been heard, while Katya, left alone in her flat, 'during everybody's absence' busied herself 'making chocolate fudges'.

At dinner when only Sophia was present, 'Chula was very excited and explained to them the reasons why the revolution had happened. Talk very well all the time in French. Looking at him, I was thinking what a wonderful leader he would be', she writes, clearly considering with maternal pride the possibility that, despite the disadvantage of having a Russian mother, her son might yet be called upon to play a part in Siam. 'On the other hand', she adds, 'I don't care of position, money and all these things; all I want is to see my child safe and happy . . . I let him talk', she concludes, 'as I knew it would be good for him.'

Later that same evening the Legation telephoned that a telegram had just come in and directly it was decoded they would ring back. When they did so it was to say that 'the official news was that a constitutional monarchy had been established and that everything in Bangkok was quiet'. Here, unfortunately, this fragment of a diary only kept from 5th to 27th June 1932 and never resumed, ends abruptly.

The situation in Bangkok that precipitated the Revolution was as follows. On ascending the throne seven years previously in 1926, Prajadhipok, who took the title of Rama VII, modestly felt that his purely soldierly career had ill-fitted him for the role of absolute monarch. He had created a Supreme Council, mostly composed of his princely brothers and relatives, to advise him in reducing the heavy debt incurred in the Privy Purse by the personal extravagance of Vajiravudh, a proportion of which had fallen to the charge of the National Exchequer. These difficulties, compounded by the world economic depression of 1929, made stringent retrenchment necessary and one economy which caused great discontent was the sweeping reduction in official salaries, particularly among officers of the armed forces.

Another factor playing a part in a potentially explosive situation was the resentment of educated commoners, numbers of whom had held high office during the two previous reigns, at their virtual exclusion from Government, a state of

King Rama VII in the ceremony at which Siam received a constitution.

King Prajadhipok who took the title King Rama VII.

mind which led them to begin questioning whether autocratic rule in the modern world was not beginning to be an anachronism.

Although Prajadhipok himself was aware of the dangerous state of affairs (which Chula had also foreseen), and had actually considered granting a constitution of his own accord, Sir Josiah Crosby, Great Britain's Minister at Bangkok from 1934 to 1941 writes in *Siam at the Crossroads* that he 'had it from the King's own lips that he was dissuaded from such a wise course by his uncles and brothers who were unable to believe that anything untoward was in the air'.

It was certainly ironic that the Supreme Council appointed by Prajadhipok himself, to help and advise him, should so signally have failed him at this crisis. Even the action of the Chief of Police, who had discovered the plot the night before the rising and had hastened to call on one of the princes of the Supreme Council for permission to arrest the ringleaders, was of no avail, for the prince in question blandly stated that he had heard such rumours before, that all had proved false, and he refused to sanction any measures whatsoever being taken.

In the event, therefore, the conspirators, consisting of young intellectuals and army and navy officers, found themselves staging a coup d'état which met with almost no resistance and the first the capital knew of it was the ominous rumble of tanks moving in to the grounds of Prince Boripatra's palace at dawn. The Prince – President of the Supreme Council – was seized and conveyed, still in pyjamas, to Dusit Palace where he was joined by several more princes and a minister or two, all rounded up as hostages. Prince Svasti escaped, having dashingly commandeered a detached railway engine and escaped in it to Hua Hin. There he found the King on holiday in his new Palace 'Klai Kangwol' whose name 'Far from Care', proved to be something of a misnomer.

The ultimatum, delivered next day by warship, informed the monarch of the formation of a Peoples' Party, whose 'principal aim' – according to the *Bangkok Times* – was 'the creation of a constitutional monarchy', and warned that, 'if members of the Peoples' Party receive any injuries, the princes held in pawn will suffer in consequence'. 'But', the document continued, 'we enjoin Your Majesty to return to the capital to reign again as King under the constitutional monarchy as established by the Peoples' Party'.

The King accepted, returned to Bangkok, and negotiations were begun. The princes were released though compelled to quit the posts they had held. Phraya Mano, Chief of the Supreme Court, was elected Prime Minister. A permanent constitution was duly signed on 10th December 1932, and a new era began.

Princess Chavlit and Prince Amorn Kitiyakara.

Prince Amorndhat Kridakorn (Tapong).

XIV
Motor-racing

*A*s not infrequently happens, dramatic coincidence can play a part in real life which would be dismissed were it written in a book or play as being unlikely or far-fetched. That same year, Katya heard to her astonishment that Chavalit, whom she had never expected to cross her path again, was actually in Paris. Married to Prince Amorn and the mother of five sons, the erstwhile pretty and lively charmer, still young, but now ravaged by illness, had been brought, as a last resort by her wealthy husband to Europe, in a despairing search for a cure.

Chakrabongse's former aide-de-camp, Tapong, was now the Siamese ambassador in Paris and being an old friend of Katya's, he frequently asked her to dine at the Siamese Legation. One day she was shocked to hear that he had seen Chavalit and was horrified to find her so changed. 'He said that she looks quite green as a dead person, that she doesn't eat, has no flesh at all, just bones, and that doctors who saw her don't give much hope'. After dinner, the door suddenly opened to admit Chavalit's husband. 'He had changed so much and got old so quick' that Katya failed to recognise him, and had to ask who he was. And she adds – feminine vanity uppermost – 'I am sure he was surprised to see me so young looking!', and goes on: 'I feel again I was in Bangkok when Chakrabongse died and the whole picture of old days passed in my brain.'

To her suggestion that she might go and see Chavalit, Tapong said diplomatically that he thought it inadvisable, since seeing her might be such a shock to Chavalit that it might kill her. Later that same evening, Amorn, who 'looked very nervous as he is terrified he may catch Chavalit's disease', asked Katya, as a trained nurse, what he should do to protect himself as his wife 'wants to kiss him every time she sees him'. To which Katya commented: 'Is it not absurd that I am the one to give him such advice?'

On her return home she could not sleep:

> *'My brain was working all the time. All the cruel action of Chavalit, all what I had to suffer through this girl, came back to me. Two feelings were fighting in me: one pity that she suffers so much, and another feeling of satisfaction that God punished her for all her selfishness. I felt rotten. Is it possible that I prayed God all these years to punish her and now when the punishment comes, I am sorry for her? All night I slept very badly. My conscience worked all the time. Oh how complicated life is!'*

On 19th June, on telephoning the Legation for news, Katya learned that Chavalit had died the day before, and that her cremation would take place privately at Père Lachaise on 20th June. Chula volunteered to attend with Tapong and when he got back to Rue Parmentier afterwards he told his mother, who wrote: 'It was awful as when the cremation was over, the men who looked after the fire came and invited them to look at the ashes! Chula said that he saw the whole body. Then to put ashes to a marble box, the men had to break the bones. He says he will never forget this cremation.'

And as a sad coda to the end of Chavalit, whom Chula had last seen as a young laughing girl in her prime, Katya adds: 'Chula says Amorn was not sad at all' – possibly because he was relieved at no longer having to fear her pathetic frightened embraces.

The revolution in Siam, coupled with the death of Chavalit, had considerable consequences for Chula for, in the summer of 1932, he was advised by King Prajadhipok that, as he was now no longer an absolute but a constitutional monarch, he had no further control over the capital and income left by hia father, Chakrabongse. It will be remembered that Chakrabongse's will in which he bequeathed his entire fortune to Chavalit, had been suspended by King Vajiravudh, who decreed that only a portion of the income from the estate should be divided between Chavalit, Katya and Chula, while the capital was to remain untouched. Now, however, due to Chavalit's death, Chula became his father's sole heir and found himself in possession of £20,000 a year instead of £1,000.

With characteristic generosity, he immediately increased his mother's allowance, and in addition bought her a charming little thatched house near Rambouillet, called Le Mesle. This was only an hour's drive from Paris and there, family and friends were entertained at weekends, and Katya was once more able to indulge her love of gardening, which she had sadly missed since her days at Paruskavan and Hua Hin. He also donated £25,000 to endow hospitals and schools in Bangkok, and was instantly accused by some in that city of 'buying popularity'.

At this time Chula was sharing a furnished flat in London with Abhas and, in midsummer, they had planned to go together with Bira on a motor-tour in Europe, in Chula's new car, a larger Voisin. But as Abhas had failed his final examinations at Cambridge, he reluctantly remained behind to prepare to re-take them in October. Chula and Bira therefore set out on their own, covering over three thousand miles in France, Switzerland and Italy, and it was during this trip that Chula became most impressed with Bira's capacity as a driver.

After Bira returned to Eton for the autumn term, Chula was in correspondence with Phraya Mano, the first Premier under the new constitution, from whom he ascertained that he was not now expected, as princes were in former times, to serve in one of the government services. As he had already decided that an army career was not for him, he decided to remain in private life and continue his work as a writer. He had already begun to establish a reputation in this field, as his book reviews and articles on political subjects had already been published and well received in Siam. In addition, his biography of *Frederick the Great* in Siamese, he explains modestly, 'had an unexpected success'.

Following the revolution, as the revenues of King Prajadhipok had been greatly reduced, the financial support hitherto enjoyed by Siamese princes abroad, including Bira, was discontinued. Consequently Chula now made himself financially responsible for Bira and, in fact, became his guardian. And when Bira left Eton aged eighteen, a private tutor was engaged to prepare him for entry into Trinity College, Cambridge, in 1934.

Bira was most engaging and talented, retaining for much of his life a childlike air of innocence and egoism – the more disarming because it was so natural. He was slender and well-built with an endearing way of seldom standing still but shifting rapidly from one foot to the other. Many of his most prized possessions were toys including a vast model railway in which he could remain absorbed for hours on end. He also had amazingly nimble fingers and, at one point, used to fashion exact replicas of different types of aircraft, tiny enough to fit into a matchbox.

During 1933, he and Chula moved into a flat in Kensington, and as Chula – unlike most of his royal relatives in whom it amounted almost to a passion – actually disliked shopping, Bira was entrusted with buying the furnishings. Unsurprisingly, his taste was in tune with the times: square deep armchairs, plenty of chromium-plate and sombre or neutral colours.

After much thought and long discussion, Bira eventually decided that an academic career was not for him, and abandoned the plan of going to Cambridge in favour of studying sculpture. After an initial trial period, he was accepted as a pupil by Charles Wheeler ARA and made excellent progress, later on exhibiting at the Royal Academy.

Meanwhile, Chula worked hard at his literary work, having two more biographies published in Siam but, although he and Bira led an active social life, going to many theatres and, above all, to performances of Russian Ballet given by de Basil's famous company, neither of them neglected their mutual great interest in motor-cars and motor-racing and, in 1935, Bira ran in some short handicap races at Brooklands, driving a Riley Imp, painted hyacinth blue – Katya's favourite colour – which soon became known as 'Bira Blue'. The Riley was superseded by a super-charged MG Magnette, but after watching the performance of cars built by a small firm, English Racing Automobiles, which became widely known as ERA, Chula, considering their productions were the best of the light car class, purchased one for Bira and presented it to him on his twenty-first birthday.

By now Chula had decided to go in seriously for racing and to act himself as Bira's manager. That the two of them, together with the first rate technicians they assembled, made a wonderful team is, of course, motor-racing history. When, in his first race in the new car at Dieppe on 20th July 1935 Bira came in second, Chula realised that the White Mouse team (so-called after Chula's Thai nickname of mouse) could be a serious contender in light car racing.

Chula had clearly inherited, along with his father's industry, his talent for organisation. This was obviously recognised by the Racing Correspondent of *The Times*, who wrote when Bira won the International Trophy at Brooklands in May 1939: 'Bira's success was as well-deserved as his frequent victories always are. As

*Prince Bira and his teacher
Charles Wheeler with the bust of
Prince Chula.*

*Prince Bira and Romulus
in June 1936 after winning
the Picardy Grand Prix.*

*Prince Bira in Hanuman winning the
Campbell Trophy, April 1938.*

a driver he possesses all the essential virtues, skill, coolness, and sympathy with
the mechanical functions of his car. But these in themselves would be unavailing
if it were not for the thoroughness with which his cousin Prince Chula attends to
every detail of the organisation. Bira's cars are beautifully turned out. There is
never a hint of last minute rush, and his pit control is what others would do well
to copy.'

In those last years before the Second World War, Bira competed in 68 long distance events, out of which he won 20 and achieved 14 seconds and 5 third places which, as Chula comments, 'was a record any amateur driver could be proud of'.

Looking ahead, Chula had initiated and begun work on a project very near his heart: a Grand Prix in Bangkok in December 1939. He was sad that this would no longer be during the reign of his uncle, King Pradjahipok, as the King had been in Europe since 1934, ostensibly for consultations about his failing eyesight. However, owing to constitutional difficulties which had arisen before his departure and which continued in his absence, a delegation from the Government had come from Siam to wait on him in his rented house in Cranleigh, Surrey, in an endeavour to find a ground of common agreement and to beg him to return. After prolonged discussion this was found impossible and the King abdicated in 1935 to be succeeded by Ananta Mahidol – the elder son of Prince Mahidol who had shown such friendship to Katya. As Ananta was only ten years old, a Council of Regency was appointed.

Bira, though beginning to be successful in his career as a racing driver, continued to work with Charles Wheeler and, deciding in 1934 that he would also benefit from taking drawing classes as well, he enrolled in the Byam Shaw School of Art in Kensington. Although he only studied there for one term, it was long enough for fate to bring into his life two fellow-students, one a pretty red-haired girl called Ceril Heycock, with whom he fell in love, and my sister Lisba Hunter.

Lisba was then only nineteen. She had silky ash-blond hair and golden skin that rendered her eyes an almost startling blue. Lisba found Bira's mercurial personality amusing and engaging and was intrigued at getting to know someone so completely different from her many English admirers as a Siamese Prince with the exotic name of Birabongse.

It is true that the word 'Siamese' conjured up in her mind that graceful enigmatic creature, the Siamese cat and then, of course, there were those twins. But about their country and origin she had only a vague notion of a mysterious

Princess Elizabeth Chakrabongse

Princess Ceril Birabongse

Eastern domain of whose history and customs, in common with most of her compatriots of that period, she knew next to nothing.

'You must meet my cousin', Bira told her, shifting restlessly from one foot to
another. 'Perhaps you could come to our flat for tea or a drink?' She replied she
would like to do so. Eventually invited to tea, she rang the bell of a small pleasant
block of flats in South Kensington and an English manservant showed her into a
sitting-room where a perfect stranger advanced to greet her.

'I am Bira's cousin', he said, shaking hands,. 'Bira told me you were coming,
but he's been detained and won't be here until later.' Unaware that his mother
was Russian, she was much surprised at how different his appearance was from
Bira: short, pale, dark-eyed, good-looking with an unusually attractive voice, she
was impressed by his considerable dignity which made him seem older than his
25 years.

While they had tea, they found much to talk about in a bantering lively way,
while each was inwardly engaged in the half defensive, half nervous attempt to
sum the other up and render manageable their mutual knowledge that this was
no ordinary casual meeting. Bira, when he arrived, added his amusing drollery to
the flow of agreeable chatter and when Lisba rose to go, he saw her out and, after
calling a taxi for her, sauntered back, ready to receive Chula's thanks for introducing him to such a charming girl. Great was his shocked astonishment therefore when Chula exclaimed vehemently: 'Keep her away from me – I never want
to see her again!', adding, 'If I do – I shall fall in love with her!'

By 1935 it was clear, not only to Lisba and Chula, but to all in their confidence,
that their attachment was not ephemeral and, by 1936, they were unofficially
engaged. Bira meanwhile had proposed to and been accepted by Ceril and, looking back on those days, it is remarkable the hostility provoked by their engagements.

In our conventional middle-class family, eyebrows were raised and voices
lowered when the matter was discussed. Of Siam, little was known and no
attempt was made to learn more – but it was readily assumed that Lisba risked
sequestration in a harem. Orientals sweeping innocent girls off their feet were all
very well on the flickering black and white cinema screens, but in real life – in
Kensington such a thing was unthinkable. For myself, while understanding the
reservations of our parents, I was in favour of the marriage.

This was the situation when, in April 1936, I went with Lisba and our mother
to Monte Carlo where Bira was to compete in what Chula called the greatest and
most popular 'round the houses' race for the Prince Rainier Cup'. This was run
over fifty laps, a distance of one hundred miles, along the twisting streets of the
little principality, still elegant before the intrusion of skyscrapers and factories.

I was happy to be there, not because I was interested in motor-racing, but
because I understood that Katya and her husband would be coming and, even
from the little I then knew of her remarkable story, I longed to meet her.

Lisba introduced us and I found myself shaking hands with an elegant lady whose still abundant severely dressed chestnut hair framed regular features that, though pleasing, seemed clouded by a pensive sadness, setting her apart from the convivial excitement around her. In consequence I felt timid, afraid of intruding on her different mood. To begin with, therefore, our conversation was rather stiff and formal; I cannot remember what I said that amused her, but suddenly and delightfully she smiled – a wide generous smile – instantly looking so animated and so much younger that I recall Queen Saowabha's long-ago praise of her 'pretty smile'. In a flash, I could now well imagine how she had once so fascinated Chakrabongse.

There was a fine, rather chilly, day for the race in which Bira managing skillfully to avoid a crash in the second lap, worked his way up the field to record his first important win.

Afterwards in Chula's hotel suite there was much champagne and many congratulations while the victor in his Bira-blue overalls sat content and happy, drinking orange juice.

Later that evening, having changed, we all met again at the Sporting Club where about twenty of us sat at a table in the centre of which glittered the resplendent cup. Many members of the elegant crowd who sauntered into the restaurant came over to greet Bira who, though obviously very happy, appeared modestly confused by all the attention. When, after an excellent meal, Chula suggested that we should all go and dance at the night club downstairs, the idea was greeted with enthusiasm.

Chula flushed and animated – he had every reason to be pleased and proud as it was his efficient management of the 'equipe' that had contributed greatly to the success, proposed to Bira that they should take the cup to their table at the night club. But Bira objected. He though it would be 'showing-off'. Chula tried to change

Prince Rainier Cup, Monaco, 11 April 1936. Prince Bira and Romulus after their first victory. Chula is at extreme right.

his mind and began to show signs of keeping anger at bay with an effort and the argument continuing as we left the restaurant, we began to feel embarrassed.

Eventually in two or three rather subdued groups, we went down in a lift into a kind of foyer, where we stood about while Chula and Bira harangued each other, oblivious of our presence. Katya was nowhere to be seen. Our spirits began to sink and the élan of the evening almost visibly drifted away. Suddenly the lift came down again and, turning towards this diversion, I saw Katya emerge. Good, I thought, she will bring them to their senses and save the party from disaster. I watched her move towards them in a quiet determined manner that promised well but, as she drew nearer, her pace quickened, she tossed her head and sprang forward, not to separate and reason with them as I had hoped, but with heightened colour and dramatic gesture, stirred the flaming quarrel higher still in furious Siamese. By now an impression was gaining ground among the forgotten guests that it would be better to depart so, with politely murmured thanks ignored by the combatants, we all stole away.

In 1937, Chakrabongse's old friend from their days together in the Corps des Pages and the last Emperor's Own Hussars, Colonel Poum, arrived in Paris, very much alone now that his great love, Madame Chrapovitzkaya, to whom he had devoted his life, had died in the South of France. In his mid-fifties, he had greying hair and moustache and an air of gentle resignation, far removed from the youthful dash and style he had shared with Chakrabongse in the last days of Imperial Russia. He gave the impression of a man somewhat withdrawn from life – courteous but absent in manner – who smiled when he saw others smile while his eyes remained grave and distant. His few clothes were always carefully brushed, pressed, and worn with elegant neatness, and he moved with the brisk precision of the soldier, contrasting with the remote sadness of his features in repose.

He had risen to the rank of Colonel in the Emperor's Own Hussars and his popularity with the men was such that on the outbreak of Revolution, though his ties with the Imperial Family were known, the Regimental Soviet voted to continue serving under him. However, probably foreseeing how wretched the plight of officers would become when, all discipline eroded, they would be powerless to command, he wisely decided on flight and took Madame Chrapovitzkaya with him. He was able to do so as, though for many years a naturalised Russian, he had retained his Siamese passport, and with it he engineered their escape. They reached eventually the South of France where, in harsh poverty but in safety, Poum worked in a bank in Monte Carlo to support them both until she died.

Chula, with his strong sense of responsibility, cast about as to how he could enable Poum to live free from financial insecurity without injuring his pride and came up with the idea of appointing him Katya's secretary. The post was diffidently accepted and, on assuming his duties, Poum took up residence in a modest hotel within easy walking distance of the Rue Parmentier. 'With him I can speak my own language', Katya writes more than once, and it would hardly seem

*Poum on a brief trip
to Thailand in 1937.*

far-fetched to infer she meant more by this than that they could merely speak Russian together, as this she could do with her relatives and many of her compatriots now in Paris.

The fact that Poum was Siamese yet spoke her language fluently and had lived in her country among her people as Chakrabongse had done, revived the already existing bond between them so that, as the months went by, the past they had shared together gradually seemed to emerge into the foreground and become part of the living present.

At the same time, his presence in Paris – as unforeseen and unlikely as Chavalit's journey there to die – must also have rekindled in Katya a painful sense of exile, not only from Russia but Siam, where her life had reached its high point only to be much reduced since.

Poum, who, as no-one else, was aware of the full secret story of her runaway marriage, reminded her of her love for Chakrabongse in all its freshness and her love for his exotic country in all its strangeness where, despite so many obstacles, she had spent her most truly happy years. For Poum, too, she was the only being he now knew, who could remember Madame Chrapovitskaya and could step back with him into that lamp-lit drawing room in the Machavaya Ulitsa in St Petersburg, where the 23 birds sang and twittered and where they could gather around them in memory the light-hearted young people drawn there by the spell of her endearing personality.

Prince Chula and Lisba on their wedding day, 30 September 1938.

An invitation to Prince Chula and Lisba's wedding luncheon.

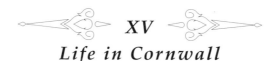

XV
Life in Cornwall

The Munich Agreement, engineered by the Prime Minister, Neville Chamberlain, in September 1938, was judged by some in Cabinet and Parliament, and by many ordinary people in Britain, to be not only shameful but ineffective: merely a temporary halt on the march of events towards inevitable war. On the other hand, there were those who welcomed it with joy and thanksgiving and believed Chamberlain when he hailed it as 'peace with honour' and 'peace in our time'.

In the year-long respite that followed, a minor effect of the still existing uneasiness – a feeling of waiting for catastrophe – was the number of couples who hurried to advance the date of their marriage. This was the case with Lisba and Chula, whose wedding took place on 30th September instead of October, as they had at first intended.

Their attachment had survived much guarded or straight-forward disapproval on both sides. Chula's uncle, King Prajadhipok, had more than once begged him not to take example from his father and marry a 'farang' and such a union was automatically frowned on by all his royal relatives, while the few among his many English friends to whom he made known his matrimonial intentions, were dubious or, at the best, cautiously lukewarm.

My parents were deeply concerned and troubled, faced with a prospect they could never have envisaged for one of their four daughters. They had also, of course, to face the pain of separation, for Lisba inevitably would spend much of her future life in a country and among people of whom they knew next to nothing. My father, in particular, felt unhappy and bereft, for he was especially fond of Lisba. For myself, as I have said, convinced that theirs was an enduring love, I gave them unreserved support, which in no way prevented me from understanding how my mother and father felt. It did mean, however, that inwardly I thought little of our relations – unanimously 'shocked' and 'dismayed', writing letters of 'condolence' instead of congratulation, telephoning their 'sympathy' and in one case calling personally to enquire if Chula was really black.

Today, over fifty years later, now that prejudice against mixed marriage has weakened, these attitudes seem strangely narrow and exaggerated, but then it made for a fraught and trying situation, which in a way was relieved when the wedding took place and became an accomplished fact. But although my father remained cordial and composed at the Registry Office and the Siamese Legation afterwards, I can still remember his lonely figure as he wandered away on his own to hide his feelings.

Katya and Hin were not among the family and few close friends who were present, and Chula explains in one of his books that 'My Mother did not come over from Paris due to the tenseness of the political situation as we expected war to be declared at any moment.'

But I wondered then and still do whether this was quite true, or whether it may have been a kind of jealousy that kept Katya from the marriage of her only son? Not so much the traditional animosity of the mother-in-law against the usurping daughter-in-law, but perhaps Katya, now plain Mrs. Stone, may have been unwilling to witness Lisba become Princess Chula, as she had become Mom Katerin so long ago.

After a brief honeymoon in the West Country, Lisba and Chula returned to the London flat and, in October, taking advantage of the still prevailing though uneasy peace, together with Bira, Ceril and Abhas, they sailed to Siam – for the last time as it happened – for they returned in March 1939 and in June that same year the country's name was changed to Thailand.

After the false promise of the Munich Agreement, the outbreak of war on 3rd September 1939 brought customary life to a standstill while people considered how to meet the occasion: what if anything could continue as before and what was irreparably changed and would never be the same again. As Thailand had declared her neutrality, Chula at first thought of returning to Bangkok, but sailings were so difficult, and even when arranged, liable to postponement or cancellation, that after packing and unpacking three or four times, he decided to stay in England.

He advised his mother, now living at her country property, Le Mesle, to take advantage of her American citizenship and depart with Hin to the States. But Katya and Hin, with blind faith in the 'impregnable' Maginot Line, at first refused to move. However, to Chula's great dismay and surprise, Thailand was invaded by the Japanese in 1941, swiftly capitulated and, worse still, declared war on Britain and the United States.

Feeling that this untoward event put him in a most delicate position, Chula came to the conclusion that his best move would be to retire from London and live quietly and unobtrusively away from the capital for the duration. Lisba and I were therefore despatched to Cornwall to search for a suitable furnished house. After some adventures and many misadventures inspecting numbers of dirty, dilapidated places, inhabited by people of repellent habits to judge by the broken furniture and grimy kitchens, or vast dank mansions unheated but for rickety oil-stoves, we began to despair and face the unenviable prospect of conveying to Chula that our mission had failed.

Hunting through our pile of glowing descriptions of properties which we had found eminently 'undesirable', we spotted 'Lynham Farm, Rock, a charming modernised farmhouse, small, well-established garden and tennis-court, overlooking a beautiful estuary'. We drove off with no confidence in the description but, as we crossed the threshold, we felt at once we had come home. It was quite delightful: low-ceilinged, thick-walled, furnished with great taste, fresh chintzes and pale unemphatic wall paper and paint; it was also roomy enough to contain a considerable household.

Ceril, Lisba, Chula and Bira on their honeymoon trip to Thailand in 1938.

Eventually after all business details had been settled, a cavalcade left London consisting of Chula and Lisba, Bira and Ceril, Shura Rahm (who had been an active member of the motor racing 'équipe'), Chula's Thai clerk Bian, a manservant, a cook, two racing-cars, two dogs and a remarkable bird, a Malaysian Grackle, black with a white waistcoat, who would puff out his chest and bow in stately fashion like a tail-coated butler.

The arrival of a Royal Highness with such an entourage caused no little stir in the village and, for weeks after they had settled in, the local house agents with the delightful and euphonious name of Button, Menhennit & Mutton, displayed a small hand-written notice in their window reading: 'Lynham Farm, let to HRH Prince Chula of Thailand by us.'

As Chula still remained convinced that Katya would be better off in America during the war, he and Lisba managed to reach Le Mesle the day before his mother's birthday, which was 10th May. Early next morning, his argument that she should leave was powerfully reinforced by the ground beneath their feet shaking with heavy gunfire – a grim warning that the 'phoney war' was over and the German invasion had begun. The fall of Sedan on 14th May finally clinched the matter, and eventually Katya and Hin, accompanied by Poum, reached the States via Spain and Portugal.

Katya's letters to her son from Portland, Oregon, are uniformly dull, unenlivened by any personal touches, and might well have been written by any one of the 'dreary middle-class people' amongst whom she found herself until the conflict ended. They abound in domestic detail: a row with the man next door about alterations to their garage; disparagement of American food; scandalously high prices. Concern over Hin's health and relief when the doctor pronounces he is not going blind and, on another occasion, that a feared heart-attack was only bad indigestion. One hopes eagerly for some word of Poum – what did he make of

Portland, Oregon? What did Portland, Oregon, make of him? But we only hear that he has been fitted with new spectacles! 'People here feel I'm different from them, from a different rank of society'. 'I don't really like their houses though they all have much more money to spend than we have'. 'There is always much work to do in the house but none offered to come to my help.'

Meanwhile at Lynham it was not long before the household was in running order, a fairly strict order so that it resembled nothing so much as a miniature court ruled by a generally benevolent autocrat. For although Chula had quite accepted his role as a private individual, he never really forgot that he came from a long line of kings and princes, and that his clear decisive mind and talent for organisation inherited from his admired father, might have been employed in a wider sphere.

He had inherited his family's penchant for rising about noon and staying up late and sometimes, after the guest or guests had begun to droop and wilt as dawn chilled and infiltrated the convivial gathering, his mind remained alert, eager to hunt a subject through all the coverts of argument to a final conclusion he found satisfactory. He was extremely industrious and devoted himself for a set period every day to his literary projects: not only historical works in Thai, but a volume of reminiscences – *Brought up in England* – and several books on motor-racing in English.

Work finished for the day, he expected to be amused not only by his immediate entourage, but by the many visitors who came to stay or were entertained to a meal. These included characters as diverse as ex-Queen Rambai of Thailand, a widow now that her husband ex-King Prajadhipok had died in 1941; Noel Coward who came to dinner, the recently widowed Duchess of Kent, who came to tea with her two children, Jack Buchanan the musical comedy star and, not only many of Chula and Lisba's friends and relations, but also those of Bira and Ceril.

Rosemary Essen-Scott, Lisba, Queen Rambai, Chula, Bira and Ceril together with Joannie the terrier and Hercules the bulldog. Lynham Farm, Rock, early 1940s.

Local people also called including the Vicar, the last being favoured with a dissertation on Buddhism and Christianity, somewhat biased in favour of the former, and leaving him in no doubt that his exotic new parishioners would not be numbered amongst his congregation. However, they did involve themselves in village activities, as Lisba and Ceril worked at the St. John's and Red Cross centre, and willingly assisted at bazaars and fêtes in aid of the war effort.

Since the Japanese occupation of Thailand and Thailand's declaration of War on Britain and the United States, Chula and Bira were, strictly speaking, classed as enemy aliens. However, Chula had been assured that neither of them would be subject to restrictions on that score and that he was to retain his GCVO. Gratifying though this undoubtedly was, Chula, still frustrated at being unable to serve his own country, began to look around to find some way in which to 'bear a share in the defence of England, the country of our refuge and our home', and decided to apply for himself and Bira to become privates in the Home Guard. Their first application in December 1941 was turned down, but Chula persisted, and in February 1942 both were accepted. The Home Guard was an auxiliary force, a million strong in 1940, and provided a welcome chance of service to veterans of the First World War and younger men in reserved occupations such as farming.

The two Princes participated fully in the strenuous training of the Rock Platoon, which included night sentry duty and coast patrols, and as there were rumours of German landings on the Cornish coast, they slept with full equipment and a rifle beneath their beds. Their duties were most loyally carried out, and

Prince Bira and Chula in their Home Guard uniforms c. 1943.

Chula, who had from quite a tender age worn immaculately tailored uniforms of no lower rank than second-lieutenant in King Chulalongkorn's Own Bodyguard, the First Cavalry Regiment of the Guards, and Fifth Cavalry Regiment of Queen Saowabha, now wore only the rough dust-coloured khaki of an English private soldier.

Later in 1942, Chula moved on to join the Army Cadet Force, greatly expanded since the war – there were three battalions in Cornwall alone - with the rank of Second-Lieutenant and, after six months, was promoted Lieutenant, retaining his operational role in the Home Guard in case of emergency. Though enthusiastic about this new departure, he records rather ruefully that when required to carry a two-inch mortar up a hill, he could only walk. 'Double, double', cried a subaltern, years younger than himself, 'You'll have to assume I'm doubling', the exhausted Prince replied.

There was dismay at Lynham when, in 1944, three months notice to leave was given them by the landlord, as they had all come to love Cornwall. In addition, Chula was reluctant to leave his Cadet Battalion, while Lisba, who had taken up work for St John's Ambulance Brigade as war-work, found it of such absorbing interest that by 1964, in recognition of her twenty-five years of devoted service, she was to be created a Dame of the Order. Therefore, instead of planning a return to London, they searched for a property not to rent but to buy.

Their final choice fell on Tredethy near Bodmin, which became their lifelong home. Tredethy was a high-standing awkward-looking house, in a magnificent setting, facing south over a wide prospect of rolling wooded countryside. It was ill-designed with large draughty rooms, lofty ceilings, old-fashioned kitchen quarters, no mains electricity or water, and completely isolated except for a neighbouring farm. Also included in the property were two or three cottages, outbuildings and old stabling built around a courtyard. It was said to be haunted, and in time to come more than one nervous guest would describe the apparition of a grey lady on the stairs; what her story was and why her spirit was uneasy, no-one knew, though it was suggested that if she were grey, she might be grey with cold, for in common with so many English country houses, Tredethy was never really warm. Oddly enough, Chula, born and brought up in a tropical climate, never felt the cold and was inclined to look down on those who did.

Tredethy was however warmed by the great hospitality of its owners. They were always looking for and finding occasion for parties and amusement for their many friends, and Lisba was adept at never being at a loss to set another place or discover room for yet another guest in the large rambling house. There were delightful musical evenings when first-rate quartets came to play. There were dances, lavish Christmas parties, country walks and swimming.

Once again, though now on an even larger scale, their home resembled a court: quite strictly organised by its presiding spirit, who in a highly charged programme of activities, kept a vigilant eye on anyone bold enough to oppose opinions or prejudices beyond certain lines – lines which might be suddenly drawn

*Tredethy, near
Bodmin, Cornwall.*

and unexpectedly halt discussion on topics ruled out of court. Royal displeasure would chill speakers, reminding them implicitly that they might amuse, interest or entertain, but not challenge their autocratic host. He sometimes went to unusual lengths to signify exasperation and recounts himself, in one of his books, how he became so enraged by a hotel manager's stupidity in Venice that 'I could only throw myself down flat on my back!'

I have also seen him do this when overcome by helpless laughter and once when he was furious. This last was when he stayed overnight with my husband and me in London to attend an important dinner. He left our house, spruce and elegant in dark blue dress uniform and decorations, but returned later in a fearful rage. Something – I forget now what it was – had greatly displeased him during the evening, and giving an account of it, he flung himself at our feet and drumming with his heels till his medals shook and jingled, consigned his host and everyone at the dinner to unutterable perdition .

Although he may at times have taken himself a little too seriously, he also possessed a sly sense of humour at his own expense. For example, he stayed with us once during the 1950s, and it cannot have been for the coronation of the present Queen, as Lisba accompanied him to the ceremony in the Abbey and to the many

Christmas 1947 at Tredethy. Front, 2nd from left is Katya, Prince Chula: holding Joan, Lisba holding 'Herc' is flanked by Nan Rahm, Ceril holds her two West Highland Terriers. A Russian samovar is visible at bottom right.

receptions and banquets of that memorable event, and I am certain that on this occasion, Chula was on his own. In any case, it came about that, splendidly attired in scarlet uniform, glittering with medals, he returned to a very late lunch. We had no help at that time, so meals were below stairs, and I had just sat him down with hot chicken casserole, wine, salad and French bread, when two German maids arrived for an interview. I showed them round the house, and when we reached the kitchen they appeared rather unnerved by the sight of this magnificent figure, calmly eating at the kitchen table. Afterwards Chula remarked: 'I bet they thought I was a cinema commissionaire!'

When Katya and Hin visited Tredethy, their presence sometimes caused a certain tension for, however hard Hin strove to maintain 'Motherrr' in an equable frame of mind, there were days when the house rang with recrimination and the sound of sharply slammed doors, as a well-rehearsed old quarrel was run through, or a brand-new one worked up from the scantiest material. Even Lisba's tact and ability to guard against giving offence sometimes failed, when the will to take it was as strong as it was in her mother-in-law. It angered her, for instance, when Lisba wore beautiful Thai jewellery because she herself had very little. And apparently obliterated from her mind was the incident long ago when she had flung in the face of King Vajiravudh's emissary the jewels the King had sent her as a personal gift. On the other hand, if Lisba wore no jewellery, she insisted obscurely that 'Lisba wished to spite her'.

Her opinions were forceful and undeviating: at a dinner where two known homosexuals were present, she spoke loudly and approvingly of a Russian nobleman, who learning one of his sons had similar inclinations, took the rather extreme step of shooting him – 'and quite right too!' Although these squalls and tempestuous huffs were afterwards lapped over by waves of maternal affection, the strewn wreckage left behind was not always easy to forget.

In 1956 came the birth of Narisa, after 18 years of marriage, and this event naturally altered the ambience of Tredethy. Although the life of the house continued to be highly organised and crowded with activities, the nursery – presided over by Miss Dorothy Thomas (always called Tommy, or Nin Nin by Narisa), a Norland nurse who was one in a thousand – became a calm refuge where the child grew and flourished. She became a source of joy to her mother who, with Tommy's invaluable help, managed not only to see much of her little daughter, but to continue to work for St John's and, above all, to be at Chula's side, knowing that her child was in good and loving hands.

More than once when I stayed at Tredethy, I met Poum and it is one of my lasting regrets that knowing nothing of his remarkable history, I accepted him as no more than a gentle and amenable guest – rather silent – an onlooker rather than a participant in the lively life around him, smiling rather anxiously at jokes he clearly found incomprehensible despite his sound English. I felt his presence there did not greatly concern him and had nothing to do with his inmost thoughts and being.

One winter's day in 1947, the house buffeted by westerly gales, he had a sudden heart attack and as quietly as he had lived since Madame Chrapovitzkaya's

Narisa on her second birthday with her beloved Norland nurse, Dorothy Thomas, known by Narisa as 'Nin Nin'.

Narisa as a baby.

Narisa, Lisba and Chula, 1957, together with Pompey the poodle.

Chula and Lisba in 1962 about to go to a royal ceremony. He is wearing the Chulachomklao chain – First Class, which he had just received.

death, he died. And so it came about that this Buddhist, Greek Orthodox, Siamese Colonel in the Russian Imperial Hussars, found his last resting place in the windswept graveyard of a Protestant church in Cornwall. Thirteen years later, Katya wrote in one of her last letters to her son, before her own death and burial in a small Russian cemetary in Paris: 'How I miss Poum you do not know. He was such a fine man and such a help and with him I could speak my own language, but we cannot change the destiny . . .'

What the extent of their relationship was or became will never be known, for their discretion was absolute. But the perceptive Henry Maxwell, who knew them both, is convinced they were lovers and when asked why said simply, 'Because of the way she regarded him.' As good a reason as any other and one hopes indeed they were.

On January 3rd, 1960, at the age of seventy-two, Katya's own adventurous life drew to a close, not accompanied by painful illness, but a calm acceptance of her end. 'Just peacefully giving up', as her doctor described it, she may have recalled from her girlhood in Russia long ago, a wise old saying: 'Never regret past happiness, but be grateful to have known it!'

How Chula reacted on learning of his mother's death later in 1960 must remain a matter for speculation. That he loved her was certain, that she exasperated him unbearably is also true, whether he ever forgave her for leaving him so abruptly all those years ago no-one dared ask, nor will ever know.

The author in the 1930s.

*I*t was not until nine years after Chula's tragic death from cancer in 1964, that I first went to Thailand with my sister. Lisba had become a Buddhist in 1952 and her life, so highly charged while Chula lived, had taken on a slower more reflective pace, enabling her to spend more time with her daughter, family and friends and to develop her considerable artistic talent.

At the airport we were met by a bevy of relations, Bisdar – childhood playmate of Chula at Paruskavan – then a good-looking man in his late fifties and his pretty wife Pungpit. Chakrabongse House, Queen Saowabha's gift to her favourite son Prince Chakrabongse, though designed on classical lines by an Italian architect, is set in about an acre of lush, tropical gardens. Dark wood panelling, polished wood or marble floors, ensure coolness within from the blazing heat outside. A wide veranda has steps down to the swimming pool and garden where palms and mangoes grow and flowering creepers and bougainvillaea shade a pergola, beyond which is the Chao Phraya river, lively and noisy with craft by day and night.

Many servants seated on the ground, saluted our arrival with clasped hands and bowed heads, men in high collared white jackets and dark trousers and women in long blue skirts and loose white blouses.

During the five weeks I spent with Lisba, our companionship seemed to have a kind of bloom on it, for it was not only truly happy but – rare indeed in the modern world – it was leisurely, for we had time to absorb the atmosphere, so new and magical to me – known but still magical to her – of this fascinating country. We had neither to cook, wash up, dust or even do the flowers, for the retinue of servants swiftly forestalled any instinctive move we might make to perform a single useful action. Even a dropped handkerchief was instantly whisked away to be laundered and with our clothes returned the same day.

My personal maid hovered speechlessly – for we had no common language – to help me into dresses, fasten zips and adroitly prevent me from tidying anything away.

Chakrabongses House seen from the river.

Such attentions left us with a generous measure of hours to savour, slowly allowing impressions to register, unblurred by distracting haste. Delicious meals were served in the pale green dining room hung with canary yellow curtains, by two young men in gold buttoned white tunics.

The food was quite exceptional: light, spicy and delicate, each dish arranged in a subtle blend of colour and taste, tempting on the hottest day as were the fruit and ices, all with the unmistakable tang of freshness, prepared with care and artistry. Well could I understand and echo Katya's exclamation: 'I like Thai food best in the world!'

Outside my bedroom was a wide tiled veranda, where I could see the sun arise and glitter on Wat Arun – Temple of the Dawn – and where I breakfasted on delicate green tea, toast, jam and sliced fresh mango and other exotic fruit. I was always brought a Bangkok newspaper in English, one of which amusingly described a 'hack journalist' as a 'Nag journalist'!

Our days were marked with small ceremonies: the moment we returned from an outing, we were brought glasses of iced fresh lime and immaculate pads of white towelling, ice cold and scented with eau-de-cologne to refresh our faces and hands after our inconsiderable exertions. And every night before retiring, Lisba lit candles in the tiny spirit house, like a pretty dolls house on a stand, to ward away evil that might molest us under cover of the dark.

No anniversary passes unnoticed or unhallowed by traditional rites and I well remember rising at five on the morning of Lisba's fifty-fourth birthday, the streets still cool and suffused with mist, the blaring traffic almost absent, when we stood in the doorway with offerings for the priests on this occasion. On a little table were curries and rice in separate containers, tied with ribbon and adorned with purple orchids, joss sticks and homely objects such as cleaning materials in western packaging. As the saffron-robed monks glided silently through the streets, I saw that other householders with an event to commemorate also awaited them with their gifts. Our offerings were accepted without thanks for 'ours was the privilege of giving'.

In a further birthday ceremony, monks had been invited to Chakrabongse House and entering the drawing room, sat cross-legged on a long bench, each holding a royal fan as Queen Rambai was present. In front of them was a narrow table with, at one end of it, a shrine bedecked with flowers and lighted candles, which held relics of Chakrabongse, Katya and Chula from which a long white cord was unwound and passed through the hands of each monk. When they began chanting it was strangely hypnotic, with a curious contrapuntal echoing sound, as though proceeding from regions far removed from earthly desires and aspirations.

After the chanting, Lisba presented each monk with robes and they were then served a splendid luncheon. Then, when each had received a tray of useful household objects, they all arose and their habitual detachment undisturbed, in silent dignity they departed.

Later that day, Lisba was brought a bowl containing 54 live fish to release into the river and 54 caged birds who, when she opened the door, soared swiftly back to freedom in the sunny sky.

Afternoon tea in the garden was delightful – like a doll's tea party: cups and plates so frail and small, cakes so tiny, some wrapped in palm leaves, their delicate flavours intriguingly unidentifiable to a western palate. One day I paused before joining Lisba at the table, for crouching at her feet was a penitent gardener, who was being admonished for larking about the shrubbery and flinging empty bottles (disgracefully intoxicated by their contents) at another gardener. As she spoke to him in Thai, she explained this afterwards, adding that on promise of future good behaviour he had been forgiven with a caution.

I had tea alone one day as Lisba had been invited to have it with Queen Sirikit, the reigning monarch's beautiful wife. But I was joined by Bisdar, who had

Eileen and Lisba in Thailand.

thought to console my solitude with a dish of fried octopus and chilli sauce which he had prepared for me himself. Although a trifle exotic for consumption in mid-afternoon, it was quite delicious. Nevertheless, he stayed to chat awhile and, though I had met and liked him in England, here in his native land, liking had deepened to affection for, though he and Pungpit supervised the complicated running of Chakrabongse House for Lisba and looked after it in her absence in England, it was his unaffected infectious delight in life's pleasures – great or small – that made him so endearing.

We spent a morning at Jim Thompson's house. He was the American who brought to profitable life the Thai silk industry, and mysteriously disappeared in 1967 in the Cameron Highlands. Lisba and Chula knew him well, used to dine there and found him a genial hospitable host. Although it now seems improbable that it will ever be known what became of him, he left as his lasting memorial, not only the thriving silk industry, but his exceptional house which, though open to the public, retains the imprint of a very personal private home.

Standing in one of the many countrified lanes on a quiet reach of the river where boats pass, piled with country produce, poled by women in traditional straw hats, the thud of looms was constant and skeins of brilliant red and purple silks hang on the balcony and reflect in the rippling water. Apparently Thompson had architectural training and assembled the house from fragments of ancient houses, fretted windows and carvings he discovered in remote parts of Thailand. The rooms are small and intimate, filled with treasures: screens, statuary, bronzes, pictures, old prints, all evidence of a refined and instinctive taste. Fresh flowers filled vases in every room and somehow the atmosphere conveyed a sense that, given up by the rest of the world, Jim Thompson's house awaits him still and has not lost faith in his return.

One evening we attended the Winter Fair – so popular in Katya's day, but no longer a social event where grand personages presided over stalls. Now obviously less refined, it was a bedlam of noise, jazz, drumming, a Ferris wheel, barkers shouting, groups squatting on the ground and frying food, spiralling smoke, smell of cooking oil, vanilla and everywhere the elusive spicy scent of Asia itself. Most remarkable of all were the Chinese fit-up theatres: two equally melodramatic plays being given within one hundred yards of the other, the actors screaming yet almost inaudible due to drums and cymbals throbbing and clashing below stage. Heavily padded garish costumes, mask-like make up ending at the jaw line, women crude white, black arched brows, carnation pink on cheekbones and voices never pitched below a sobbing shriek. Warriors in gold, emerald and scarlet, in weighty head-dresses topped by a single emotionally wagging feather. A blasé shirt-sleeved stage manager came on stage to lay down matting on which in dreadful throes of tongue wagging and eyeball rolling, a dying hero could more comfortably expire, the matting promptly removed when the corpse arose and exited. Clearly visible throughout were characters backstage, smoking, chewing, spitting, occasionally cuffing or kicking small boys who hung about, no less entranced than we were.

We lunched and dined out frequently: with Queen Rambai, and at several embassies. The British Embassy is a fine building with an impressive double staircase and a real punkah swishing above the dinner table. In the centre of the front courtyard sits a coal black statue of Queen Victoria. And once, when paving was being relaid to guard Her Majesty from harm, she was protected by a wooden cover. The Thai workmen on hearing the statue was that of a great queen, made two slits on a level with her eyes so that she might see out!

Although it is true that much of the old city of Bangkok, laid out by Chulalongkorn with tree-lined boulevards and rimmed with canals has been intruded upon by the West, its civilised plan defaced by huge cinemas, grotesque advertisements, modern hotels, massage parlours and the everlasting screech and grind of traffic, its original elegance still asserts itself in places as a reminder of that illustrious monarch.

The countless brilliantly glittering temples are seldom empty but full of people of all ages who make offerings, light candles, prostrate themselves or chat quietly to one another, seated gracefully on the ground. For here, the full inner life of the soul is not set apart but always present and acknowledged as though Thailand, pervaded by guardian spirits, maintains ties with her past that, like silken cords, twine and thread their way through daily life.

Other evenings we spent at home, out on the veranda, while darkness hid the glossy-leaved trees and shrubs, frogs croaked and touk-kae – a giant frilly-necked lizard - appeared, then shyly disappeared. Smaller lizards remained motionless on the walls while we listened dreamily to music played on Bisdar's record-player, or laughed and gossiped together, as we had in our youth. I can only remember one instance during those happy, happy weeks when I felt not sadness but an intimation of sorrow. I was awaiting Lisba in the garden, my mind idling and feeling agreeably blank but, as she came towards me, it struck me like a blow that the tone of her golden skin had changed – was a bad colour – and I was afraid. In a flash I rationalised and exorcised it: she was wearing green – a sharp green that did not suit her – of course, that explained it. I put my arm around her and realised, for all her energetic and radiant vitality, how slight she was. A year later, she fell ill and two years later she was dead.

It was 13 years later before I would visit Thailand again. Chakrabongse House remained much as I remembered it though Narisa's vital personality had imposed itself and made the rooms less formal, introducing delightful alterations in the previously rather austere bedrooms. A curious aspect of my stay which still haunts me was that, although Lisba had died in England, I had never felt so aware of her after her death as I now felt in Thailand. The strange form this awareness took was that, in the way Narisa moved, in the cadence of her voice, I often saw and heard Lisba to the point of almost calling her daughter by her name; and once or twice, hearing Narisa's young decisive footsteps approach the room where I was, I expected to see my sister enter through the door when she opened it.

A memorable visit was to Vimanmek, 'Residence in the Clouds' which has a singular history. Planned by one of King Chulalongkorn's brothers, Prince Narisarasuwaitiwong, who was also architect of the most superb temple in Bangkok, Wat Benjamabopitr. Vimarnmek, constructed of a rare golden teak, was an enchanting palace of exquisite design, started in 1893 on Koh Si Chang Island in the Gulf of Thailand. But, owing to a blockade by French gunboats in 1894, the building was abandoned, still incomplete, until, in 1901, Chulalongkorn, impressed by its deserted beauty, ordered its removal to the vast gardens of Suan Dusit, another of his many palaces, where it was rebuilt as the main royal residence in a mere seven weeks! Chulalongkorn lived there for six years, delighting in its airy serenity and spacious gardens reflected in four canals to north, south, east and west. But eventually, he moved to another palace just across the park where he died in 1910.

Once more Vimanmek was forsaken and forgotten until, in 1982, Thailand's present Queen Sirikit, aided by one of her daughters, Princess Sirindhorn, lovingly restored it, arranging with unerring taste the treasures of furniture, paintings, porcelain and sculpture collected not only by Chulalongkorn, but by his royal predecessors. Here, in this magical ambience, Narisa and I wandered for the length of a golden afternoon, so enfolded in a gentle calm that memory returns to it gratefully long afterwards.

On another occasion after I had gone, Narisa was once again at Vimanmek, this time conducted by a female guide who repeatedly and ingratiatingly expressed her amazement at her fluent command of Thai. 'How is it that you speak our language so well?' she asked once too often, whereupon Narisa, pointing to a full length portrait of Chakrabongse, replied rather shortly, 'Because that's my grandfather!'

One morning we were admitted as a special favour to the Chapel only opened for a royal lying-in-state where, within the golden urn, glimmering with diamonds in the soft effulgent light, was the body of Queen Rambai (whom I met more than once with Lisba in 1969) guarded by two officers, motionless and uniformed in white. On an easel her portrait, wreathed in flowers, smiled in the bloom of youth and the calm beauty of the scene seemed to breathe both acceptance of the young woman in the prime of life and the acquiescence in the end.

It was not without difficulty that Narisa arranged for me and Bisdar – who knew it well as a boy – to accompany her to Paruskavan, as it is now a top-security Government Department, and we were therefore prepared to find it greatly changed – and greatly changed it was. The magnificent gardens, so beloved by Katya, had long since disappeared beneath modern administrative buildings and only a solitary waterfall and the strange ugly 'folly', built by Chakrabongse, remained. Within, the house has suffered the inevitable neutering of its character by conversion to official use.

The original shallow marble stairs lead not to lofty palatial rooms but to rooms small and cramped in size, filled with office desks, filing cabinets and clacking typewriters. Only the dark teak, carved and fretted fanlights remain from the past, as do a profusion of art-nouveau light fittings, in one of which Narisa noticed a birds nest – lending an informal touch – but which would certainly have been swept away by industrious servants in Chakrabongse and Katya's day. We found it difficult to identify, even with the help of Bisdar and the faded snapshots taken by Katya almost eighty years ago with such enthusiasm. But we did recognise her sitting-room where she had her piano and where the lamp burned before her icon, and also the window from where, alas, poor Cham fell to her death.

Before we left, saddened in spite of the kindness with which we had been received, we were taken to a large room on the ground floor arranged as a shrine where, before a garlanded statue of Chakrabongse, we knelt and burned joss-sticks in his memory. The fact that this shrine exists in a high-powered Government department is characteristic of the respect for the past which is a way of life in Thailand, for there is no wish to obliterate the time when Chakrabongse and Katya lived there, but to honour and remember it.

As for me, my mind retreated from reality to recreate Paruskavan as I had long imagined it, when Chakrabongse, Katya and Chula, who 'loved it more than words can say' were happy there; before Katya went abroad; before Chavalit appeared.

The house is full and humming with life. There is bustle in the kitchens. Fountains play and waterfalls splash and sparkle in the gardens brilliant with exotic blooms and flowering shrubs. The slow-paced baby-elephant waits for Katya's visit with his favourite fruit. The horses stamp and whinny in the stables where perhaps Ramushka is being groomed and the sun has risen, shining on another day, bright with the promise of felicity.

SIMPLIFIED FAMILY TREE

SHOWING MEMBERS OF CHAKRABONGSE FAMILY

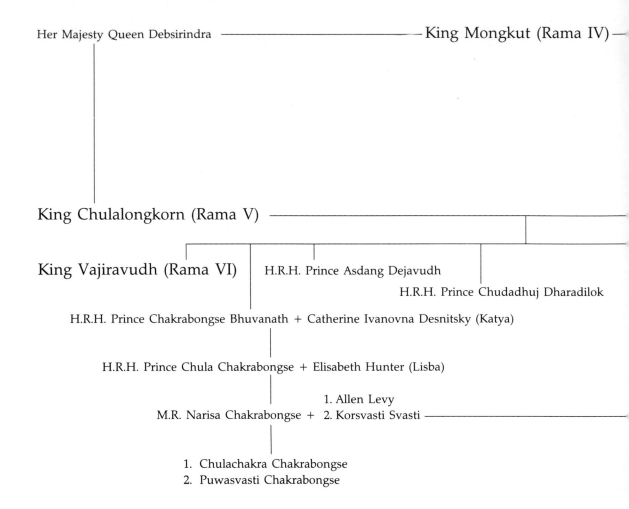

Her Majesty Queen Debsirindra ———————————— King Mongkut (Rama IV)—

King Chulalongkorn (Rama V)

King Vajiravudh (Rama VI)   H.R.H. Prince Asdang Dejavudh

H.R.H. Prince Chudadhuj Dharadilok

H.R.H. Prince Chakrabongse Bhuvanath + Catherine Ivanovna Desnitsky (Katya)

H.R.H. Prince Chula Chakrabongse + Elisabeth Hunter (Lisba)

1. Allen Levy
M.R. Narisa Chakrabongse + 2. Korsvasti Svasti ————————————

1. Chulachakra Chakrabongse
2. Puwasvasti Chakrabongse

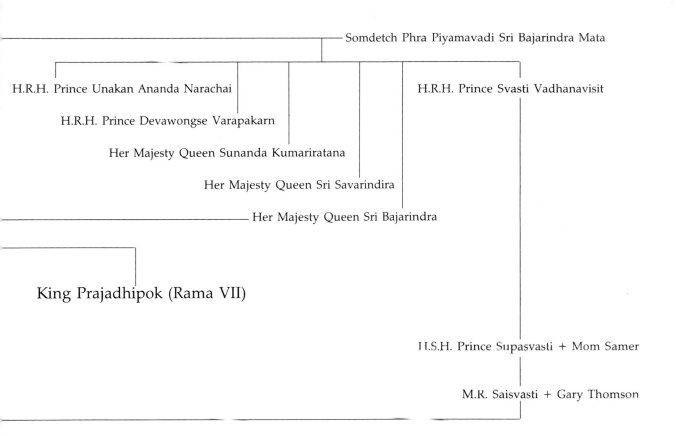

Somdetch Phra Piyamavadi Sri Bajarindra Mata

H.R.H. Prince Unakan Ananda Narachai

H.R.H. Prince Devawongse Varapakarn

Her Majesty Queen Sunanda Kumariratana

Her Majesty Queen Sri Savarindira

Her Majesty Queen Sri Bajarindra

H.R.H. Prince Svasti Vadhanavisit

King Prajadhipok (Rama VII)

H.S.H. Prince Supasvasti + Mom Samer

M.R. Saisvasti + Gary Thomson

BIBLIOGRAPHY

SIAM

Bowring, Sir John, *The Kingdom and People of Siam*; (1875), London.

Bristowe, W S, *Louis and the King of Siam*; (1976), Chatto & Windus, London.

Chakrabongse, HRH Prince Chula, *Brought up in England*; (1943), G L Foulis, London.

Chakrabongse, HRH Prince Chula, *Lords of Life*; (1960), Alvin Redman, London.

Chakrabongse, HRH Prince Chula, *The Twain Have Met*; (1956), G T Foulis, London.

Chakrabongse, M R Narisa, *Desnitsky Family Archives*; (unpublished).

Chakrabongse, M R Narisa, *Prince Chakrabongse Diaries*; (unpublished).

Crosby, Sir Josiah, KCMG, CIE, KBE, *Siam: The Crossroads*; (1945), Hollis & Carter, London.

Leonowens, A H, *The English Governess at the Siamese Court*; (1870), Trubner, London.

Poum, Nai, *The Education of Prince Chakrabongse in Russia*; (unpublished).

Pramoj, Kukrit, *Four Reigns*; (1981), Éditions Duang Kamol, Bangkok.

Smith, Dr Malcolm, *A Physician at the Court of Siam*; (1947), Country Life Ltd, London.

RUSSIA

Brook-Shepherd, Gordon, *Royal Sunset*; (1987), Wiedenfeld & Nicholson, London

Bruce Lockhart, R H, *Memoirs of a British Agent*; (1932), Putnam, New York & London.

Buxhoeveden, Baroness Sophie, *Left Behind*; (1929), Longman Green, London.

Cassini, Countess Marguerite, *Never a Dull Moment*; (1956), Harper, New York.

Crankshaw, Edward, *Shadow of the Winter Palace*; (1976), Macmillan, London.

Deutscher, Isac, *The Prophet Armed*; (1954), Oxford University Press.

Dolgorouky, Princess Stephanie, *Russia Before the Crash*; (1926), Herbert Clark, Paris.

de Grunvald, Constantin, *Les Nuits Blanche de St Petersburg*; (1968), Berger-Levrult, Paris.

Herzen, Alexander, *My Past Thoughts*.

Herzen, Alexander, *From Another Shore*.

Karsavina, Tamara, *Theatre Street*; (1947), Constable, London.

Knox, Major General Sir Alfred, *With the Russian Army, 1914–1917*; (1921), Hutchinson, London.

Kochan, Lionel, *The Making of Modern Russia*; (1962), Jonathan Cape, London.

Massie, Robert K, *Nicholas & Alexandra*; (1968), Gollancz, London.

Obolensky, Serge, *One Man in His Time*; MacDowell Obolensky, New York.

Paleologue, George Maurice *An Ambassador's Memoirs, 1914-1917;* 3 Volumes 1923-1924 & 1925. (Trans. A Holt) Huchinson, London.

Romanov, Princesse Pavalovic, *Éducation d'une Princesse*; (1931); Grevin, Paris.

de Stoecle, Agnes, *Not All Vanity*; (1950), John Murray, London.

Summers, Anthony and Mangold, Tom, *The File on the Tsar*; (1976). Gollancz, London.

Youssoupoff, Prince Felix, *Lost Splendour*; (1953), Jonathan Cape, London.

Journal de Nicholas II, 1914–1918; (1934), Payat, Paris.

Journal Secret de Anna Viroubova, 1909–1917; (1928), Payat, Paris.

 # INDEX